HK Sport Science Monograph Series

The *HK Sport Science Monograph Series* is another endeavor to provide a useful communication channel for recording extensive research programs by sport scientists. Many publishers have discontinued publishing monographs because they have proven uneconomical. It is my hope that with the cooperation of authors, the use of electronic support systems, and the purchase of these monographs by sport scientists and libraries we can continue this series over the years.

The series will publish original research reports and reviews of literature that are sufficiently extensive not to lend themselves to reporting in available research journals. Subject matter pertinent to both the broad fields of the sport sciences and to physical education are considered appropriate for the monograph series, especially research in

- sport biomechanics,
- sport physiology,
- motor behavior (including motor control and learning, motor development, and adapted physical activity),
- sport psychology,
- sport sociology, and
- sport pedagogy.

Other titles in this series are:

- *Adolescent Growth and Motor Performances: A Longitudinal Study of Belgian Boys*
- *Biological Effects of Physical Activity*
- *Growth and Fitness of Flemish Girls: The Leuven Growth Study*
- *Athletes and the American Hero Dilemma*
- *Kinanthropometry in Aquatic Sports: A Study of World Class Athletes*

Authors who wish to publish in the monograph series should submit two copies of the complete manuscript to the publisher. All manuscripts must conform to the current *APA Publication Manual* and be of a length between 120 and 300 doublespaced manuscript pages. The manuscript will be sent to two reviewers who will follow a review process similar to that used for scholarly journals. The decision with regard to the manuscript's acceptability will be based on its judged contribution to knowledge and on economic feasibility. Publications that are accepted, after all required revisions are made, must be submitted to the publisher on computer disk for electronic transfer to typesetting. No royalties will be paid for monographs published in this series.

Authors wishing to submit a manuscript to the monograph series or desiring further information should write to: Monograph Editor, Human Kinetics, P.O. Box 5076, Champaign, IL 61825-5076 for further details.

Rainer Martens

Preface

The longitudinal data reported in this HK Sport Science Monograph are from the Amsterdam Growth Study. This 15-year multidisciplinary investigation was carried out between 1976 and 1991 with a group of almost 100 males and 100 females in the Netherlands living in and around Amsterdam. The study is in progress and will continue with repeated measurements in the near future.

The general purposes of this longitudinal study are to describe the physical and mental development of a group of males and females from the teen years to adulthood and to find out whether there are periods of change in health status and, if so, to elaborate their possible causes. We monitored aspects of lifestyle, such as nutrition and physical activity, and several psychosocial variables. These factors are thought to have an impact on the development of health in young people. Four yearly measurements were made in teenagers aged 13 to 17 years, and later two measurements were made at ages 21 and 27.

After a general introduction the purpose and setup of this study are described in Part I. We pay special attention to the "multiple longitudinal design" and to the measures taken to prevent selective dropout and to promote the adherence of the subjects. We describe the multidisciplinary methods that are used, including the assessment of body growth, body composition, physical fitness, physiological and psychological characteristics, nutritional intake, and daily physical activity.

Part II describes the longitudinal changes of (a) body growth and body composition in terms of body mass and fat mass; (b) physiological fitness in terms of maximal oxygen uptake, muscle force, speed, flexibility, and indicators for cardiovascular diseases; and (c) psychological traits, such as personality, attitude, type A or B behavior, and life events over the 15-year period.

The important lifestyle patterns under review in this study are described in Part III, which concerns the changes in dietary intake (including alcohol and smoking behavior), daily habitual physical activity, stress, behavioral style, and health complaints that subjects reported. Six points in time are available, giving a fairly good pattern of change over the 15-year period of these males and females.

Part IV contains six chapters describing relations between lifestyle and health in the study's population. Chapter 9 describes the relationship between physical activity level and fitness parameters, and chapter 10 concerns the relationships between physical fitness and the incidence of sports injury and the health of subjects. Chapter 11 concerns tracking analyses of cardiovascular risk indicators (such as hypercholesterolemia, hypertension, percentage of body fat, smoking) and psychological characteristics (such as stress, Type A or B behavior) and the incidence of daily hassles and life events. In the last year of measurement (1991) bone mineral density was also measured in the lumbar spine of subjects

HK SPORT SCIENCE MONOGRAPH SERIES
Volume 6

The Amsterdam Growth Study

*A Longitudin... * Term-time opening hours: *lth,*
Fitness, and Lifestyle

Han C.G. Kemper, PhD
Universiteit van Amsterdam

Editor

Human Kinetics

Library of Congress Cataloging-in-Publication Data

The Amsterdam growth study : a longitudinal analysis of health,
fitness, and lifestyle / Han C.G. Kemper, ed.
    p. cm. -- (HK sport science monograph series ; v. 6)
    ISBN 0-87322-507-4
    1. Youth--Health and hygiene--Netherlands--Amsterdam--Longitudinal
studies. 2. Life style--Health aspects--Netherlands--Amsterdam-
-Longitudinal studies. I. Kemper, Han C.G. II. Series.
RA564.5.A57 1995
362.1'083--dc20   94-33964
                                                    CIP

ISBN: 0-87322-507-4
ISSN: 0894-4229

Acquisitions Editor: Richard A. Washburn; **Developmental Editor**: Larret Galasyn-
Wright; **Assistant Editors**: Julie Marx Ohnemus, Dawn Roselund, and John Wentworth;
Copyeditor: Jay Thomas; **Proofreader**: Jim Burns; **Production Manager**: Kris Ding;
Typesetting and Text Layout: Sandra Meier; **Text Designer**: Keith Blomberg; **Layout
Artist**: Tara Welsch; **Cover Designer**: Jody Boles; **Printer**: Versa Press

Printed in the United States of America

10 9 8 7 6 5 4 3 2 1

Human Kinetics
P.O. Box 5076, Champaign, IL 61825-5076
1-800-747-4457

Canada: Human Kinetics, Box 24040, Windsor, ON N8Y 4Y9
1-800-465-7301 (in Canada only)

Europe: Human Kinetics, P.O. Box IW14, Leeds LS16 6TR, England
(44) 532 781708

Australia: Human Kinetics, 2 Ingrid Street, Clapham 5062, South Australia
(08) 371 3755

New Zealand: Human Kinetics, P.O. Box 105-231, Auckland 1
(09) 309 2259

Contents

at age 27. This is the age at which peak bone density is thought to occur. In chapters 12 and 13 the possible influence of calcium intake and weight-bearing activities (measured during the previous 15 years) on the development of peak bone density in the lumbar spine is assessed. The last chapter is devoted to an analysis of the effects on adult health of physical condition and lifestyle in the adolescent period.

In the final section the main conclusions of the longitudinal study are drawn. Preventive strategies for increasing health and avoiding diseases at young-adult age and even in older years are suggested. The four parts of this book are divided into chapters written by one or more authors in the form of a scientific article with references listed at the end.

The members who participated in this long-term study did a great job: They measured and remeasured subjects year after year and gave their utmost to publish these important longitudinal data. We hope that this publication will be of value for all who are interested in the health of teenagers and young adults, and especially for the authorities who are responsible for, and can have impact on, the prospering of future youth.

Han C.G. Kemper

Acknowledgments

It is obvious that a complex project as the long-term multidisciplinary study described in this monograph could never have been realized without the support and cooperation of many people and institutions. First we would like to thank all the men and women who served as our longitudinal subjects since their early teenage years. Following their secondary school years, most of them have finished further education, started professional education, begun jobs, and/or raised children. They are now living not only in and around Amsterdam but all over the Netherlands. Some of them who live abroad even used their vacation to visit our laboratories for a full day to continue their participation. Without their enthusiasm this longitudinal study could never have been so successful.

We are also grateful for the cooperation of our colleagues from various institutions in the Netherlands:

M.A. van't Hof (Catholic University of Nijmegen) was of great importance in the design of the longitudinal study.

The Department of Psychonomics (Vrije Universiteit, J. Orlebeke) and the Department of Psychonomy (Universiteit van Amsterdam, A. Kok) assisted us in the psychological aspects of the study.

The Department of Health Science for Occupational and Environmental Health (Universiteit van Amsterdam, F.J.H. van Dijk) lent us their analyst for taking blood samples.

The laboratory of the Department of Human Nutrition (Landbouw Universiteit Wageningen, J.G.A.J. Hautvast) performed the analysis of all blood samples.

The Technical University in Eindhoven (C.J. Snijders and T. Seroo) constructed the instrument for measuring the forward/backward curvature of the spine during the adolescent period.

The Institute of Child Health (J.M. Tanner) in London advised and trained us in the scoring of X-rays of the hand and wrist made during the first 4 years in order to estimate skeletal age of the subjects.

The Catholic University of Leuven (G. Beunen) advised us in the choice and measurement of physical fitness tests.

The Department of Nuclear Medicine (G.J.J. Teule) and Endocrinology (P. Lips) of the Academic Hospital of the Vrije Universiteit advised us concerning the measurements of bone mineral density and also made available their dual X-ray absorptiometry facilities.

Technical assistance was given by Hans du Jour, Karin ten Kroode, Paul Kuijer, Jan van Leeuwen, Tony Lewis, Peter Lowie, Ton Meulemans, John

Nunumete, Martijn Overzier, Anneke van Schijndel, Wim Schreurs, and Frank Wijkhuizen.

We would also like to thank the following students who did their research work within the scope of this project: Marc van der Berg, Berthel Blom, Gerda Dorreboom, Louisanne Gemen, Hans Gosselink, Jeroen Jekel, Pieter Kempe, Cor Koning, Alexander Molendijk, Annet Postma, Maurits van Tulder, Joop van Velzen, Tim Winkler, Adrie van Zundert.

This longitudinal study has been supported by grants from

De Stichting voor Onderzoek van het Onderwijs (Foundation for Educational Research, SVO nr.0255).

Het Praeventiefonds (Dutch Prevention Fund; proj.nr. 28-189a, 28-1106, 28-1106-1).

De Nederlandse Hart Stichting (Dutch Heart Foundation, proj.nr. 76051-79051 and 90-312).

Het Ministerie van Welzijn en Volksgezondheid (Dutch Ministry of Well-Being and Public Health, nr. 90-170).

Stichting Voeding Zuivel en Gezondheid (Dairy Foundation on Nutrition and Health).

Last but not least we acknowledge our own universities, the Universiteit van Amsterdam and Vrije Universiteit, which gave us on a long-term basis the freedom to do this research within the financial and personnel facilities available.

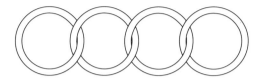

Introduction to the Amsterdam Growth Study

Han C.G. Kemper

"A longitudinal study will be done only once in your life." This was one of the well-intentioned warnings given by some colleagues in 1973 when we started to think about setting up a longitudinal study of boys and girls in their teenage years. Indeed, in 1993—20 years later—we are still in progress with that longitudinal study and have covered more than the teenage period. Information is now available from young adulthood (age 21) and from age 27. And we are still busy!

Although children are generally thought to be physically active by nature, in recent years the extent of physical activity among youngsters has greatly concerned health officials. Up to a generation ago, physical activity was a natural part of life for most children. Because this is no longer the case, one may wonder whether a particular child or adolescent performs the physical activity necessary for normal, healthy development. In many ways the lifestyles of children and adolescents will resemble those of adults. The necessity for physical activity has been greatly reduced, owing to the mechanization and automatization of work and leisure time (Shephard, 1982). The absence of sufficient physical activity is a direct or indirect cause of many pediatric diseases and an important risk factor for chronic behavioral diseases that appear in adulthood, such as cardiovascular and musculoskeletal diseases (Bar Or, 1983).

It is believed that there are critical periods in the course of development that determine whether individuals will live physically active lives later on:

- Childhood (ages 4-12), when children in the Netherlands attend school for the first time and the school hours impose restrictions on a naturally physical, active lifestyle
- Adolescence (ages 13-19), when teenagers enter secondary school, where homework further restricts leisure time and there is a shift from bicycles to engine-driven transport means at age 18

At about age 12 children enter puberty. In the Netherlands girls have their peak height velocity at about 12.5 years and boys at about 14 years. At the same time sexual development begins (Falkner & Tanner, 1978).

Originally, it was planned the Amsterdam Growth and Health Study would have four subsequent annual measurements covering the school-age period (Kemper & van't Hof, 1978). The results are published in a review article (Kemper et al., 1983) and as a monograph (Kemper, 1985).

The results showed clearly that although physical fitness and health parameters do not decline during the adolescent period in either boys or girls (Kemper, 1991; Kemper et al., 1990a; Kemper & Verschuur, 1990b; Kemper et al., 1989; Snel & Gosselink, 1989), habitual physical activity changes dramatically: The amount of physical activity decreased 25% in boys and 20% in girls (Verschuur, 1987). Their eating habits, that is, the proportion of nutrients, were typically Western, with content too high in fat and protein and too low in carbohydrates (Post, 1989). In addition, an increase was seen in the percentages of smokers (at age 17, 38% of the girls and 25% of the boys) and alcohol drinkers (from 5% at age 12 to 65% at age 17 in both sexes).

These data impelled us to continue this longitudinal study to find out whether a continuation of these lifestyles would be manifested ultimately in unfavorable physical and psychosocial characteristics at a young-adult age and to find out what direction the changes would have taken at a young-adult age. Grants from several organizations in the Netherlands enabled us to continue the study, and we measured the same subjects again at age 21 in 1985 and at age 27 in 1991.

Different ages invite a critical update, and we included some new measurements (e.g., stress measurements in 1985 and 1991 and bone density determination in 1991) and left out others (such as skeletal age, once full maturity was reached in all subjects).

One of the crucial aspects in a longitudinal study is the subjects' adherence. We are proud that the dropout rate of our subjects was very low: We lost 14% between 1980 and 1985 and only another 9% in 1991.

Thank to the subjects' continuous efforts, this monograph contains data for a sample of young Dutch men and women. The results give a highly interesting ''motion picture'' (Paffenbarger, 1988) of the ongoing development of physical and mental health from childhood to adulthood in the Netherlands.

This longitudinal investigation, continuing over a period of more than 15 years, has been carried out with the help of many colleagues. A list of investigators who gave their utmost till 1985 has already been published (Kemper, 1985). Since 1985 the research group has consisted of the following persons:

Ronald van Aalst, human movement scientist (till 1986)
Nora Brouwer, secretary (till 1986)
Ingrid Buitendijk, human movement scientist (1990-1991)
Han C.G. Kemper, exercise physiologist (principal investigator since 1974)
Annemieke Kerkhof, secretary (1992)
Bram Knaap, secretary (since 1992)

Irene Kooiman, secretary (1987)
Langha de Mey, data analyst (till 1987)
Frank van Lenthe, human movement scientist (since 1992)
Willem van Mechelen, occupational physician and epidemiologist (project
    leader since 1989)
G. Bertheke Post, nutritionist (since 1975)
Harry Schlatmann, human movement scientist (1985-1986)
Wouter Schouten, biologist (till 1987)
Jan Snel, psychologist (since 1974)
Lucienne Storm-van Essen, data analyst (till 1987)
Jos Twisk, human movement scientist (since 1990)
Robbert Verschuur, exercise physiologist (till 1988)
Desiree C. Welten, nutritionist (since 1992)
Adrie van Zundert, human movement scientist (till 1988)

The Amsterdam Growth and Health Study is a multidisciplinary longitudinal
study carried out in and around Amsterdam. The study was initiated by the
University of Amsterdam as a joint research project of the Department of Health
Science for Occupational and Environmental Health (Coronel Laboratory) and
the Laboratory of Psychophysiology. Since 1985 the project has been undertaken
by the Department of Health Science (with respect to human movement) of the
Faculty of Human Movement Sciences at Vrije Universiteit, Amsterdam, and
the Medical Faculty and Faculty of Psychology of the University of Amsterdam.

References

Bar-Or O. (1983). Pediatric sports medicine for the practitioner: From physiologi-
    cal principles to clinical applications. Springer, New York.
Falkner F., J.M. Tanner. (1978). Human Growth, vols. 1-3. Plenum Press,
    New York.
Kemper H.C.G. (ed.). (1985). Growth, health and fitness of teenagers: Longitudi-
    nal research in international perspective. Vol. 20 of: Medicine and sport
    science. Karger, Basel.
Kemper H.C.G. Sources of variation in longitudinal assessment of maximal
    aerobic power in teenage boys and girls: The Amsterdam Growth and Health
    Study. Hum Biol 63:4 (1991) 533-546.
Kemper H.C.G., C. van der Bom, H. Dekker, G. Ootjers, G.B. Post, J. Snel, P.G.
    Splinter, L. Storm-van Essen, R. Verschuur. Growth and health in teenagers
    in the Netherlands: Survey of multidisciplinary longitudinal studies and
    comparison with recent results of a Dutch study. J Sports Med 4 (1983)
    202-234.
Kemper H.C.G., M.A. van't Hof. Design of a multiple longitudinal inter-
    disciplinary study of growth and health in teenagers. Eur J Pediatr 129
    (1978) 147-155.

Kemper H.C.G., J. Snel, R. Verschuur, L. Storm-van Essen. Tracking of health and risk indicators of cardiovascular disease from teenager to adult: Amsterdam Growth and Health Study. Prev Med 19 (1990a) 642-655.

Kemper H.C.G., R. Verschuur. Longitudinal study of coronary risk factors during adolescence and young adulthood: The Amsterdam Growth and Health Study. Pediatric Exercise Science 1 (1990b) 359-371.

Kemper H.C.G., R. Verschuur, L. de Mey. Longitudinal changes of aerobic fitness in youth ages 12 to 13. Pediatric Exercise Science 1 (1989) 257-270.

Paffenbarger R.S. Contribution of epidemiology to exercise science and cardiovascular health. Med Sci Sports Exerc 20:5 (1988) 426-438.

Post G.B. (1989). Nutrition in adolescence: A longitudinal study in dietary patterns from teenager to adult. Thesis, Landbouw Universiteit Wageningen, de Vrieseborch, Haarlem, SO 16.

Shephard R.J. (1982). Physical activity and growth. Year Book Medical Publishers, Chicago.

Snel J., H. Gosselink. Health, personality and physiological variables as discriminators of the Type A behaviour pattern in young adults. Journal of Psychophysiology 3 (1989) 291-299.

Verschuur R. (1987). Daily physical activity and health: Longitudinal changes during the teenage period. Thesis, Universiteit van Amsterdam, de Vrieseborch, Haarlem, SO 12.

Part I

Purpose, Setup, and Methods
of the Study

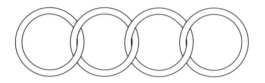

Chapter 1

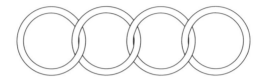

Design of the Amsterdam Growth Study

Jos Twisk & Han C.G. Kemper

In studies of growth and development, three types of designs have been used to a great extent: cross-sectional, longitudinal, and time-lag designs. In these designs each measurement taken on a subject at a particular point in time is influenced by three factors:

- Age of the subject
- Birth cohort to which the subject belongs (group of subjects born in the same year)
- Time of measurement

Each of the designs has its problems. Cross-sectional designs are confounded by age and cohort effects because different groups are measured at the same point in time. Longitudinal designs are confounded by age and time-of-measurement effects because one cohort is studied at different times and therefore at different ages. Time-lag designs, on the other hand, are confounded by cohort and time-of-measurement effects, because different cohorts with the same age are measured at different points in time (Magnusson & Bergman 1990).

Multiple Longitudinal Design

To study these confounding effects separately we used a *multiple longitudinal design* (Kemper and van't Hof, 1978), which means that we did repeated measurements in more than one cohort with overlapping ages (Fig. 1.1). Because of this we were able to distinguish age, cohort, and time-of-measurement effects, all described in earlier publications (Kemper, 1985).

We have not mentioned another confounding factor that can play an important role in repeated measurement studies: learning, or test, effects. These

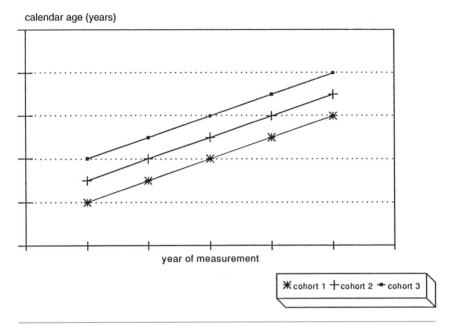

calendar age (years)

year of measurement

✳cohort 1 ✚cohort 2 ➤cohort 3

Figure 1.1   Principle of a multiple longitudinal design. Different cohorts with overlapping ages are measured at different points in time.

effects introduce differences between repeated measurements, differences that are due only to a changing attitude toward the measurements themselves. If test effects occur, they will seriously hinder the interpretation of individual and group development. Test effects can be analyzed when one selects suitable control groups without repeated measurements. Therefore, during the first 4 years of the study we performed a second study at a comparable school with subjects from identical cohorts. In this school, instead of repeated measurements, independent samples were taken at each of the four times of measurement. Comparisons between the data of both populations can demonstrate test effects (Fig. 1.2).

In 1985 and 1991 we continued our study with the longitudinal group, which was measured in 1977, 1978, 1979, and 1980. For the last two measurements we did not use a control group. The main reason for this was the practical problems in selecting a representative group of controls; secondly, we did not expect a test effect to take place because of the long time lag (5 years) between successive measurements.

To demonstrate the way cohort effects, time-of-measurement effects, and test effects were measured in our multiple longitudinal design, let us look at the measurement of maximal oxygen uptake ($\dot{V}O_2$max). $\dot{V}O_2$max was measured by a maximal running test on a treadmill, continued until complete exhaustion (Kemper & Verschuur, 1980). The three possible confounding factors were tested with multivariate analysis of variance (MANOVA) for repeated measurements

performance

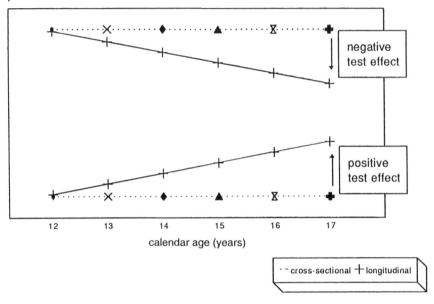

calendar age (years)

Figure 1.2   Test, or learning, effects, can be studied by comparing repeated measurements in the same population with nonrepeated measurements in a comparable population (different symbols indicate different subjects).

and Student's *t*-test (Kemper, 1991). Because of the design, time-of-measurement effects and test effects could be measured only during the first 4 years of measurements.

In Figure 1.3 the longitudinal development of $\dot{V}O_2$max of the three different cohorts for both males and females is shown. Statistical testing of the differences between the three cohorts did not reveal any cohort effects.

In Figure 1.4 time-of-measurement effects are displayed. Comparison of $\dot{V}O_2$max values among subjects of the same age, measured in two different years, can show possible time-of-measurement effects. In our example we were only able to compare two groups with the same ages (13, 14, and 15 years), measured at different times, because other same-age groups were too small (the number of subjects was less than 5). No differences between same-age groups could be shown.

Relative to test effects, repeated measurements of $\dot{V}O_2$max is a good example, because physical performance tests, where maximum motivation is needed, are particularly threatened by these effects. In Figure 1.5 the $\dot{V}O_2$max values of the longitudinal groups are shown in comparison with the $\dot{V}O_2$max of the control groups. No significant differences can be demonstrated in either sex.

Dropouts

Another possible confounding factor in longitudinal studies is the dropout effect. In the case of selective dropout, it is possible that subjects who dropped out

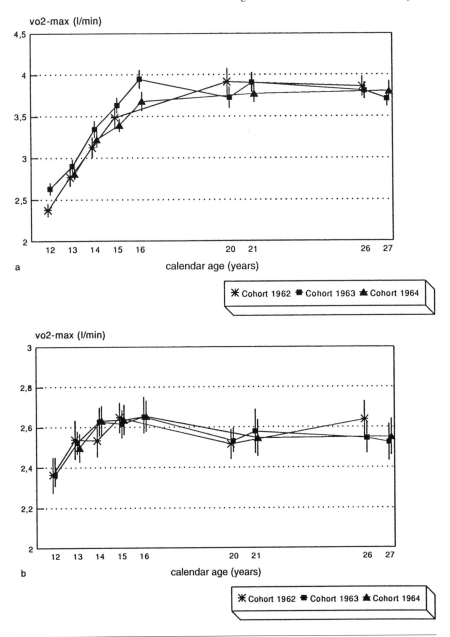

Figure 1.3   Longitudinal development of $\dot{V}O_2$max for three different cohorts for (a) males and (b) females.

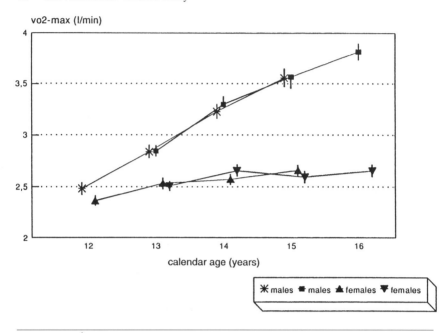

Figure 1.4 V̇O₂max of males and females of the same age, measured at different times.

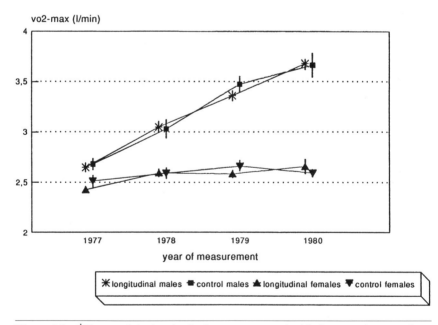

Figure 1.5 V̇O₂max of the longitudinal group compared with the control groups for both males and females.

scored at an earlier measurement significantly higher (or lower) than the subjects who stayed in the study. We could easily investigate these effects using Student's t-test. For example, we analyzed the possible dropout effects on $\dot{V}O_2$max measurements. No dropout effect was found in each of the three measurement periods (Table 1.1). The number of dropouts is quite low. During the school period (1977-1980) only 74 subjects left the study, mostly because of leaving school. Of the longitudinal group ($n = 233$), 200 subjects returned for the 1985 investigation and 182 of them visited the laboratory for the sixth measurement in 1991. The two most important reasons for leaving the study at the last two measurements were "not interested" and "too busy."

Not all the subjects who participated in 1991 were measured in all the earlier years. Some subjects missed one of the first four measurements, some subjects missed the measurement in 1985, but all these persons were nevertheless longitudinally analyzed. Thus, the analysis was performed on all subjects who participated in the 1991 measurement ($n = 182$).

Table 1.1   Number of Dropouts and Comparison of the $\dot{V}O_2$max of the Longitudinal Group With the Groups That Dropped Out During Three Measurement Periods for Both Males (M) and Females (F)

Year of measurement	Dropout period		Number (%) of dropouts	$\dot{V}O_2$max ($M \pm SD$)		p
				Dropouts	Longitudinal	
1977	1977-1981	M	46 (30.8%)	2.67 ± 0.42	2.68 ± 0.42	0.97
		F	28 (17.6%)	2.44 ± 0.29	2.42 ± 0.32	0.67
1980	1980-1985	M	9 (8.8%)	3.77 ± 0.49	3.67 ± 0.55	0.60
		F	14 (18.4%)	2.52 ± 0.37	2.66 ± 0.35	0.08
1985	1985-1991	M	15 (15.5%)	3.80 ± 0.70	3.83 ± 0.55	0.86
		F	17 (16.5%)	2.56 ± 0.43	2.54 ± 0.36	0.83

Interperiod Correlations

The purpose of longitudinal studies is to investigate individual changes over time. This becomes difficult when the stochastic measurement error exceeds the change over time. The degree to which this occurs for a variable may be studied on the basis of interperiod correlation (IPC) matrices. An IPC is a correlation coefficient between two times of measurement for one variable. Van't Hof and Kowalski (1979) showed that under fairly realistic conditions, correlation coefficients can be approximated by a linear function of the time interval. The intercept of the straight line is the correlation coefficient between two independent measurements and has an intermediate time interval equal to zero; this may be interpreted as the instantaneous measurement-remeasurement reproducibility. The slope of the line is a measure of interindividual growth difference. Comparison of the slope and intercept gives an impression of the usefulness of the variable for longitudinal purposes:

• If the intercept is small (e.g., .5) and there is not a steep descent, the reproducibility of the variable is so poor that individual changes over time are overruled by measurement errors. In this case, for each individual the mean value of the variable over time is a more accurate measurement of the level of the variable than each of the single measurements separately.

• If the intercept is about 1.0 and there is a steep descent, the variable has a high degree of reproducibility accompanied by large differences in growth between the individuals. When no other confounding factor is present, the variable is very suitable for the study of individual growth patterns.

In Figure 1.6 the regression lines of the IPCs for V̇O₂max are given for both males and females. The estimated intercept is about .65 for males and .7 for females, and the descent over a period of 14 years is from .65 to .25 for males and from .7 to .4 for females.

Analysis of Longitudinal Changes

We analyzed differences in longitudinal development between several groups (for instance, females vs. males, low-activity group vs. high-activity group, smokers vs. nonsmokers, drinkers vs. nondrinkers) with MANOVA for repeated

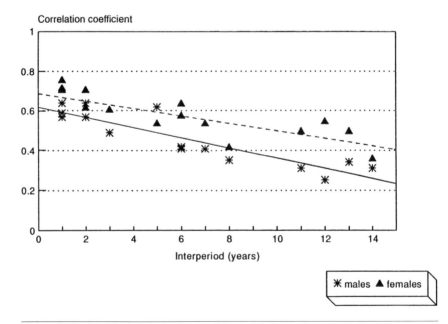

Figure 1.6   Interperiod correlation coefficients and estimated regression lines of V̇O₂max for both males and females over a measurement period of 14 years.

measurements. In our longitudinal study we were able to take measurements six times over an age period of 15 years. The first four measurements occurred annually (1977, 1978, 1979, and 1980) and covered the *adolescent period* (ages 13-17). The fifth measurement was in 1985 at age 21. The period between 1980 and 1985 covered the *young-adult period*. The sixth measurement was in 1991 at age 27. This last period, between 1985 and 1991, covered the *adult period*.

First we observed the whole period of 15 years (1977-1991) and analyzed two possible main effects: a time effect (Is there a significant change in time for the population considered as a whole?) and a group effect (Is there a significant difference at one of the measurements between the groups under consideration?). We also looked for a possible time-group interaction (Is the change in time different for the distinguished groups?) (Figs. 1.7 and 1.8). If there was a significant time effect for the whole population or a significant time-group interaction, then the same analysis was done for the groups separately to see in which group there was a significant change in time (Fig. 1.9).

After analyzing the whole measurement period of 15 years, we checked whether any significant effect found for the whole period also appeared in a shorter period. To do so, we analyzed the longitudinal development of the first five measurements, over the 8-year period between 1977 and 1985 (the adolescent and young-adult periods). If we found, for example, a significant group effect over the whole measurement period, we checked whether the groups also differed in the shorter interval of 8 years between 1977 and 1985 (Fig. 1.10). If we found

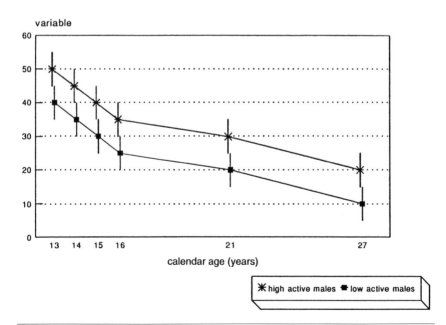

Figure 1.7   An example of a group effect and a time effect for the whole measurement period of 15 years. There was no time-group interaction.

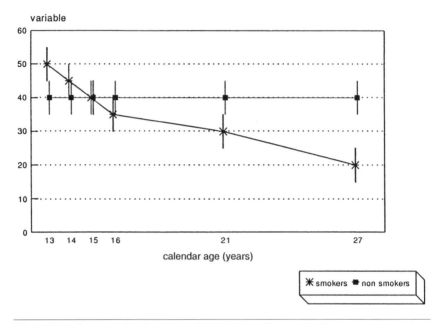

Figure 1.8   An example of a group effect, a time effect, and a time-group interaction for the whole measurement period of 15 years.

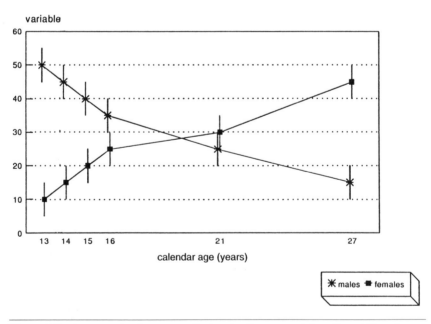

Figure 1.9   An example of a group effect and a time-group interaction. Although there is no time effect for the whole population, the separate groups show significant time effects.

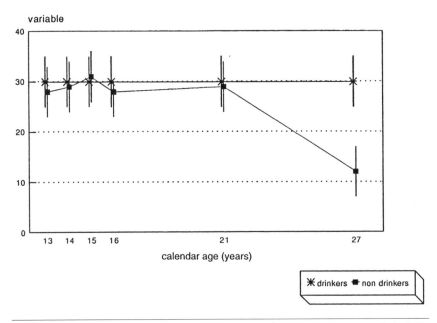

Figure 1.10   An example of a group effect over the whole measurement period of 15 years, but not over the shorter period of 8 years.

any significant effects in the period between 1977 and 1985, we continued our analysis by observing the longitudinal development of the first four measurements, from 1977 to 1980 (the adolescent period). If one of the steps in the analysis did not reveal any significance, we discontinued the analysis (i.e., if there was no time effect or time-group interaction in analyzing the whole measurement period of 15 years, we did not look for possible time effects or time-group interactions in the shorter time periods).

Data Cleaning

Data cleaning was a very intensive process, but a necessary one. Quality control of longitudinal data is very important, because intrasubject differences are generally more subtle than intergroup differences. We used three data-cleaning procedures:

1. First, after editing the data, a second or third person not involved in this process checked the data for errors.
2. Second, data on outliers were checked by comparing the data with biologically plausible values.
3. The third data-cleaning method was available because of the longitudinal design of the study. Errors were detected by observing the longitudinal sequence of the data. For example, a decrease in height throughout this age range is not possible; if one apparently occurred, we knew we had found an error.

Data Analysis

Numerous statistical techniques were used to describe and analyze the longitudinal data. These are described in the respective chapters. For all analyses, the Statistical Package for Social Sciences (SPSS) was used (Norussis, 1990; SPSS-X User's Guide, 1988).

References

Hof M.A. van't, C.J. Kowalski. (1979). Analysis of mixed longitudinal data sets. In: B. Prahl-Andersen (ed.), A mixed longitudinal interdisciplinary study of growth and development. Academic Press, New York.

Kemper H.C.G. (ed.). (1985). Growth, health and fitness of teenagers: Longitudinal research in international perspective. Vol. 20 of: Medicine and sport science. Karger, Basel.

Kemper H.C.G. Sources of variation in longitudinal assessment of maximal aerobic power in teenage boys and girls: The Amsterdam Growth and Health Study. Hum Biol 63:4 (1991) 533-547.

Kemper H.C.G., M.A. van't Hof. Design of a multiple longitudinal study of growth and health of teenagers. Eur J Pediatr 129 (1978) 147-155.

Kemper H.C.G., R. Verschuur. (1980). Measurement of aerobic power in teenagers. In: K. Berg and B.O. Erikson (eds.), Children and exercise IV. University Park Press, Baltimore.

Magnusson D., L.R. Bergman (eds.). (1990). Data quality in longitudinal research. Cambridge University Press, Cambridge.

Norussis M.J. (1990). SPSS advanced statistics user's guide. SPSS, Chicago.

SPSS-X user's guide, 3rd ed. (1988). SPSS, Chicago.

Chapter 2

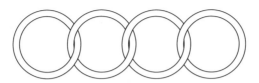

Procedures and Subjects Used in the Longitudinal Study

G. Bertheke Post & Han C.G. Kemper

The current study is a continuation of the Growth and Health of Teenagers study begun in 1977 and carried out in two secondary schools in and around Amsterdam (Kemper, 1985). The two schools were coeducational for pupils with a level of intelligence above the average for their age (one "higher secondary school," or HAVO in Dutch, and one "highest secondary school," or VWO).

Periods of Measurement

The population described herein comprises girls and boys of the longitudinal sample who started in 1977, were followed over the years, and completed the study in 1991; they were 13 years old at the outset and 27 at the conclusion. We should note, however, that the population may not be representative of the general population either of Amsterdam or of the Netherlands as a whole (Kemper et al., 1983).

1977-1980: The Adolescent Period

During the adolescent period, four annual measurements took place. During each school year the measurements were spread throughout the whole year. A special Mobile Research Unit was placed near the school to perform most of the measurements during school hours (Fig. 2.1): anthropometric measurements, treadmill tests, X-ray photographs of hand and wrist, forward/backward curvature of the spine, nutrition and activity interview, lung function tests, and blood sampling. Personality inventories took place in classrooms, and the motor performance tests in the gymnasium (Kemper et al., 1983).

Figure 2.1   The Mobile Research Unit.

1980-1985: The Young-Adult Period

In 1985, 5 years after the last measurement at school, the subjects were asked to continue their participation by visiting our laboratories for one full day. The measurements took place from February to June. In principle, the same measurements were repeated, and some additional ones were included (Kemper et al., 1987), such as questionnaires about personality, stress, and perceived health and measurements of stimulant drugs in the urine and immunoglobulins in the saliva (Schouten et al., 1988a, 1988b).

1985-1991: The Adult Period

Following the adult period (1985-1991), we took mostly the same measurements as in 1985, with the exception of urine and saliva sampling. Measurements were taken in February to June, 1991. Also, for the first time measurement of bone mineral density was done, using dual X-ray absorptiometry of the lumber spine region (L2-L4). This measurement took place in the Academic Hospital of Vrije Universiteit, Department of Nuclear Medicine.

Dropout Rate

Adolescent Period

A longitudinal group was selected from one school in Amsterdam (Pius X Lyceum; since 1985 known as Katholiek College Amsterdam) and started in 1977 with 307 pupils, among whom 233 completed the first 4 years of the study (131 girls and 102 boys).

One of the serious drawbacks of longitudinal studies is the number of subjects lost in time from the original sample. In the first 4 years of the study the main reason for withdrawal was leaving school, especially between the first and second years of measurements. The total dropout percentage in the longitudinal group between 1977 and 1980 was 24.1% (girls, 17.6%; boys, 31.1%) (Kemper et al., 1985). Because of the possibility of selective dropout, the dropout group was compared to the group that stayed in the study for 4 years. Virtually no dropout effects were found in anthropometric, physiological, and nutritional variables. Striking differences were found in both girls and boys in their popularity (as a homework partner): Female and male dropouts were regarded significantly less popular than those who stayed in the study (Snel & Ritmeester, 1985).

From 1977 to 1980 a second school, located at some distance from Amsterdam (Ignatius College, in Purmerend), acted as a control school. A similar population, 292 pupils (159 girls and 133 boys), was selected, but during the first 4 years of the study measurements were made of a randomly selected sample, a different 25% of the population, each year. Thus, after 4 years all the pupils had been measured on only one occasion. These control data were used to detect test effects caused by repeated testing in the longitudinal sample (Kemper, 1985).

Young-Adult Period

In 1985, 200 subjects (107 females and 93 males) from the original sample were remeasured. This represents a dropout rate of 14% with considerably more females (18.4%) than males (8.8%) leaving (Table 2.1). To ensure that the dropouts did not represent a selective group of the total sample, a comparison was made between the dropouts and the group that remained. This comparison was based on the measurements from the first year of the study. No dropout effects could be demonstrated in relation to anthropometric variables, maximal oxygen uptake, habitual physical activity, and nutrition. The mean age of the dropouts (21.7 ± 0.8 years) was comparable with that of the longitudinal group (21.5 ± 0.8 years) (Kemper & van Aalst, 1987).

Table 2.1 Number of Longitudinal Participants and Dropouts Over the Years of Measurement

Year of measurement	Females		Males		Total	
	n	%	n	%	n	%
1977	159		148		307	
1980	131		102		233	
Dropouts	28	17.6	46	31.1	74	24.1
1985	107		93		200	
Dropouts	24	18.4	9	8.8	33	14.1
1991	98		84		182	
Dropouts	9	8.4	9	9.7	18	9.0
1977-1991						
Dropouts	61	38.4	64	43.2	125	40.7

The possibility of selective dropout was further examined by asking the 33 subjects who did not come for measurements at the laboratory to fill in a questionnaire concerning biographical and anthropometric characteristics; 79% (26 subjects) returned a completed questionnaire. Table 2.2 indicates that females in both groups did not differ in anthropometric variables. The mean height of the males that dropped out is somewhat higher, but their body mass index (weight per height squared), as a measure of fatness, is the same. In females the body mass index is slightly lower.

A difference was found in the percentage of those who were studying or had a paying job (Table 2.3). The dropouts had more paying jobs (77.5% vs. 61.5%) and consequently were less involved in studies (38.5% vs. 62.5%). This may be the explanation why dropouts claimed to have no time to participate

Table 2.2   Means and Standard Deviations of Three Anthropometric Characteristics of the Longitudinal Group and the Dropouts in 1985

		Longitudinal group	Dropout group
Height (cm)	Females	170 ± 6	170 ± 6
	Males	183 ± 6	189 ± 5
Weight (kg)	Females	62.5 ± 9	61 ± 9
	Males	71.5 ± 9	73 ± 7
Body mass index (kg/m²)	Females	18.3 ± 0.2	18.0 ± 0.5
	Males	19.5 ± 0.2	19.5 ± 0.7

Table 2.3   Distribution of Some Biographical Characteristics of the Longitudinal Group and the Dropout Group in 1985

		Longitudinal group (%)	Dropout group (%)
Marital status	Single	71	85
	Married	4	4
	Living together	18	12
	Other	6	0
Housing	Single	17	23
	With parents	54	42
Education	Secondary school	90	91
Study	Present	62	38
Employment	Paid	62	77
	Unpaid	6	4

in the study (50% said "no time," 27% said "no interest") (Kemper & van Aalst, 1987).

Adult Period

In 1991 we were able to measure 182 subjects (98 females and 84 males) of the original sample. Since the measurement in 1985, this accounted for a dropout rate of 9% (8.4% of females and 9.7% of males). (See Table 2.1 for a summary of the dropout rates over the six measurements.)

Calendar Age of the Subjects

All pupils included in the study were in the first 2 years of the secondary school. In 1977 the age range of the subjects was 12 to 15 years. The mean calendar age in 1991 was 27.1 ($\pm$0.8) years. The distribution of calendar age in the population over the years is shown in Table 2.4.

Health Status of the Subjects

Adolescent Period

Before the study started in 1977, all the subjects were given a medical examination. This examination had two purposes: to determine the level of health and

Table 2.4   Number of Females and Males in the Different Age Groups of the Study Population in 1977, 1985, and 1991

Year of measurement	Age (y)	Females	Males	Total
1977	12	31	26	57
	13	68	48	116
	14	31	24	55
	15	1	4	5
Total		131	102	233
1985	20	24	23	47
	21	56	45	101
	22	26	21	47
	23	1	4	5
Total		107	93	200
1991	26	21	19	40
	27	50	40	90
	28	26	21	47
	29	1	4	5
Total		98	84	182

to judge whether a maximal stress test on a treadmill could be made. Each pupil was classified as good, doubtful, or bad for 28 medical criteria (Kemper et al., 1985). In general, the percentages of pupils scoring in bad and doubtful were very small, and no subject was rejected as medically unfit. During the study, when a health risk indicator was found, the school physician was informed.

Young-Adult Period

In 1985 information was gathered about subjects' consultation of public health services and frequency of the use of medications. A general practitioner was consulted most often, but significantly more by the women (36%) than the men (20%). Some 63% of the women were using a preservative. A consultation with a medical specialist was found in 16% of the women and 12% of the men. Nonprescription medication was being used in 32% of the women and 20% of the men, while prescription medication was being used by 10% of the women and 7% of the men. Compared to the total population of the Netherlands, a significant difference was found only for the nonprescription medication. No differences could be demonstrated in frequency of consultations in relation to general practitioners and specialists.

Adult Period

In 1991, 40% of the women and 26% of the men had consulted a general practitioner during the 2 months prior to questioning, while 17% of the females and 19% of the males visited a specialist. The use of nonprescription medicines was found in 37% of the women and in 17% of the men, while 26% of the women and 17% of the men were using prescription medication. Preservative medication was used by 60% of the women. In Table 2.5 the data from 1985 and 1991 are compared. Overall, an increase in medical consumption was demonstrated in 1991.

Table 2.5 Percentages of Participants Using the Most Important Public Health Services

Health service	Females		Males	
	1985 ($n = 107$)	1991 ($n = 98$)	1985 ($n = 93$)	1991 ($n = 84$)
General practitioner (in last 2 months)	36	40	20	26
Specialist (in last 2 months)	16	17	12	19
Prescription medication (in last 2 weeks)	10	26	7	17
Nonprescription medication (in last 2 weeks)	32	37	20	17
Preservative	63	60		

Socioeconomic Status

Adolescent Period

The socioeconomic background of the subjects was ascertained at the beginning of the study (1977) by means of a questionnaire to parents. As regards profession, education, and income the parents of children at both schools were above the average compared with the total Dutch population at that time (Kemper et al., 1985).

Young-Adult Period

Using a questionnaire, the socioeconomic background of the study population in 1985 was examined. Of the total population, 71% were living on their own, 4% were married, and 25% were living with some other person. Four percent of women and 16% of men had not finished advanced elementary education; 95% of the women and 82% of the men had finished their higher educational/ preuniversity schooling. Fifty percent of the females and 77% of the males were pursuing a higher vocational education or studies at university, while, respectively, 73% and 48% also had a paying job.

Adult Period

In 1991 the subjects again filled out a questionnaire about their education level, profession, and income.

Education Level

Table 2.6 shows the school education finished following primary school of the 182 subjects in the study in 1991. Two percent of the women and 5% of the

Table 2.6   Highest Level of Secondary School Education Finished (After Primary School) by the Study Population by 1991

Level	Females		Males		Total
	n	%	n	%	n
None	2	2	4	5	6
Lower vocational school (LBO)	—	—	1	1	1
Intermediate secondary school (MAVO)	—	—	2	2	2
Higher secondary school (HAVO)	40	41	18	21	58
Highest secondary school (preuniversity) (VWO)	52	53	47	56	99
Unknown	4	4	12	14	16
Total	98		84		182

Note. Acronyms are for the Dutch terms for the schools.

men had not finished their secondary schooling, whereas 86.3% of the population had finished their HAVO or VWO school, the school they started with in 1977. After secondary school, 64% of the women and 61% of the men had finished a follow-up vocational course, whereas 31% of the women and 44% of the men had a polytechnical or university level education; see Table 2.7. In 1991 35% of the women and 33% of the men were pursuing courses, but full time in only about 7% of both sexes.

Profession and Income

Table 2.8 shows that the proportion of women in 1991 with full-time jobs was 54%, and 24% had part-time jobs; 21% had no paying jobs (21 cases, of whom 7 were pursuing full-time studies). Among men, 75% had a full-time job, 12% a part-time job; 13% had no paying jobs (11 men, 4 of whom were pursuing full-time studies). Two percent of the women and 6% of the men lived on government relief.

Marital Status

In 1991 more women, 74%, than men, 57%, were living together with a partner (30% of the women and 17% of the men were married). In 1991, 4 out of 98 women (4%) were pregnant; 21% had had at least one child.

Table 2.7   Postsecondary School Finished by the Study Population by 1991

	Females		Males		Total
Level	n	%	n	%	n
Intermediate vocational education (MBO)	18	18	10	12	28
Polytechnical education (HBO)	21	21	24	29	45
University (WO)	9	9	13	16	22
Course	5	5	4	5	9
Total	53		51		104

Note. Acronyms are for the Dutch terms for the schools.

Table 2.8   Percentages of the Study Population Involved in Jobs and Education

	Job		Education	
	Full time	Part time	Full time	Part time
Females	54	24	8	28
Males	75	12	7	25

Maximizing Adherence

In order to motivate the subjects to adhere to the longitudinal study, we took special measures in the different periods.

Adolescent Period

The administration of the participating schools permitted us to perform measurements during regular school hours. Therefore, classrooms and the gymnasium were used, and our Mobile Research Unit was parked in front of the school.

For parents and pupils a 20-minute 16-mm color movie was made to explain the aims of the study (Busken & van Gijzel, 1976). Each year a small report was made in language understandable to pupils of the ages in question, focusing on the several measurements and containing practical suggestions on such items as estimation of adult height and percentage of body fat. After the maximal exercise tests, a photograph was given to each student; another year a T-shirt with the project logo (Fig. 2.2) was presented. To express our appreciation for their participation in the study, all girls and boys of both schools were invited to a dinner on board a boat in the harbor and canals of Amsterdam, at the end of the four annual measurements in 1980.

In 1982 a 300-page book was finished (Kemper et al., 1982a), written for the subjects to report to them the general results of the total study in understandable language. Separately, they received a special report of their own results, indicated

Figure 2.2   A stimulation reward of the longitudinal study: T-shirt with the project logo.

with graphs and tables (Kemper, 1981). Parents and pupils, together with professionals in different fields, were invited to attend a presentation of the results by the investigators. These presentations were recorded on video (Kemper et al., 1982b).

Young-Adult and Adult Periods

After the decision to continue the longitudinal measurements in 1985 and 1991, the problem was tracing all the participants and to motivate them to come to our university laboratory in Amsterdam from all over the Netherlands. (Two participants, living in Switzerland and Spain, even agreed to come when they were on holiday in the Netherlands.) To optimize participation, all the measurements for a given subject were scheduled in a single day, starting at 8:30 a.m. and lasting until 5:00 p.m. Measurements were taken all days of the week, except Sundays. The participants were offered free drinks and lunch, and free travel costs, and they received an honorarium for their effort. In 1986 and 1992 the subjects received a personal report of their own results compared to the mean values and the sex- and age-specific norms of the whole longitudinal group.

References

Busken J.M. van den, B. van Gijzel. (1976). How healthy is growth? [Film]. Universiteit van Amsterdam, C.A.V.D.

Kemper H.C.G. (ed.). (1981). [Growth and health of teenagers]. Unpublished manuscript, Universiteit van Amsterdam.

Kemper H.C.G. (ed.). (1985). Growth, health and fitness of teenagers: Longitudinal research in international perspective. Vol. 20 of: Medicine and sport science. Karger, Basel.

Kemper H.C.G., R. van Aalst. (1987). Characteristics of the subjects that dropped out in 1985. In: Van Tiener tot Volwassene. Unpublished manuscript, Universiteit van Amsterdam and Vrije Universiteit, Amsterdam.

Kemper H.C.G., C. van der Bom, H. Dekker, G. Ootjers, G.B. Post, J. Snel, P.G. Splinter, L. Storm-van Essen, R. Verschuur. (1982a). Growth and health of teenagers: Results of a four year investigation. De Vrieseborch, Haarlem.

Kemper H.C.G., H. Dekker, G. Ootjers, G.B. Post, J.W. Ritmeester, J. Snel, P.G. Splinter, L. Storm-van Essen, R. Verschuur. (1983). Growth and health of teenagers: A multiple longitudinal study in Amsterdam, the Netherlands. Universiteit van Amsterdam.

Kemper H.C.G., J. Snel, R. Verschuur, W. Schouten, G.B. Post, L. Storm-van Essen, R. van Aalst, L. de Mey, A. van Zundert. (1987). [From teenager to adult: Health and lifestyle in longitudinal perspective]. Unpublished manuscript, Universiteit van Amsterdam and Vrije Universiteit, Amsterdam.

Kemper H.C.G., L. Storm-van Essen, P.G. Splinter. (1985). Procedures and subjects. In: H.C.G. Kemper (ed.), Growth, health and fitness of teenagers: Longitudinal research in international perspective. Vol. 20 of: Medicine and Sport Science. Karger, Basel.

Kemper H.C.G., R. Verschuur, G.B. Post, J. Snel, P.G. Splinter, L. Storm-van Essen. (1982b). Growth and health of teenagers [Videotape (VHS)]. Universiteit van Amsterdam, C.A.V.D.

Schouten W.J., R. Verschuur, H.C.G. Kemper. Habitual physical activity, strenuous excercise and salivary immunoglobulin A levels in young adults: The Amsterdam Growth and Health Study. Int J Sports Med 9 (1988a) 289-293.

Schouten W.J., R. Verschuur, H.C.G. Kemper. Physical activity and upper respiratory tract infections in a normal population of young men and women: The Amsterdam Growth and Health Study. Int J Sports Med 9 (1988b) 451-455.

Snel J., J.W. Ritmeester. (1985). Sociometric status. In: H.C.G. Kemper (ed.), Growth, health and fitness of teenagers: Longitudinal research in international perspective. Vol. 20 of: Medicine and sport science. Karger, Basel.

Chapter 3

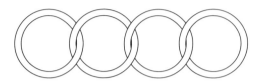

Methods of Measurements Used in the Longitudinal Study

Han C.G. Kemper & Willem van Mechelen

The measurement methods included in this longitudinal study are summarized in this chapter to give a general overview of what we measured in the subjects during the course of the whole investigation and when measurements were made. The measurements can be divided into five general categories:

- Physical measurements of body build, body growth, and body composition
- Physiological measurements of functional and performance characteristics
- Psychological measurements of personality traits
- Lifestyle measurements, concerning dietary habits, habitual physical activity, psychosocial behavior, and stress
- Health measurements, concerning both physical and mental aspects

Table 3.1 provides an overview of measurements taken during the three time periods of measurement. Although the main goal of a longitudinal study is to take all measurements at all stages, this was not always possible. Sometimes the measurements were not feasible, applicable, or useful; thus, new measurements were introduced in several situations and others deleted:

- In 1985 (the fifth measurement period), the population reached young adulthood (age 21), and several measurements used during the adolescent period were not useful or relevant. This was the case regarding skeletal age when full maturity was reached.

- During the adolescent period all subjects were measured at school on several occasions spread out over the school year, whereas at ages 21 and 27 the subjects came in small groups (6 subjects) for one whole day to our laboratory. Therefore, it was not feasible to monitor their physical activity with pedometers and heart rate integrators.

**Table 3.1   Overview of the Methods Used in
the Amsterdam Growth and Health Study at the Different Times of Measurement**

	Years of measurement		
	1977-1980 Age (yr) 13-17	1985 Age (yr) 21	1991 Age (yr) 27
Physical measurements			
Anthropometrics	x	x	x
Waist : hip ratio	—	—	x
Skeletal age	x	—	—
Forward/backward bending of spine	x	—	—
Dual X-ray of lumbar spine	—	—	x
Physiological measurements			
Motor performance tests	x	x	x
12-minute endurance run	x	—	—
Treadmill test	x	x	x
Isokinetic leg force	—	x	x
Lung function	x	x	x
Blood pressure	x	x	x
Blood analyses	x	x	x
Stimulant drugs in urine	—	x	—
Immunoglobulin in saliva	—	x	—
Psychological measurements			
Personality traits	x(y)	x(a)	x(a)
Sociometrics	x	—	—
Lifestyle measurements			
Habitual food intake			
Dietary history interview	x	x	x
Smoking, alcohol	x	x	x
Habitual physical activity			
Activity interview	x	x	x
Pedometers	x	—	—
Heart rate	x	—	—
Sports injuries	—	—	x
Psychosocial behavior/stress	—	x	x
Health measurements			
Physical health			
Back pain	x	x	x
Health questionnaire	—	x	x
Mental health			
Health complaints	—	x	x
Sleep/waking problems	—	x	x

Note. x = measurement done; (y) and (a) refer to youth and adult versions of the
measurement instrument.

• Some questionnaires measuring personality traits have different versions for different age groups. This was the case in the Achievement Motivation Test (AMT) and the Dutch Personality Inventory (DPI), which have youth versions, for ages 12 to 18, and adult versions for age 18 on. After the first four measurements, we had to change to the adult versions (see Table 3.1).

• One final reason to include extra measurements was that new technology enabled us to perform measurements on the population that were not available at the start of the study. This occurred with the dual X-ray measurements of bone mineral density in the lumbar spine.

Physical Measurements

Anthropometrics

The anthropometric measurements followed the guidelines of the International Biological Program (IBP) (Weiner & Lourie, 1968).

Height and Weight

• Standing and sitting height were measured with a Harpenden digital readout, wall-mounted or portable stadiometer (Holtain, UK; van Rietschoten & Houwens, the Netherlands).

• Body weight was measured with a spring balance (van Vucht, the Netherlands)

• The body mass index is the weight divided by standing height squared.

• During the adolescent period, height and weight were measured three times per year (every 4 months) in order to calculate height and weight velocity (Kemper et al., 1984, 1985).

Bone Diameter

• Biacromial and bi-iliacristal diameters were measured using a sliding caliper with widened jaws (Mauser, Germany; van Rietschoten & Houwens, the Netherlands).

Skinfold Thickness

• Bicipital, tricipital, subscapular, and suprailiacal skinfolds were measured with a Harpenden skinfold caliper (Holtain, UK; van Rietschoten & Houwens, the Netherlands).

Circumference

• Upper arm, thigh, and calf circumferences were measured with a flexible steel tape (Martin circumeter, Franken & Itallie, the Netherlands).

• The fat-corrected upper-arm diameter was calculated from upper-arm circumference and bicipital and tricipital skinfolds (Novak, 1963).

During the adolescent period five extra circumferences and three skinfolds of the upper and lower leg were added to calculate the total and lean leg volume (according to Jones and Pearson, 1970). Fat mass as a percentage of body weight and lean body mass was calculated from the sum of the four skinfold thicknesses (according to Durnin and Rahaman, 1967), but at ages 21 and 27 it was calculated according to the regression equation from Durnin and Womersly (1974). In order to make comparisons over the 15-year period we used the sum of four skinfolds.

At age 27 two additional circumferences were included: torso (at nipple height) and hip. The torso- to hip-circumference ratio was used as a measure of fat distribution (Garn, 1957).

The anthropometric variables were limited to the left side of the body, and the subjects were barefooted and clothed in gym shorts and shirt.

Skeletal Age

During the adolescent period only, biological age was determined by measuring skeletal age from X-rays of the left hand, according to the Tanner-Whitehouse II method. Ratings of 20 bones of the hand and wrist were assigned by comparing the ossification stage of each bone with plates, diagrams, and a description of the bone in question (Tanner et al., 1975). Using X-ray apparatus (Utilis 15/18; Enraf-Nonius, the Netherlands), photographs were taken of the hand with the palm facing downward. To restrict the radiation to the subject's left hand, a wooden box was used, covered on the inside with lead. The entrance for the hand at the base of the box was covered by flexible lead-filled rubber. The X-ray tube at the top of the box was centered at a distance of 80 cm above the hand, which rested on double-wrapped film (Osray T-4; Agfa-Gevaert). Exposure time varied from 0.3 to 0.5 s, with a tube voltage of 53 kV, thus restricting the local radiation to less than 30 mR. All X-rays were rated by the same examiner, who was previously trained in the Tanner-Whitehouse II method at the Institute of Child Health, University of London. The X-rays were made in each of the four adolescent years but discontinued thereafter as soon as full maturity was reached (in boys at skeletal age 18 and in girls at skeletal age 16) (Kemper et al., 1987b).

Forward/Backward Curvature of the Thoracolumbar Spine

During adolescence four annual measurements were made of thoracic kyphosis and lumbar lordosis of the spine. Because these forward and backward curvatures are hidden behind the shoulder blades and back muscles and X-rays of the trunk could not be used from an ethical point of view in this healthy population, an optical method was used. This method was developed by Snijders (1971) and reconstructed by Aarts and Janssen (1976). A mathematical approach calculated the curve of the spine (Seroo et al., 1982).

Bone Mineral Content of the Lumbar Spine

At the age of 27 years in all subjects, the bone mineral content and bone mineral density of the lumbar region (L2, L3, and L4) were measured by dual X-ray absorptiometry using the Norland XR-26. The scanning was performed in the Department of Nuclear Medicine, Academic Hospital of Vrije Universiteit, Amsterdam, while the subject was recumbent. A photomultiplier tube recorded transmission from a narrowly collimated X-ray source located under the scanning table. The whole procedure was finished within 10 to 15 minutes.

Physiological Measurements

The physiological measurements can be divided into motor performance fitness tests and measurement of maximal aerobic power, maximal isokinetic muscle power, blood pressure, and lung function.

Motor Performance Fitness Tests

In the Netherlands from 1975 to 1981 a Motor Performance (MOPER) Fitness Test battery was developed (Kemper et al., 1979), and reference scales were constructed for boys and girls aged 9 to 18 years (Bovend'eerdt et al., 1980; Leyten et al., 1982). The MOPER Fitness Test consists of eight test items that have been selected to represent the more important measurable aspects of physical fitness. In this test battery, four strength tests, two speed tests, one flexibility test, and one test for aerobic endurance were included:

Strength Measurements
> *Arm pull*—maximal pull (in kilograms) with the subject's "best" arm, measured by a dynamometer (Bettendorff, Belgium)
> *Standing high jump*—maximal jumping height (in centimeters), measured with jump board, measuring tape, and girdle (belt)
> *10 leg lifts*—the time (in seconds) to lift the legs 10 times from horizontal to vertical position with extended knees
> *Flexed-arm hang*—maximal time (in seconds) that the subject's eyes stay above a horizontal bar

Speed Measurements
> *10 x 5-m sprint*—time (in seconds) to run 10 times between two lines 5 m apart
> *Plate tapping*—time (in seconds) to tap 50 times with the subject's "best" hand between two plates 75 cm apart

Flexibility Measurement
> *Sit-and-reach*—maximal reach (in centimeters) in sitting position with the legs fully stretched

Measurement of Aerobic Endurance
> *12-minute endurance run*—maximal distance covered on a 150-m track in 12 minutes

All tests were performed according to the instructions in the manual (Bovend'eerdt et al., 1980), using standard equipment (Jansen & Fritsen, the

Netherlands). The first seven tests were measured indoors by trained experimenters. The 12-minute endurance run was measured only during the adolescent period by a physical education teacher outdoors in the school yard.

Maximal Aerobic Power and Maximal Isokinetic Muscle Power

Maximal aerobic power—the maximal rate of delivery of oxygen by the cardiovascular and respiratory system and utilization by the skeletal muscles—was measured by a direct method using a standard running test. Running took place on a treadmill (Quinton, model 18-54, the Netherlands) in our Mobile Research Unit. The subjects were asked not to eat for 1.5 hours prior to testing. The oxygen uptake ($\dot{V}O_2$) of each subject was measured during the treadmill test, and the maximal oxygen uptake ($\dot{V}O_2max$) was used as the criterion for maximal aerobic power.

Treadmill Running

We used a procedure with a submaximal test preceding a maximal test, slightly modified after the method of Bar-Or and Zwiren (1975). The submaximal test consisted of three 2-minute runs at a constant speed of 8 km/h, with slopes of 0%, 2.5%, and 5% (in that order). During practice for this submaximal test, the subjects got accustomed to running on a treadmill and got acquainted with the mouthpiece plus noseclip; at the same time, they were warming up. After a short period of rest (10-15 minutes) running was continued on the treadmill at the same constant speed of 8 km/h. In this maximal test the slope was increased every 2 minutes by 2.5% or 5%, depending on the heart rate of the subject. Heart rate, minute ventilation, and $\dot{V}O_2$ were measured continuously. This maximal test was continued until complete exhaustion had been reached. Each subject was encouraged verbally to exercise to his or her maximum. The maximal slope was the mean slope reached in the last 2 minutes of running.

Cardiovascular Measurements

Heart rate was monitored telemetrically (Telecust 36, Siemens, the Netherlands) before the test at rest (sitting on a chair) and throughout the test using chest electrodes in conjunction with an oscilloscope, cardiotachometer, and electrocardiographic pen recorder (Sirecust BS 1, Siemens, the Netherlands). Heart rate was calculated as the mean from 15 R-R intervals in the last 15 seconds of the minute. We selected the mean heart rate in the last minute of each 2-minute period of the submaximal test at slope 0%, 2.5%, and 5%, and the maximal heart rate (beats per minute) as that reached during the treadmill test.

Ventilation Measurements

Expired air was measured by a 10-L high-speed, low-resistance dry-gas meter (Parkinson Cowan CD4, Instrumentation Associates, New York) via a two-way low-resistance breathing valve with a dead air space of 35 ml (Terpoorten; Coronel Laboratory, the Netherlands). We selected the following from the last full minute of the maximal treadmill test:

- Respiratory rate (f_R), measured as the total number of expirations per minute
- Ventilation volume ($\dot{V}_E$), measured in liters per minute and corrected for body temperature and barometric pressure saturated
- Tidal volume (TV), calculated from the ratio of ventilation volume to maximal respiratory rate

Oxygen Uptake and Carbon Dioxide Production Measurements

$\dot{V}O_2$ was measured each minute throughout the test, using the open-circuit method. Samples of mixed expired air were continuously withdrawn from the gas meter, dried by tampons (Amira-extra), and analyzed for the fractional concentration of oxygen in expired gas (F_{EO_2}) by a paramagnetic oxygen analyzer (Servomex) and for carbon dioxide (F_{ECO_2}) by an infrared carbon dioxide analyzer (Mijnhardt BV). The gas meter, two gas analyzers and a number of electronic calculators were incorporated into a movable 19-in. unit called an Ergoanalyzer (Mijnhardt BV, the Netherlands). The Ergoanalyzer continuously and automatically analyzed the collected expired air and printed the calculated $\dot{V}O_2$, standardized for temperature, humidity, and barometric pressure (STPD).

Measurement of the $\dot{V}O_2$ with the Ergoanalyzer has proven to be comparable to the classical method of collecting expired air in Douglas Bags and analyzing carbon dioxide and oxygen content with the Scholander technique (Kemper et al., 1976). Both analyzers were calibrated daily using gases (Air Liquide), controlled by the Scholander technique. We selected the following:

- Oxygen fraction (difference between inspiratory and expiratory air) (F_{IO_2}-F_{EO_2})
- Carbon dioxide fraction (F_{ECO_2})
- Respiratory gas exchange ratio (R)
- $\dot{V}O_2$max at STPD, using the equation of Hurzeler et al. (1972) and corrected for STPD conditions (Kemper & Verschuur, 1980)

Maximal Isokinetic Torque

Since 1985 the maximal isokinetic torque of knee flexion and knee extension in both legs was measured at four speeds (30°, 60°, 180°, and 300°/second). The measurements were performed on a Cybex II isokinetic dynamometer (Lumex, New York; Lameris, the Netherlands). The subjects were fixed and stabilized on the Cybex chair with girdles at the pelvis, upper leg, and trunk. The sequence of the testing was at random for left and right legs and for each of the four velocities. Before each test a warm-up of at least 1 minute was provided at the specific extension/flexion velocity. Each test consisted of four trials at the same velocity in which the subject continuously applied to the lever arm of the instrument a maximal torque from flexion (lower leg in 90° flexion) to extension (lower leg in 180° extension). The highest value of the four trials was selected. The peak torque (in Newton-meters) and the hamstrings:quadriceps ratio for each leg and each speed were calculated (Velzen & Kemper, 1988).

Blood Pressure and Lung Function

Blood pressure was measured at rest prior to the treadmill test. No attempt was made to obtain basal conditions. Blood pressure was measured using an indirect method. The subject was seated in a chair, and a standard pressure cuff (12 cm) was placed around the left upper arm. With a sphygmomanometer (Speidl-Keller No. 2010; Franken & Itallie, the Netherlands), systolic and diastolic pressures (phase V) in the arteria brachialis were measured. These pressures were measured twice and the lower values were recorded, systolic blood pressure in kilopascals and diastolic blood pressure in kilopascals and millimeters of mercury.

A lung function test was carried out using an electronic spirometer (Monaghan 403, Medicare; Vica test, Mijnhardt B.V., the Netherlands). The subject, wearing a noseclip, was asked, following a maximal inspiration, to complete an expiration as fast as possible in a mouthpiece and sustain it for 6 seconds. The best of three correct attempts was used for analysis.

- Vital capacity (VC) measured in liters per minute
- Forced expiratory volume in 1 second (FEV_1) in liters per minute
- Maximal expiratory flow (peak flow)
- FEV_1 divided by VC and expressed in a percentage ($FEV_\%$)

Analyses of Blood, Urine, and Saliva

For the determination of cholesterol in blood from each subject, approximately 10 ml of venous blood was taken from the vena antecubitus with a vacutainer. Blood sampling and serum preparations were done between 8:30 a.m. and 12:30 a.m. with subjects in a nonfasting state. Analyses were carried out in the Department of Human Nutrition of the Agricultural University in Wageningen. External quality control took place with samples from a World Health Organization (WHO) reference laboratory (Lipid Standardization Laboratory, USA). The following information was obtained:

- Total cholesterol (TC), analyzed according to Huang et al. (1961) and Abell et al. (1952) in mmol/L
- High-density lipoprotein (HDL) cholesterol fraction, analyzed according to Burnstein and Samaille (1960)
- TC:HDL-cholesterol ratio in blood

At the young-adult age, triglycerides and the very low density lipoprotein (VLDL) cholesterol fraction were determined in the venous blood, as was the stress hormone cortisol.

The urine concentration of catecholamines was measured. The Jellinek Centre (Amsterdam) inspected the urine samples on drugs—opiates, amphetamines, barbiturates, methadone, metabolites of cocaine, methaqualon, benzodiazepines, and cannabinoides (Kemper et al., 1987a).

The salivary concentration of immunoglobulin A (Mancini, 1965) was measured before and after a maximal running test in order to investigate the relation between physical stress and upper respiratory tract infections (Schouten et al., 1988a and 1988b).

Psychological Measurements

Measurement of Personality Traits

The Dutch Personality Inventory, youth version (DPI-y) (Bücking et al., 1975), was employed. It measures the following:

- Inadequacy (28 items)—feelings of malfunctioning, anxiety, vague physical complaints, depression
- Social Inadequacy (13 items)—neurotic shyness, uncomfortable feelings in social situations, avoidance of unfamiliar people and situations
- Rigidity (25 items)—the need for regularity, having fixed habits and principles, sense of duty, positive task appraisal
- Self-Sufficiency (24 items)—mistrust of others, desire to solve problems alone
- Dominance (15 items)—self-reliance, trying to be the boss

The DPI-y was derived from the adult version of the DPI (Luteijn, 1974), which contains two additional scales. Bücking et al. (1975) experienced difficulties in the construction of the Dominance scale. The construct validity of the Inadequacy, Social Inadequacy, and Rigidity scales was supported, although Luteijn et al. (1981) and van Dijk and Luteijn (1982) mentioned that the rigidity concept in adults and children has a different content; they therefore suggested the term *Perseverance* for the scale in the youth version with this additional description: ''well adapted to work demands, keeping appointments.'' The validity of the Self-Sufficiency scale received only minimal support; the authors proposed *Recalcitrance* as a new name for this scale. The Dominance scale received no support whatsoever on construct validity.

The Achievement Motivation Test for children (AMT-y) (Hermans, 1971) was also employed. It measures the following:

- Achievement Motivation (33 items)—the need to achieve and the will to make achievements
- Debilitating Anxiety (15 items)—a fear of failure, leading to lower achievements, especially in unstructured task situations
- Facilitating Anxiety (17 items)—a fear of failure, leading to higher achievements, especially in unstructured task situations
- Social Desirability (16 items)—a tendency to give the most socially acceptable answers

With the exception of the Social Desirability scale, the construct validities were satisfactory (Hermans, 1971).

Both inventories were taken each year in the classroom during regular school hours, with one teacher and one or two testers present. In the fifth and in some classes of the fourth form, the school classes were regrouped to this aim, since classes at this school level contained both pupils from the subject and nonsubject groups. To prevent sequence effects, the inventories were presented in random order among the classes during the years of investigation.

Because of the subjects' ages at the fifth (21 years) and sixth (27 years) measurements, the youth version of the two inventories could not be used and the adult versions of the DPI (Luteijn et al., 1985), and the AMT (Hermans, 1976) were used (see Table 3.1). The adult inventories were completed by each subject on the day when they visited the laboratory for testing activities.

Sociometric Status

In the adolescent period another inventory was used to measure sociometric status—the Amsterdam Sociometric Scale, a modified version of the Syracuse-Amsterdam-Groningen Scale of Gardner and Thompson (Defares et al., 1968). All pupils were asked to rate each of their classmates on a five-point scale in terms of (a) how much they liked to cooperate on doing homework or work at school with each classmate and (b) how much they liked to accept each classmate on a school sports team. To take into account the individual's sociometric status of ratings from popular and unpopular pupils and of direct and indirect ratings, the Katz (1960) Status Index was used.

Lifestyle Measurements

Habitual Food Intake

The adolescent and young-adult periods are life stages in which the intake of energy and nutrients appears to be of special importance for realizing full growth potential and influencing the state of health of the developing child. Therefore, we considered it necessary within the scope of this study to be informed about the quantitative and qualitative aspects of food habits of the subjects.

Method

It is very difficult to collect data about individual food habits of adolescents and young adults, since they themselves are not quite aware of their eating and drinking habits. Therefore, we had to look for a special approach for accurately determining the normal daily diet of the subjects. The most important requirements in choosing a suitable method were that (a) the technique should not interfere with the subject's dietary habits, (b) the data collected should be representative of the true intake, and (c) the technique should be applicable in field investigations with large groups of normal teenagers.

On the basis of a pilot study we decided to choose the cross-check dietary history interview for the determination of dietary habits (Post and Kemper, 1980). A modification of the cross-check dietary history interview (Beal, 1967; Marr, 1971) was used to ascertain the individual food intake of the teenagers. The interview lists a series of items covering the entire range of food and drink, making allowance for teenagers. Data on foods eaten during regular meals as well as between-meal snacks were collected separately for normal school days and for weekend days. Only food items eaten at least twice monthly were recorded. The amounts were reported in household measures and dimensions. Models were used to illustrate common portion sizes (glasses, bowls, spoons, etc.) and also imitations of such foods as potatoes, apples, and other fruit. To estimate the amount of sugar in tea and coffee and of butter on bread, we used small scales to weigh the amounts (Post, 1989). The main items of the dietary history interview are summarized in Table 3.2. This interview took 60 to 90 minutes and was carried out during all years of measurements.

Parents' Dietary Questionnaire
Because it was assumed that adolescents do not know everything about their food consumption and how to prepare food, during the first four measurements we also developed a questionnaire for their parents concerning details of several food items consumed by their children—e.g., skimmed or whole milk, kind and quantity of meat, and addition of butter or sauce to vegetables and potatoes. An outline of the parents' dietary questionnaire is given in Table 3.3.

For each individual, all amounts were converted into grams for the 5 week-days and the 2 weekend days. The subjects in this study did not have a fixed pattern of meals. In the Netherlands, hot lunches are not served at school or at work. Most of the subjects brought sandwiches to school with them or bought snacks for lunch, and had a hot meal at home in the evening.

Coding
The coding and calculation of the food characteristics were based on the Dutch Food and Nutrition Table, known as the NEVO Table (1979). The following food characteristics were calculated:

- *Energy*—as kilocalories and kilojoules, and percentage obtained from carbohydrate, fat, protein, and alcohol
- *Protein*—vegetable origin (grams), animal origin, total of vegetable and animal (grams)
- *Fat*—polyunsaturated fatty acids (grams), total of saturated and polyunsaturated fatty acids (grams)
- *Carbohydrate*—mono- and disaccharides (grams); nondigestible polysaccharides (dietary fiber) (grams); total mono-, di-, and polysaccharides (grams)
- *Alcohol*—in grams
- *Minerals*—calcium (milligrams), iron (heme and nonheme, milligrams)
- *Vitamins*—thiamine (milligrams), per 1,000 kilocalories of energy (milligrams); riboflavin (milligrams); pyridoxine (milligrams), per gram of protein; ascorbic acid (milligrams)

Energy and nutrient value per mean day was calculated as follows:

$$\frac{(5 \times \text{weekday value}) + (2 \times \text{weekend value})}{7}$$

Table 3.2   Main Items of the Dietary History Interview

Questions covered
- Average number of times used during 5 weekdays
- Average number of times used during 2 weekend days

Questions concerned
1. Breakfast/lunch food items
   - Kind of bread
   - Kind of butter/margarine
   - Kind of sandwich filling (cheese, meat, egg, sweets)
   - Raw vegetable items
2. Cooked meal/dinner food items
   - Kind of soup
   - Kind of meat
   - Kinds of potatoes or substitutes
   - Kinds of vegetables/legumes; cooked or raw
   - Kinds of sauces
   - Meal substitutes like pancakes/fondue
3. Fruit
   - Kind of citrus fruit
   - Kind of other fruit; cooked or raw
4. Milk products/desserts
   - Kind of milk product
   - Kinds of additives (cereals, sugar, cream, sweet sauces)
5. Drinks
   - Kinds of drinks (milk, chocolate milk, coffee, tea)
   - Kinds of additives (cream, sugar)
   - Kinds of soft drinks/juices
   - Kinds of alcoholic drinks (with/without soft drink)
6. Pastries and sweets
   - Kinds of cookies/cakes
   - Kinds of sweets (chocolate, candy bars, licorice)
7. Snacks
   - Kinds of salty items (crackers, chips, cheese, nuts)
   - Kinds of snack bar items (french fries, sausages, rolls)
   - Kind of ice cream

Score: Mean amount (grams) of the 5 weekdays and the 2 weekend days.

Smoking and Alcohol Intake

Because it is evident that tobacco smoking and alcohol intake are health hazards, we gathered information about the development of the subjects' smoking and drinking habits. Subjects were asked during the dietary history interview whether and how much they smoked (cigarettes, pipe, cigars, and shag) or drank (alcohol), and, if so, how many cigarettes per day and how many alcoholic beverages per day they consumed.

Table 3.3   Main Items of the Parents' Dietary Questionnaire

Questions were directed to the parents, but concerned the food consumption of their child.

Questions covered
- Ingredients used
- Amount used (grams)
- Average number of times served in a week or month

Questions concerned
- Bread
- Fat used for bread/cooking
- Meat/fish/cheese as sandwich filling
- Soup
- Meat/fish/egg/cheese for dinner
- Stews
- Sauces/gravy/salad dressing
- Desserts
- Kind of milk (whole, low-fat, cream)

Habitual Physical Activity

The best indication of the level of physical activity is the energy expended during the activity. This energy is liberated by anaerobic and aerobic metabolic processes in the active muscle cells. The anaerobic processes play a role at the onset of any activity and dominate intensive activities of short duration. Over a period of 24 hours, however, the aerobic processes deliver approximately 98% of all the energy. In daily life situations only the measurement of the aerobic part of the energy expenditure is feasible. The assessment of habitual physical activity is usually undertaken to obtain a measurement of all daily activities and an estimate of the kind, intensity, duration, and frequency of the physical activities. Because of their pronounced health effects on the human body, a distinction was made between energy expenditure of these activities (metabolic equivalent) and the biomechanical load on the skeletal system (weight-bearing activities).

Selection of Measurements of Physical Activity

When selecting methods one must keep in mind that the measurements should (a) not interfere with the person's normal activity pattern and (b) obtain an estimate of the energy expenditure, which also reflects the intensity of the activity. To get an impression of the daily activity pattern, the measurements should ideally include

- school, work, and leisure-time activities and thereby be applicable for at least 24 hours;
- all days of the week, including weekends; and
- all seasons of the year (Edholm, 1966).

Also, in large group studies, such as this one, the method has to be simple, cheap, and time-efficient.

These requirements and the fact that we had to limit the extent of the activity measurements led us to the selection of three methods during the adolescent period:

- The 8-level heart rate integrator, which has proven to be a reliable and simple method of recording heart rate (Saris et al., 1977)
- The pedometer, which has been reduced in sensitivity (Verschuur and Kemper, 1980) to exclude measurement during walking and to give a reliable indication of energy expenditure during running
- A questionnaire/interview, aimed at tracing activities with a minimal energy expenditure of 4 times the basal metabolic rate (4 METs) over a period of 3 months prior to the interview

These three methods were applied in winter and spring, from January through May. Physical activities during two randomly selected weekdays (about 48 hours) were measured simultaneously with the heart rate integrator and the pedometer. After school hours, approximately 15 pupils came to our Mobile Research Unit, where electrodes, heart rate integrator, and pedometer were attached. Just before and after school hours, scores on both instruments were collected and the instruments checked. Thus, separate scores were collected for school and leisure-time activities. Because electrode attachment requires regular functional inspection, measurement of heart rate during the weekend without control did not seem meaningful. Therefore, only the pedometer was used to measure activities during the weekend, from Friday afternoon until Monday morning just before school started. The activity interview took place during the period of rest between the submaximal and maximal treadmill test, and lasted 10 to 15 minutes (Verschuur, 1987).

The Activity Interview

For practical reasons the activity interview was also given only at ages 21 and 27. This standardized activity interview was based on a questionnaire developed for this study and covered the 3 months prior to the interview. To classify activities according to their energy expenditure independent of body size (i.e., body weight), the ratio of work metabolic rate to basal metabolic rate was used (Lange Andersen et al., 1978).

The interview was limited to activities with a minimal intensity level of approximately 4 times the basal metabolic rate (4 METs), which is equivalent to walking at a speed of approximately 5 km/h. Below this level of intensity, physical activities will hardly contribute to a "reasonable" level of physical fitness (American College of Sports Medicine, 1978). The main items of this activity interview are summarized in Table 3.4.

The scored activities were subdivided into three levels of intensity—light, medium-heavy, and heavy activities—in accordance with the three highest activity levels used by the WHO (Lange Andersen et al., 1978). They correspond to a

Table 3.4   Main Items of the Activity Questionnaire/Interview

Activities in Relation to School or Work

I. Activities in relation to school or work

A. All transportation

Means: 1st and 2nd possible choice (walking, cycling, or public transport) and average number of times used
Active time per means (both ways)
Score = mean active transportation time in minutes per week (intensity = 1)

B. Physical education and extracurricular sport activity

Average active time per lesson
Obligatory number of lessons per week
Real number of lessons participated in
Real extracurricular activity
Score = mean active physical education or sport time in minutes per week (intensity = 2)

C. Work-related activities like walking, cycling, lifting, and stair climbing

Average active time per working day above minimum intensity
Score = mean activity plus active transportation time in minutes per week

II. Organized activities

A. Activities in sport clubs

Kind of sport club membership

1. Training (club 1; repeat in case of more memberships)
   Average active time per training
   Number of training sessions per week
   Real number of training sessions participated in
   Score = mean active training time in minutes per week (intensity = 1, 2, or 3)
2. Matches (club 1; repeat in case of more memberships)
   Average active playing time per match
   Number of matches per week
   Real number of matches participated in
   Score = mean active playing time in minutes per week (intensity = 1, 2, or 3)
3. Transportation
   Score = mean active transportation time in minutes per week of all organized sports activities (intensity = 1)

B. Activities in other clubs

Kind of membership
Average active time per meeting above minimum intensity (club 1)
Real number of meetings participated in
Score = mean activity plus active transportation time in minutes per week (intensity = 1)

Activities in Relation to School or Work

III. Unorganized activities

   A. General leisure time activities (unorganized sports, gardening, etc.)

      Monday through Sunday: average active time in minutes per week (intensity = 1, 2, or 3; see Table 3.5)

      Score = mean active leisure time in minutes per week (intensity = 1, 2, or 3; see Table 3.5)

   B. Activities in jobs (housekeeping, shopping, voluntary work)

      Kind of job

      Average active time per working day above minimum intensity

      Score = mean activity plus active transportation time in minutes per week (intensity = 1)

Note. A classification list of intensity Levels 1, 2, and 3 is given in Table 3.5.

relative energy expenditure of 4 to 7 METs for light physical activities, 7 to 10 METs for medium-heavy activities, and 10 METs or more for heavy activities. This classification was based on data from the literature (Bink et al., 1966; Durnin & Passmore, 1967; Hollmann & Hettinger, 1976; Lange Andersen et al., 1978; Reiff et al., 1967; Seliger, 1966). The interview collected the average weekly time with a minimum of 5 minutes spent over the previous 3 months in each of the three activity categories. The classification of activities in the level of intensity was indicated either in the questionnaire itself (Table 3.4) or in a coded list (Table 3.5).

In addition to the information derived directly from the questionnaire/interview, we calculated (a) the active sports time for light, medium-heavy, and heavy sports separately, as well as the total time spent on training and matches, and (b) the active time separately for all light, medium-heavy, and heavy activities, as well as the total of these three categories.

The energy expenditure per week above a level of 4 METs and expressed as multiples of the basal metabolic rate (METs) was estimated by multiplying the time spent per level of intensity by a fixed value for the relative energy expenditure at that level—5.5 METs for the light activities, 8.5 METs for the medium-heavy activities, and 11.5 METs for the heavy activities. The scores of the three levels were added to obtain a total MET score. This score is called the *weighted activity score.*

For some purposes not only the energy expenditure, but also the biomechanical stress that goes along with physical activity, is important. In particular, weight-bearing activities are thought to be important to the activity of the skeletal system.

Table 3.5   Classification of the Intensity Level of Work, Sports, and Leisure Activities Into Four Categories on the Basis of Their Average Intensity

Intensity		Activity
Very light < 4 METs	Domestic:	Washing dishes, dusting, sweeping floors
	Outdoor:	Sitting, standing, strolling
	Sport:	Billiards, bowling, bridge, checkers, chess, cricket, fishing, gliding, golf, sailing, shooting, skittle, t'ai chi ch'uan
Light 4-7 METs (Level 1)	Domestic:	Beating carpets, carrying groceries, hammering, polishing floors, sawing, scrubbing floors, lifting
	Outdoor:	Bicycling, canoeing, rowing, walking
	Sport:	Ballet, baseball, bodybuilding, dancing (ballroom, modern, folk), gymnastics (rhythmic, remedial, jazz), hiking, horseback riding, softball, table tennis, tug-of-war, volleyball, waterskiing, weight lifting
Medium-heavy 7-10 METs (Level 2)	Domestic:	Stair climbing
	Outdoor:	Basketball (dribbling, shooting), playing active games, skating, soccer (dribbling, kicking), swimming
	Sport:	Track and field (field events), badminton, fencing, gymnastics, mountaineering, scuba diving, skating (figure, speed), skiing (alpine), tennis (outdoor, indoor)
Heavy ≥ 10 METs (Level 3)	Outdoor:	Basketball (game), running, soccer (game)
	Sport:	Track and field (track events), basketball, canoeing, conditioning exercises, cycling (race), handball (European; indoor, outdoor), hockey (field, ice, roller; indoor, outdoor), jogging, kick-boxing, netball (indoor, outdoor), martial arts (judo, jujitsu, karate, aikido, kendo, kung fu, tae kwan do), rowing, rugby, skiing (cross-country), soccer (indoor, outdoor), squash, swimming, trampolining, water polo, wrestling

Note. Domestic = at home; Outdoor = unorganized recreational activity; Sport = activity in sport clubs.

All activities during walking, running, and stair climbing were considered weight-bearing activities. Cycling, swimming, rowing, diving, and canoeing were considered non-weight-bearing activities.

Sports Injuries

At age 27, the incidence of sports injuries over the previous year was measured retrospectively by means of a questionnaire.

Psychosocial Behavior and Stress

The variables listed below were measured in 1985 and 1991 only.

• *Coronary-prone behavior pattern.* The Type A/B behavior pattern was measured with the Dutch version of the Jenkins Activity Survey (JAS) (Appels et al, 1979). The 36 items with three to five response alternatives and scores of 1 to 5 result in a scoring range of 36 to 180.

• *Coping style.* Coping style was evaluated using the Dutch version of the Ways of Coping Checklist (WCC) (Vingerhoets & Flohr, 1984); this list is based on the WCC of Folkman & Lazarus (1980). The WCC counts 67 dichotomous items; 24 refer to problem-focused coping and 40 items to emotion-focused coping. Both scores are found by summation.

• *Life events.* The Life Event List (LEL), a translated version of the Life Events Survey of Sarason et al. (1978), has 89 life events in five domains of life. These domains are health (8 events), work (14), home and family (38), personal and social relations (23), and finances (6). Each event is scored on the intensities of impact. The subject indicates only those events that he or she has experienced during the past year and assesses them in terms of negative or positive impact. For the present study, the incidence of scores was used.

• *Daily hassles.* Daily hassles were assessed with the Everyday Problem Checklist (EPCL) (Vingerhoets et al., 1989). Each of the 114 items with four alternatives is scored from 0 ("Doesn't mind at all") to 3 ("Do mind very much"). The score used in the present study was the sum of daily hassles that occurred during the past 2 months.

Health Measurements

The health measurements we made can be classified as mental aspects of health (such as sleep problems and feelings of malfunctioning) and physical aspects (such as back pain, chronic diseases, and health services consumption). Back pain was measured at each measurement period and the other health measurements at age 21 and 27 only.

Mental Health

• *Mild health complaints.* The Check-list on Experienced Health (CLEH), based on the original list of Dirken (1967), is an index of long-term health or physical malaise. Jansen & Sikkel (1981) have shown that the their shortened version of the scale is responsive to situational stress. The 13 dichotomous items have each a weighing factor. The mean score for 15- to 22-year-old men is 2.44 and for women of the same age range, 3.25.

• *Sleep-wake problems.* Sleep-wake problems were assessed with the Sleep-Wake Experience List (SWEL) (van Diest et al, 1989). The scale contains 14 items, asking for problems in falling asleep, staying asleep, waking too early, waking in the morning, and functioning during the day. The answers, based on the past 3 months, are summed.

• *Vital exhaustion.* Defined as feelings of depression, malfunctioning, apathy, and anxiety, vital exhaustion was measured with the Maastricht Questionnaire (MQ) (Appels et al., 1979, 1987). The 21 items have a score range of 0 to 42 and load on one factor, that is, vital exhaustion. The reliability (Cronbach's α) is .89.

• *Inadequacy.* The Inadequacy scale of the DPI (Luteijn et al., 1985) contains 21 items with three response alternatives, the score ranging from 0 to 63. The Inadequacy scale asks for vague physical complaints, depressed mood, and vague feelings of anxiety and malfunctioning. The reference value for men is 7 to 13 and for women, 11 to 17.

Physical Health

• *Back pain.* Complaints about backache were recorded every year by retrospective questioning about the prevalence of back complaints over the preceding period. Each subject was asked to indicate if he or she experienced pain in the back for more than 2 or 3 days. External causes such as injuries or menstruation were excluded. Three regions were discerned: the cervical, thoracic, and lumbar parts of the spine.

• *Health questionnaire.* At ages 21 and 27 a health questionnaire was given to the subjects (Centraal Bureau voor de Statistiek, 1983) to determine the prevalence of health complaints and health services consumption over the prior 12 months. In this questionnaire, more than 25 diseases came under review. Also, the usage of health facilities (including general practitioners, dentists, medical specialists, physiotherapy, hospitals, and medication) was ascertained.

References

Aarts B., E. Janssen. (1976). Het ontwerpen en volledig detailleren van een opstelling voor het meten en registreren van de vorm van de wervelkolom. Afstudeerprojekt HTS Den Bosch, afd. Werktuigbouwkunde.

Abell L.L., B.B. Levy, B.B. Brody, F.E. Kendall. Simplified method for estimation of total cholesterol in serum and demonstration of its specificity. J Biol Chem (1952) 357-366.

American College of Sports Medicine. Position statement on the recommended quantity and quality of exercise for developing and maintaining fitness in healthy adults. Medicine Sport Sci 10 (1978) vii-x.

Appels A., W. de Haes, J. Schuurman. Een test ter meting van het 'coronary prone behaviour pattern' Type A. Nederlands Tijdschrift voor de Psychologie 34 (1979) 181-188.

Appels A., P. Höppner, P. Mulder. A questionnaire to assess premonitory symptoms of myocardial infarction. Int J Cardiol 14 (1987) 15-24.

Bar-Or O., L.D. Zwiren. Maximal oxygen consumption test during arm exercise: Reliability and validity. J Appl Physiol 38 (1975) 424-426.

Beal V.A. The nutritional history in longitudinal research. J Am Diet Assoc 51 (1967) 426-432.

Bink B., F.H. Bonjer, H. van der Sluys. (1966). Assessment of the energy expenditure by indirect time and motion study. In: Evang, Lange Andersen (eds.), Physical activity in health and disease. Scandinavian University Books, Oslo.

Bovend'eerdt J.H.F., H.C.G. Kemper, R. Verschuur. (1980). The MOPER Fitness Test: Manual and performance scales. De Vrieseborch, Haarlem.

Bücking H., J. van Egmond, S. Elsenga, F. Haanstra. De konstruktie van een jeugdversie van de Nederlandse Persoonlijkheidsvragenlijst, de NPV-J. [Construction of the Dutch Personality Inventory, youth version], Heymans Bull. (1975), report no. HB-75-190.

Burnstein M., J. Samaille. Sur un dosage rapide du cholesterol lié aux alpha-et aux bétalipoprotéines du serum. Clin Chim Acta 5 (1960) 609-611.

Centraal Bureau voor de Statistiek. (1983). Gezondheidsenquête, Heerlen.

Defares P.B., G.N. Kema, E. van Praag, J.J. van der Werff. (1968). Syracuse-Amsterdam-Groningen sociometrische schaal. Uitgave voor Research-doeleinden.

Diest R. van, H. Milius, R. Markusse, J. Snel. De Slaap-Waak Ervaring Lijst. Tijdschrift voor Sociale Geneeskunde 10 (1989) 343-347.

Dijk H. van, F. Luteijn. The validity of a new children's personality inventory: The DPI-y. Nederlands Tijdschrift voor de Psychologie 37 (1982) 241-256.

Dirken, J.M. (1967). Arbeid en stress. Wolters-Noordhoff, Groningen.

Durnin J.V.G.A., R. Passmore. (1967). Energy, work and leisure. Heinemann, London.

Durnin J.V.G.A., M.M. Rahaman. The assessment of the amount of fat in the human body from measurements of skinfold thickness. Br J Nutr 21 (1967) 681-689.

Durnin J.V.G.A., J. Womersly. Body fat assessed from total body density and its estimation from skinfold thickness: Measurements on 481 men and women aged from 16-72 years. Br J Nutr 32 (1974) 77-97.

Edholm O.G. (1966). The assessment of habitual activity. In: K. Evang, K. Lange Anderson (eds.), Physical activity in health and disease. Universitetsforlaget, Oslo.

Folkman S., R.S. Lazarus. An analysis of coping in a middle-aged community sample. J Health Soc Behav 21 (1980) 219-239.

Garn S.M. Fat weight and fat placement in the female. Science 125 (1957) 1091-1092.

Hermans H.J.M. (1971). Achievement motivation and anxiety in family and school. Swets & Zeitlinger, Amsterdam.

Hermans H.J.M. (1976). Prestatie Motivatie Test, Handleiding PMT. Swets & Zeitlinger, Lisse.

Hollman W., T. Hettinger. (1976). Arbeits- und Trainingsgrundlagen. Schattauer, Stuttgart.

Huang T.C., C.P. Chen, V. Wefler, A. Raftery. A stable reagent for the Lieberman Buchard reaction: Application to rapid serum cholesterol determination. Anal Chem 33 (1961) 1405-1407.

Hurzeler P.A., W.Z. Gualtiere, L.R. Zohman. Time-saving tables for calculating oxygen consumption and respiratory quotient. Res Q Exerc Sport 43 (1972) 121-124.

Jansen M.E., D. Sikkel. Verkorte versie van de voegschaal. Gedrag & Samenleving 2 (1981) 78-82.

Jones P.R.M., J. Pearson. Anthropometric determination of leg and muscle plus bone volumes in young male and female adults. J Physiol (Lond) 204 (1970) 63-64.

Katz, L. (1960). A new status index derived from sociometric analysis. In: J.L. Moreno, The sociometry reader. Free Press, New York.

Kemper H.C.G., R.A. Binkhorst, R. Verschuur, A.C.A. Visser. Reliability of the Ergoanalyzer. Journal of Cardiovascular Technology 4 (1976) 27-30.

Kemper H.C.G., L. Storm-van Essen, M.A. van't Hof. (1984). Measurement of growth velocity and peak height velocity in teenagers. In: J. Borms, R. Hauspie, A. Sand, C. Suzanne, M. Hebelinck (eds.), Human growth and development. Plenum, New York.

Kemper H.C.G., L. Storm-van Essen, R. Verschuur. Height velocity in a group of teenage boys. Ann Hum Biol 12:6 (1985) 545-549.

Kemper H.C.G., R. Verschuur. (1980). Measurement of aerobic power in teenagers. In: K. Berg, B.O. Erikson (eds.), Children and exercise IX. University Park Press, Baltimore.

Kemper H.C.G., R. Verschuur, J. Bovend'eerdt. The MOPER Fitness Test: I. A practical approach to motor performance tests in physical education in the Netherlands. S Afr J Res Sport Phys Educ Recreat 2 (1979) 81-93.

Kemper H.C.G., R. Verschuur, J.W. Ritmeester. Longitudinal development of growth and fitness in early and late maturing teenagers. Pediatrician 14 (1987b) 219-220.

Kemper H.C.G., R. Verschuur, J. Snel, W. Schouten, G.B. Post, L. Storm-van Essen. (1987a). [From teenager to adult: Health and lifestyle in longitudinal perspective]. Unpublished manuscript, Universiteit van Amsterdam and Vrije Universiteit, Amsterdam.

Lange Andersen K., J. Rutenfranz, R. Masironi, V. Seliger. Habitual physical activity and health. WHO Reg Publ, Eur Ser no. 6 (1978).

Leyten C., H.C.G. Kemper, R. Verschuur. (1982). The MOPER Fitness Test for 9-11 years olds: Manual performance scales. De Vrieseborch, Haarlem.

Luteijn F. (1974). The construction of a personality inventory—DPI. Swets & Zeitlinger, Amsterdam.

Luteijn F., H. van Dijk, E.A.E. van der Ploeg. (1981). Dutch Personality Inventory, youth version. Swets & Zeitlinger, Lisse.

Luteijn F., J. Starren, H. van Dijk. (1985). Nederlandse Persoonlijkheids Vragenlijst. Handleiding, Herziene uitgave. Swets & Zeitlinger, Lisse.

Mancini G., A.D. Carbonara, J.F. Heremans. Immunochemical quantitation of antigens by single radial immunodiffusion. Immunochemistry 2 (1965) 235-254.

Marr J.W. Individual dietary surveys: Purpose and methods. World Rev Nutr Diet 13 (1971) 105-164.

Novak L.P. Age and sex differences in body density and creatinine excretion of high school children. Ann N Y Acad Sci 110 (1963) 545-577.

Post G.B. (1989). Nutrition in adolescence: A longitudinal study in dietary patterns from teenage to adult. Thesis, Wageningen, de Vrieseborch, Haarlem SO 16.

Post G.B., H.C.G. Kemper. Cross-check dietary history and 24-hour dietary recall. Voeding 41 (1980) 123-129.

Reiff C.G., H.J. Montoye, R.D. Remington, J.A. Napier, H.L. Metzener, F.H. Epstein. (1967). Assessment of physical activity by questionnaire and interview. In: Karvonen, Barry, Physical activity and the heart. Charles C Thomas, Springfield, IL.

Sarason, I.G., J.H. Johnson, J.M. Siegel. Assessing the impact of life changes: Development of the Life Experience Survey. J Consult Clin Psychol 46 (1978) 932-946.

Saris W.H.M., P. Snel, R.A. Binkhorst. A portable heart rate distribution recorder for studying daily physical activity. Eur J Appl Physiol 37 (1977) 19-25.

Schouten W.J., R. Verschuur, H.C.G. Kemper. Habitual physical activity, strenuous exercise and salivary immunoglobulin A levels in young adults. Int J Sports Med 9 (1988a) 289-293.

Schouten W.J., R. Verschuur, H.C.G. Kemper. Physical activity and upper respiratory tract infections in a normal population of young men and women. Int J Sports Med 9 (1988b) 451-455.

Seliger V. (1966). Circulatory responses to sport activities. In: Evang, Lange Andersen (eds.), Physical activity in health and disease. Scandinavian University Books, Oslo.

Seroo T., L. Storm-van Essen, H.C.G. Kemper. De voor- en achterwaartse krommingen van de rug bij tieners. Geneeskunde en Sport 15:2 (1982) 78-82.

Snijders C.J. (1971). On the form of the human thoracolumbar spine and some aspects of its mechanical behaviour. VAM, Voorschoten.

Tanner J.M., R.H. Whitehouse, W.A. Marshall, M.J.R. Healy, H. Goldstein. (1975). Assessment of skeletal maturity and prediction of adult height (TW 2 method). Academic Press, London.

Velzen J.H.A. van, H.C.G. Kemper. Maximal isokinetic torque of knee flexion and extension in young adults. Geneeskunde en Sport 21:2 (1988) 59-66.

Verschuur R. (1987). Daily physical activity and health: Longitudinal changes during the teenage period. Thesis, Universiteit van Amsterdam, de Vrieseborch, Haarlem, SO 12.

Verschuur R., H.C.G. Kemper. Adjustment of pedometers to make them more valid in assessing running. Int J Sports Med 1 (1980) 87-89.

Vingerhoets A.J.J.M., P.J.M. Flohr. Type A behavior and self-reports of coping preferences. Br J Med Psych 57 (1984) 15-21.

Vingerhoets A.J.J.M., A.J. Jeninga, L.J. Menges. The measurement of daily hassles and chronic stressors: The development of the Everyday Problem Checklist. Gedrag & Gezondheid 17:1 (1989) 10-17.

Weiner J.S., J.A. Lourie (eds.). (1968). Human biology: A guide to field methods. Blackwell, Oxford.

Part II

Descriptive Longitudinal Results

Chapter 4

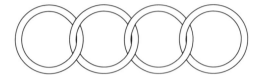

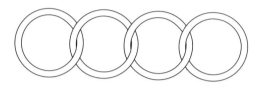

Body Growth, Body Composition, and Physical Fitness

Willem van Mechelen & Han C.G. Kemper

As described in chapter 3, measurements in the longitudinal study included indices of body growth and body composition at each year. Also, both motor fitness and cardiorespiratory fitness were monitored and resting systolic and diastolic blood pressures and serum cholesterol levels were measured.

The purpose of this chapter is to describe the longitudinal development of these variables in both males and females. We also describe the stability of motor and cardiorespiratory fitness. For information on the stability of body growth and body composition variables, systolic and diastolic blood pressure, and serum cholesterol, refer to chapter 11, where tracking of these variables is discussed in relation to the risk for cardiovascular disease.

Subjects and Methods

We measured 98 females and 84 males in 1991. However, not all of these subjects were measured at each year of measurement. Table 4.1 indicates the numbers

Table 4.1 Numbers of Subjects Present at the 1991 Measurements Who Were Also Present During the Preceding Years of Measurement

	1985	1980	1979	1978	1977
Males ($n = 84$ in 1991)	78	80	84	80	83
Females ($n = 98$ in 1991)	94	98	98	97	97

of subjects measured in 1991 who were present for these measurements. (For practical reasons during 1991 not all subjects performed all tests.) The resulting small variations in numbers of subjects were accounted for when any of the statistical procedures described in this chapter were performed.

Although described in depth in chapter 3, for each of the variables discussed in this chapter the method of measurement is briefly described again here. In the first 4 years, height and weight were measured every 4 months. From this information, the body mass index (BMI, in kilograms per meter squared) was calculated. Skinfold thickness was measured at four sites according to the method described by Weiner and Lourie (1968). In 1991 the measurement of waist and hip circumferences was added to the measurements. From these circumferences a waist:hip ratio was calculated. A high ratio indicates a "central" fat distribution, and a low ratio, a "peripheral" fat distribution (Ashwell, 1992).

Motor fitness was assessed by means of the Motor Performance (MOPER) Fitness Test. Details of the MOPER Fitness Test, a field test for the assessment of motor fitness, are described extensively elsewhere (Kemper, 1982). We performed the following seven standardized fitness tests:

- *Arm speed*, expressed in seconds, was measured by the best time needed to alternately tap two plates at the umbilical level, using the hand of preference, as fast as possible for 25 complete cycles; the midpoints of the plates lie 75 cm apart.

- *Explosive leg strength*, expressed in centimeters, was measured by vertical jump height.

- *Running speed*, expressed in seconds, was the time needed to perform a 10 × 5-m run.

- *Static arm strength*, expressed in kilograms of pulling force, was measured with an arm-pull test in which the subject was asked to pull a calibrated dynamometer using the preferred arm. The dynamometer was fixed to a wall in such a way that its handgrip was in the plane of the stretched supporting arm, which is held horizontally against the wall.

- *Flexibility of the trunk*, expressed in centimeters, was measured using the sit-and-reach test. Reaching the toes with straight legs gave a score of 25 cm.

- *Trunk/leg strength*, expressed in seconds, was measured as the time scored on a leg lift test in which the subject was asked to lift the legs as quickly as possible 10 times from the horizontal to the vertical with extended knees.

- *Endurance strength of the arms*, expressed in seconds, was measured by the maximal time that the subject was able to keep the eyes above a horizontal bar in a bent-arm hang position.

Cardiorespiratory fitness was assessed by measuring submaximal and maximal oxygen uptake ($\dot{V}O_2$max) while the subject performed a graded maximal running test on a treadmill. The treadmill test protocol has been described by Kemper and Verschuur (1981; see also chapter 3). Before starting the protocol, resting diastolic and systolic blood pressures and resting heart rate were measured. The treadmill protocol consisted of two parts: a 6-minute submaximal test separated by a rest period from a maximal test. The running speed was 8 km/h for both tests. Starting horizontal, the slope of the treadmill increased every 2nd minute by 2.5% for the submaximal test and by 2.5% or 5% (depending on the heart rate) for the maximal test. The subject's electrocardiogram (ECG) was monitored telemetrically throughout the test. Heart rate was calculated from 15 R-R intervals in the last 15 seconds of every minute. Oxygen uptake ($\dot{V}O_2$) was measured directly every minute using an Ergoanalyser. The following results will be presented: resting diastolic and systolic blood pressures (in millimeters of mercury); $\dot{V}O_2$ at 0%, 2.5%, and 5%; and $\dot{V}O_2$max (expressed in both absolute values [liters per minute] and relative to body weight [milliliters per kilogram per minute]).

Total serum cholesterol (TC) and high-density lipoprotein (HDL) cholesterol were assessed from a fasting blood sample taken from the antecubital vein and expressed in millimoles per liter. Furthermore, the TC:HDL ratio was calculated.

If applicable, insight into the longitudinal pattern of the various variables was obtained by applying a multivariate analysis of variance (MANOVA) for repeated measurements, in which sex and time, as well as the interaction between those two variables, were entered. This procedure, when applicable, was always performed in the following way: First, the MANOVA was applied taking the entire period of study (1977-1991) into consideration, then the period covering 1977 to 1985, followed by the time period covering 1977 to 1980. Statistical significance was accepted at the 5% level. If for the first (1977-1991) or the second (1977-1985) time period either of the analysis variables, or their interaction, proved to be not significant, then the analysis was not repeated for the next time period. This is indicated in the various tables with "NA" (not applicable).

Stability of motor and cardiovascular fitness was assessed by calculating interperiod coefficients (IPCs).

Development of Body Growth and Body Composition in Longitudinal Perspective

Longitudinal development of height is presented in Figures 4.1 (males) and 4.2 (females) by the 10th, 50th and 90th percentiles. Longitudinal development of body weight is presented in Figures 4.3 (males) and 4.4 (females), also by the 10th, 50th, and 90th percentiles. A MANOVA for repeated measurements both in males and females indicated that body height and weight did not increase significantly between the ages of 21 and 27.

As a measure of body composition, the BMI was calculated (Fig. 4.5). Over the entire period of measurement (1977-1991), the BMI of males differed significantly from that of females. Both for males and females there was between ages 13 and 27 a significant increase in BMI, from 17.3 ± 0.2 to 22.5 ± 0.3 for males and from 18.1 ± 2.1 to 21.9 ± 2.5 for females. The interaction between time and sex was significant, indicating that the longitudinal pattern of the

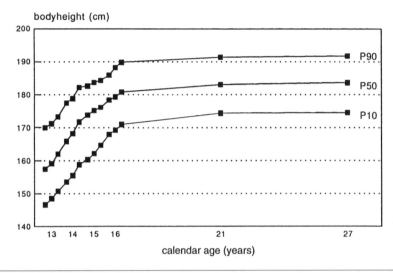

Figure 4.1   Height of males. P_{50} = median; P_{10} = 10th percentile; P_{90} = 90th percentile.

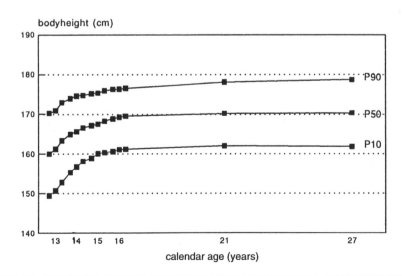

Figure 4.2   Height of females. P_{50} = median; P_{10} = 10th percentile; P_{90} = 90th percentile.

males

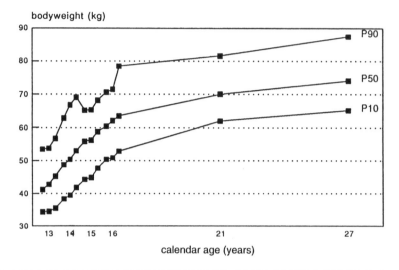

Figure 4.3   Weight of males. P_{50} = median; P_{10} = 10th percentile; P_{90} = 90th percentile.

females

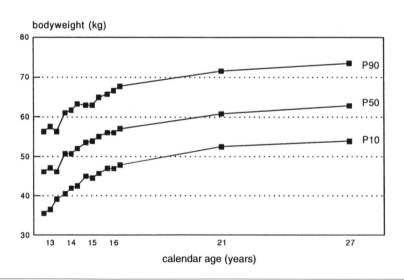

Figure 4.4   Weight of females. P_{50} = median; P_{10} = 10th percentile; P_{90} = 90th percentile.

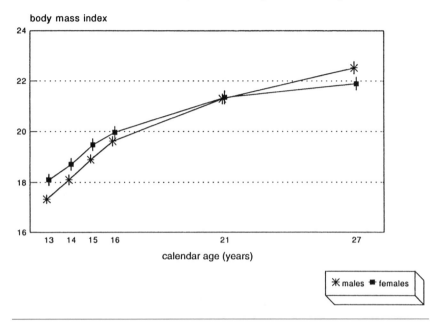

Figure 4.5   Mean and standard error of body mass index of males and females.

development of BMI was different for males and females, and showing for males a higher value during the adolescent years and a lower value at adult age.

Skinfolds were also assessed as a measure of body composition. The biceps, triceps, subscapular, and suprailiac skinfolds were measured. The mean results are presented in Figures 4.6 through 4.9. The sum of skinfolds is given in Figure 4.10. A MANOVA showed for each separate skinfold for each period of measurement significantly greater values for females. For both males and females there was an increase over time. Also, a significant interaction between sex and time was found. The results are seen in Table 4.2.

Over the entire longitudinal period females had a significantly greater sum of four skinfolds than males. For both sexes a significant time effect was found, as well as a significant interaction between sex and time. In females there was from the start of the adolescent period until age 21 a gradual increase from 37.5 ± 1.3 mm to 52.3 ± 1.7 mm; this was followed by a decrease to 46.3 ± 1.7 mm at age 27. In males there was a gradual increase in the sum of skinfolds from age 12 until age 27, from 28.3 ± 1.2 mm to 38.5 ± 2.5 mm.

From these results we may conclude the following.

1. Females had significantly thicker skinfolds than males throughout the entire period of study, except for the two skinfolds at the trunk at adult age; the suprailiac and subscapular skinfold were no longer significantly different.

2. The longitudinal pattern was significantly different for males compared with females:

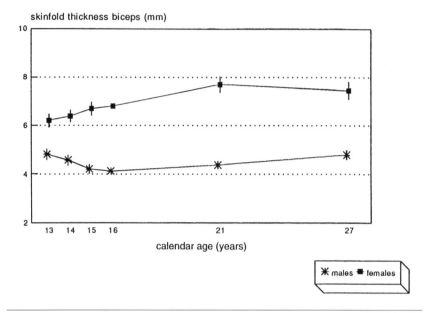

Figure 4.6   Mean and standard error of biceps skinfold thickness of males and females.

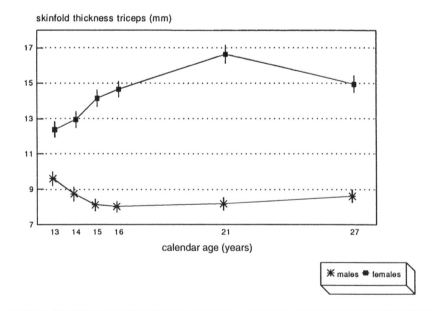

Figure 4.7   Mean and standard error of triceps skinfold thickness of males and females.

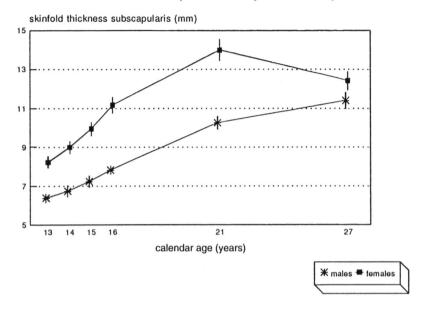

Figure 4.8   Mean and standard error of subscapular skinfold thickness of males and females.

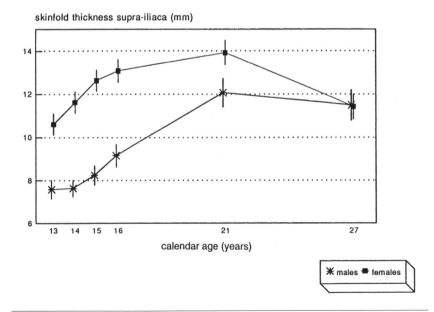

Figure 4.9   Mean and standard error of suprailiac skinfold thickness of males and females.

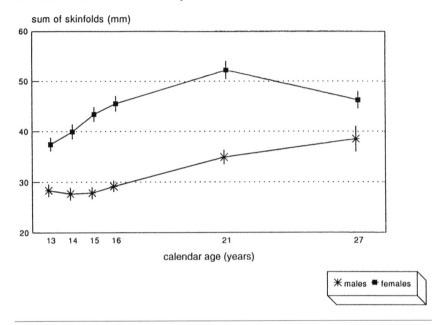

Figure 4.10   Mean and standard error of sum of four skinfolds of males and females.

• For females there was a significant increase for all skinfolds from age 13 until age 21, stabilizing at age 27.

• In males there was between ages 13 and 17 a significant decrease in the thickness of the biceps and triceps skinfold, stabilizing at the ages of 21 and 27. The thickness of the subscapular skinfold increased significantly between ages 13 and 27. The suprailiac skinfold thickness increased significantly between the ages of 13 and 21, but not at age 27.

3. For females the sum of skinfolds showed an increase between ages 13 and 21, followed by a decrease at age 27, whereas for males there was a stable pattern during the adolescent years followed by a gradual increase at age 27.

The measurement of hip and waist circumferences at age 27 resulted in the calculation of the following mean and standard deviations of the waist:hip ratios: for males, 0.90 ± 0.72; and for females, 0.79 ± 0.66.

Development of Motor Fitness in Longitudinal Perspective

Changes in motor fitness were monitored by repetitive performance of the MOPER Fitness Test. Mean results for the test are shown in Figures 4.11 to 4.17. For each of the tests of the MOPER Fitness Test, the longitudinal results were analyzed by a MANOVA for repeated measurements in which sex, time, and their interaction were entered as variables. The results of the MANOVA are summarized in Table 4.3.

Table 4.2   Results of MANOVA and Subsequent Post Hoc Analysis for Skinfolds

Skinfolds	1977-1991		1977-1985		1977-1979	
	Males	Females	Males	Females	Males	Females
Biceps						
Time	$p < .001$	$p < .001$	$p < .001$	$p < .001$	$p < .001$	$p < .001$
Sex		$p < .001$		$p < .001$		$p < .001$
Time by sex		$p < .001$		$p < .001$		$p < .001$
Triceps						
Time	$p < .001$	$p < .001$	$p < .001$	$p < .001$	$p < .001$	$p < .001$
Sex		$p < .001$		$p < .001$		$p < .001$
Time by sex		$p < .001$		$p < .001$		$p < .001$
Subscapularis						
Time	$p < .001$	$p < .001$	$p < .001$	$p < .001$	$p < .001$	$p < .001$
Sex		$p < .001$		$p < .001$		$p < .001$
Time by sex		$p < .001$		$p < .001$		$p < .001$
Suprailiac						
Time	$p < .001$	$p < .001$	$p < .001$	$p < .001$	$p < .001$	$p < .001$
Sex		$p < .001$		$p < .001$		$p < .05$
Time by sex		$p < .001$		$p < .001$		$p < .001$
Sum of skinfolds						
Time	$p < .001$	$p < .001$	$p < .001$	$p < .001$	NS	$p < .001$
Sex		$p < .001$		$p < .001$		$p < .001$
Time by sex		$p < .001$		$p < .001$		$p < .001$

Note. NS = not significant.

Plate Tapping

The result of the plate-tapping test is expressed as the time (in seconds) needed to complete 25 full cycles. Figure 4.11 shows the results of the test. The MANOVA indicated no significant differences in performance between males and females. The longitudinal pattern of the performance on the test differed significantly ($p < .001$) between males and females for each of the three periods of measurement. Also, both for males and females, significant ($p < .001$) time effects were discerned for the three periods.

At age 13, females scored 11.3 seconds on the plate-tapping test and males 12.1 seconds. At age 27, females scored 9.2 seconds and males 8.8 seconds, an improvement in performance of about 23% and 38%, respectively.

10 × 5-m Run

Performance on the 10 × 5-m run is expressed in seconds. The MANOVA showed that for each of the three periods there was a significant ($p < .001$) difference in performance between males and females. Significant ($p < .001$) time effects

Table 4.3   Results of MANOVA and Subsequent Post Hoc Analysis for All Motor Performance Fitness Test Items

	1977-1991		1977-1985		1977-1979	
	Males	Females	Males	Females	Males	Females
Plate tapping						
Time	$p < .001$	$p < .001$	$p < .001$	$p < .001$	$p < .001$	$p < .001$
Sex	NS		NA		NA	
Time by sex	$p < .001$		$p < .001$		$p < .001$	
10 × 5-m run						
Time	$p < .001$	$p < .001$	$p < .001$	$p < .001$	$p < .001$	$p < .001$
Sex	$p < .001$		$p < .001$		$p < .001$	
Time by sex	$p < .001$		$p < .001$		$p < .001$	
Sit-and-reach						
Time	$p < .001$	$p < .001$	$p < .001$	$p < .001$	$p < .001$	$p < .001$
Sex	$p < .001$		$p < .001$		$p < .001$	
Time by sex	$p < .01$		$p < .001$		$p < .01$	
Standing high jump						
Time	$p < .001$	$p < .01$	$p < .001$	$p < .01$	$p < .001$	$p < .05$
Sex	$p < .001$		$p < .001$		$p < .001$	
Time by sex	$p < .001$		$p < .001$		$p < .001$	
Arm pull relative to body weight						
Time	$p < .001$	$p < .001$	$p < .001$	$p < .001$	$p < .001$	$p < .001$
Sex	$p < .001$		$p < .001$		$p < .001$	
Time by sex	$p < .01$		$p < .001$		$p < .01$	
Bent-arm hang						
Time	$p < .001$	$p < .001$	$p < .001$	$p < .001$	$p < .001$	NS
Sex	$p < .001$		$p < .001$		$p < .001$	
Time by sex	$p < .001$		$p < .001$		$p < .001$	
Leg lift						
Time	$p < .001$	$p < .001$	$p < .001$	$p < .001$	$p < .001$	$p < .001$
Sex	NS		NA		NA	
Time by sex	$p < .001$		$p < .01$		NS	

Note. NA = not applicable; NS = not significant.

were found, as well as a significant ($p < .001$) interaction between sex and time. During the adolescent period there was an increase in performance of 12% in males and 5% in females, followed by a decrease in performance of 6% in males and 9% in females by the end of the young-adult period. No further changes were observed until age 27 (Fig. 4.12).

Sit-and-Reach Test

Performance on the sit-and-reach test is expressed in centimeters. The MANOVA indicated that for each period, there was a significant ($p < .001$) difference in

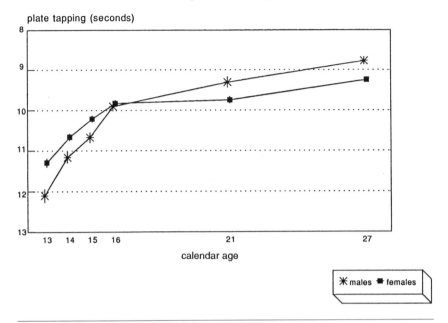

Figure 4.11   Mean and standard error of plate-tapping score of males and females.

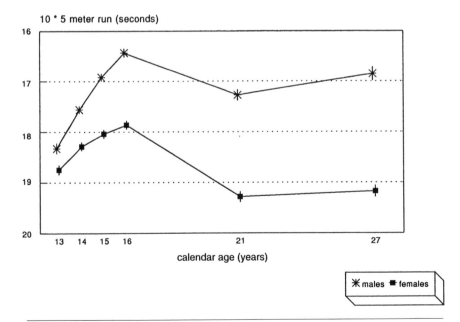

Figure 4.12   Mean and standard error of 10 × 5-m run scores of males and females.

performance between males and females. A significant ($p < .001$) time effect was found in both males and females, as well as a significant interaction between time and sex. From the start until the end of the adolescent period, males' performance on the sit-and-reach test improved by 15% and that of females by 10%, followed by a further improvement during the young-adult period of 7% in males and 3% in females. At age 27 the performance had declined again, 4% in males and 1% in females (Fig. 4.13).

Standing High Jump

Performance on the standing high jump test is expressed in centimeters. The MANOVA indicated that there was a significant ($p < .001$) difference in performance between males and females for each of the three periods. The MANOVA also indicated a significant ($p < .001$) time effect for both sexes, as well as a significant ($p < .001$) interaction between time and sex. From Figure 4.14 it can be seen that males consistently performed better than females. During the adolescent period there was among males an increase in performance of 13%, followed by another 9% and 2% in 1985 and 1991. In females, too, a significant time effect was noted, but not one that resulted in a change in actual performance; the changes were between 42.2 and 43.2 cm.

Arm Pull Relative to Body Weight

Static strength is related to body weight. Therefore, the result of the arm pull test is expressed as kilograms of force per 100 g body weight. The MANOVA

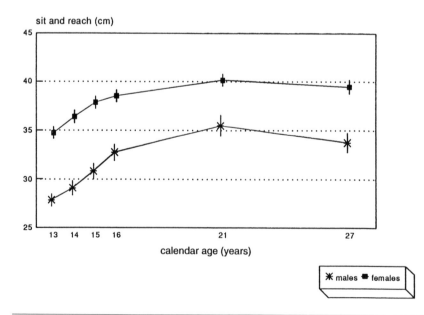

Figure 4.13 Mean and standard error of sit-and-reach scores of males and females.

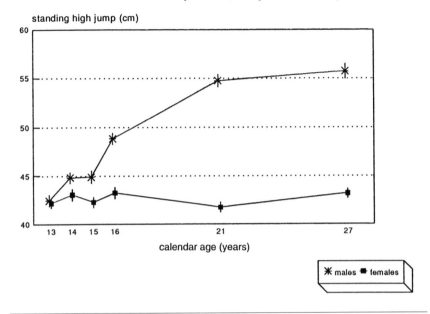

Figure 4.14   Mean and standard error of standing high jump scores of males and females.

indicated a significant ($p < .001$) difference between males and females for each of the three periods. Significant time effects were found, as well as significant interactions between time and sex. Throughout the adolescent period an increase in arm pull performance of 22% was seen in males (mean score at age 13 = 84.4 ± 15.3) and one of 15% in females (mean score at age 13 = 72.7 ± 12.3), followed by a steady decrease of 16% in males and of 31% in females by age 27 (Fig. 4.15).

Bent-Arm Hang

Performance on the bent-arm hang test is expressed in seconds. The MANOVA revealed a significant ($p < .001$) difference between males and females for each of the three periods, as well as a significant ($p < .001$) interaction between sex and time, indicating a male-female difference in the longitudinal pattern of performance on the test. The time effect was in general significant both for males and females, although there was no time effect among females during the adolescent period. As can be seen in Figure 4.16, over time males showed a significant gradual increase in performance of 39%, from 23.6 seconds at the start of the adolescent period to 38.8 seconds at age 21, a value that remained constant until age 27. The performance of females on the bent-arm hang stayed more or less constant throughout the entire longitudinal period: 17.3 seconds at age 13 and 16.2 seconds at age 27.

Leg Lifts

Performance on the leg lift test is expressed in seconds. The MANOVA showed a significant ($p < .001$) time effect for each of the three periods, in both males

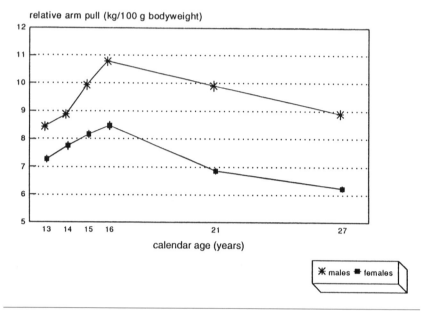

Figure 4.15   Mean and standard error of score of arm pull relative to body weight of males and females.

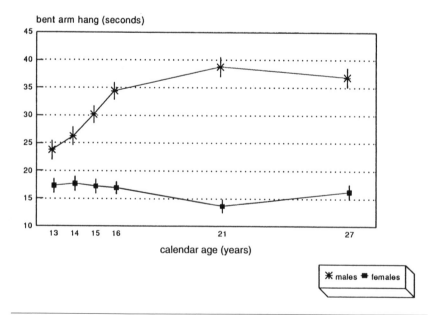

Figure 4.16   Mean and standard error of bent-arm scores of males and females.

and females. The differences in performance between males and females were not significant. The MANOVA discerned a significant ($p < .001$) interaction between time and sex, but only for the entire period of study and for the period between 1977 and 1985. Both males and females showed an improvement in performance of 6% during the adolescent period. This was followed by further improvement in performance of 2% in males in 1985, which was followed by a 2% decrease in 1991. In females over the same period a 4% decrease in performance was noted, followed by a 2% decrease (Fig. 4.17).

In conclusion, over the entire longitudinal period of study, males performed significantly better with regard to running speed, explosive leg strength, static arm strength, and endurance strength of the arms. Females showed a significantly better performance in flexibility. No significant differences between males and females were observed for arm speed and trunk/leg strength. All tests showed a time effect between 1977 and 1991, as well as a significant interaction between time and sex.

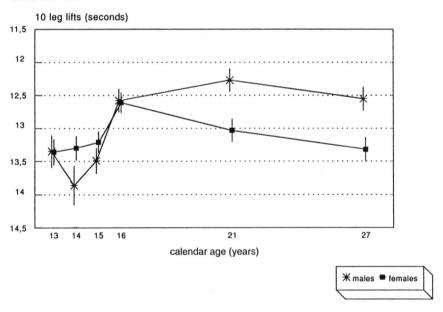

Figure 4.17   Mean and standard error of leg lift scores of males and females.

Development of Cardiorespiratory Fitness
in Longitudinal Perspective

Measures Obtained at Rest

Resting diastolic (Fig. 4.18) and systolic (Fig. 4.19) blood pressures were obtained longitudinally as indices of cardiorespiratory fitness. Additionally, a fasting blood sample was taken from which the TC (Fig. 4.20) and the HDL cholesterol (Fig.

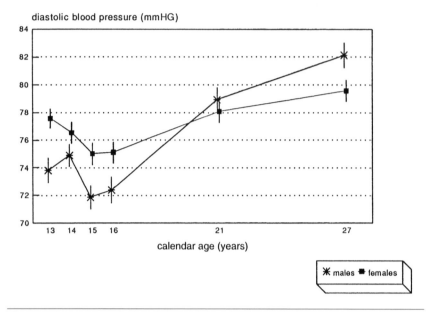

Figure 4.18   Mean and standard error of resting diastolic blood pressure of males and females.

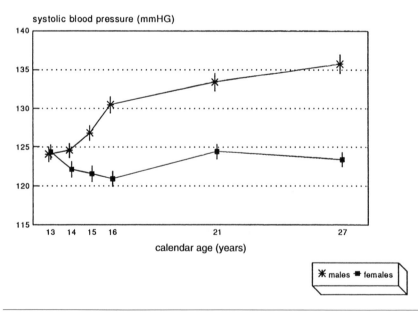

Figure 4.19   Mean and standard error of resting systolic blood pressure of males and females.

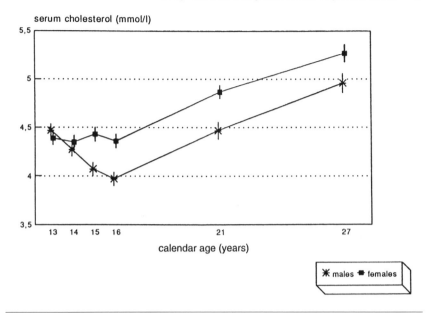

Figure 4.20   Mean and standard error of serum total cholesterol concentration of males and females.

4.21) concentrations were assessed. From these values the TC:HDL-cholesterol ratio was calculated (Fig. 4.22).

Over the entire period of study there was no significant difference between males and females in resting diastolic blood pressure. However, a MANOVA showed an interaction of time by sex, indicating a significantly different longitudinal pattern between males and females in resting diastolic pressure. For both sexes a significant time effect was found (Table 4.4). During the adolescent period, resting diastolic pressure in females was significantly higher than that of males. The opposite was found at age 27, when resting diastolic pressure was found to be higher in males than in females; however, the differences at age 27 were not significant. At age 27 the mean and standard deviation of resting diastolic blood pressure in males was 82 ± 8 mmHg and in females, 80 ± 8 mmHg.

The resting systolic blood pressure was for each of the three periods of measurement significantly higher among males than females. For both males and females a significant time effect was found, and the interaction between time and sex was significant. In 12-year-old males a mean resting systolic pressure of 124 ± 9 mmHg was found; this steadily increased to 136 ± 11 mmHg by age 27. In females the resting systolic pressure remained more or less constant throughout the entire period of study, with mean values ranging from 121 ± 9 mmHg to 124 ± 10 mmHg. The differences at age 27 between males and females were statistically significant.

Regarding cholesterol, the TC of females was for each of the three periods of measurement significantly higher than that of males. For both males and

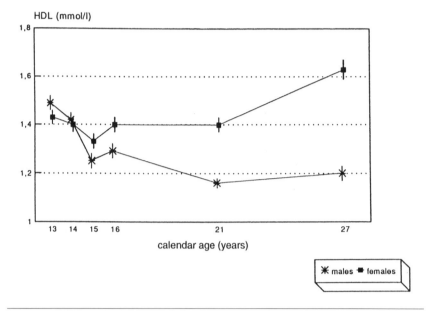

Figure 4.21   Mean and standard error of serum HDL cholesterol concentration of males and females.

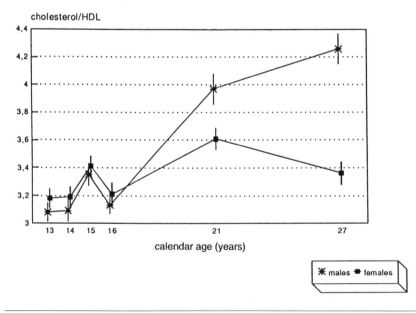

Figure 4.22   Mean and standard error of TC:HDL-cholesterol ratio of males and females.

Table 4.4   Results of MANOVA and Subsequent Post Hoc Analysis for Blood Pressure and Lipoproteins

	1977-1991		1977-1985		1977-1979	
	Males	Females	Males	Females	Males	Females
Resting diastolic blood pressure						
Time	$p < .001$	$p < .001$	$p < .001$	$p < .01$	$p < .01$	$p < .01$
Sex	NS		NA		NA	
Time by sex	$p < .001$		$p < .05$		NS	
Resting systolic blood pressure						
Time	$p < .001$	$p < .001$	$p < .001$	$p < .001$	$p < .001$	$p < .01$
Sex	$p < .001$		$p < .001$		$p < .001$	
Time by sex	$p < .001$		$p < .001$		$p < .001$	
Serum total cholesterol (TC)						
Time	$p < .001$	$p < .001$	$p < .001$	$p < .001$	$p < .001$	NS
Sex	$p < .01$		$p < .01$		$p < .05$	
Time by sex	$p < .001$		$p < .001$		$p < .001$	
Serum HDL cholesterol						
Time	$p < .001$	$p < .001$	$p < .001$	$p < .01$	$p < .001$	$p < .001$
Sex	$p < .001$		NS		$p < .001$	
Time by sex	$p < .001$		$p < .001$		$p < .001$	
TC:HDL ratio						
Time	$p < .001$	$p < .001$	$p < .001$	$p < .001$	$p < .001$	$p < .001$
Sex	NS		NS		NS	
Time by sex	$p < .001$		$p < .001$		NS	

Note. NA = not applicable; NS = not significant.

females a significant time effect was found, with the exception of the adolescent period in females. The interaction between time and sex was also significant. In females during the adolescent period, TC was about 4.4 mmol/L, increasing to 5.3 ± 0.9 mmol/L by age 27. In males initially there was a significant decrease between ages 13 and 17, from 4.5 ± 0.6 mmol/L to 4.0 ± 0.6 mmol/L; this was followed by a significant increase, to 5.0 ± 0.9 mmol/L by age 27.

For serum HDL-cholesterol concentrations, no significant differences were found between the two sexes. For both sexes a significant time effect was found, as well as a significant interaction between time and sex. Between ages 13 and 21 in males a significant decrease was noted: 1.5 ± 0.3 mmol/L down to 1.2 ± 0.2 mmol/L. No further significant changes were noted by age 27. In females, serum HDL-cholesterol concentration varied around 1.4 mmol/L between ages

13 and 21, with the exception of a dip at age 15. By age 27 the serum HDL-cholesterol concentration had significantly increased to 1.6 ± 0.4 mmol/L.

The TC:HDL-cholesterol ratio showed a significant time effect among both males and females. No significant differences were found between males and females. The interaction between time and sex was significant, but only after the adolescent period. In males at age 13 the ratio was found to be 3.1 ± 0.6, significantly increasing to 4.3 ± 1.1 by age 27. In females between ages 13 and 21 a significant increase was observed, from 3.2 ± 0.7 to 3.6 ± 0.8. At age 27 the ratio had significantly decreased, to 3.4 ± 0.8.

Measures Obtained During Submaximal Treadmill Testing

$\dot{V}O_2$ was measured for 6 minutes of a submaximal treadmill test at three different slopes (0%, 2.5%, and 5%) (Fig. 4.23-4.25). The results of a MANOVA are presented in Table 4.5.

At all three slopes, the longitudinal pattern of $\dot{V}O_2$ per kilogram of body weight is similar for males and females. Both males and females show for each slope a significant decrease in $\dot{V}O_2$ while running at a speed of 8 km/h. Only at inclinations of 0% and 2.5% was a significant interaction between time and sex found. Males showed significantly higher $\dot{V}O_2$ values than females at all years of measurement for all three slopes (about 1-2 ml · kg^{-1} · min^{-1}) while running at the same speed of 8 km/h. The decrease in $\dot{V}O_2$ with age averaged 5 ml · kg^{-1} · min^{-1} during the adolescent period, and another 2 ml · kg^{-1} · min^{-1} till adult age in both sexes.

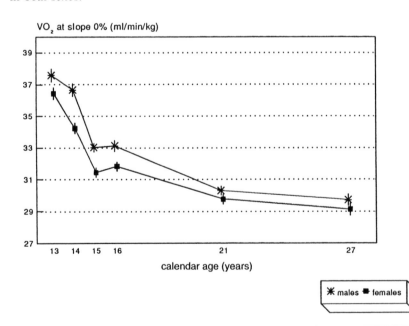

Figure 4.23   Mean and standard error of $\dot{V}O_2$ of males and females obtained during submaximal running at a speed of 8 km/h at 0% slope.

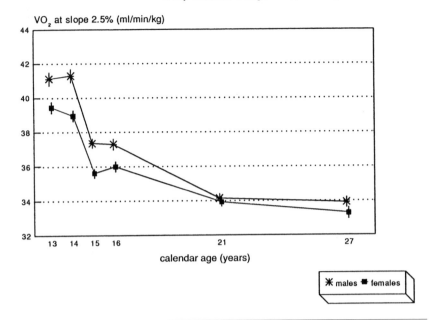

Figure 4.24   Mean and standard error of V̇O₂ of males and females obtained during submaximal running at a speed of 8 km/h at 2.5% slope.

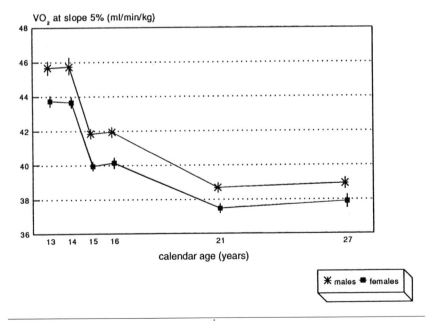

Figure 4.25   Mean and standard error of V̇O₂ of males and females obtained during submaximal running at a speed of 8 km/h at 5% slope.

Table 4.5   Results of MANOVA and Subsequent Post Hoc Analysis for $\dot{V}O_2$ Relative to Body Weight

	1977-1991		1977-1985		1977-1979	
	Males	Females	Males	Females	Males	Females
$\dot{V}O_2$ at 0% slope						
Time	$p < .001$	$p < .001$	$p < .001$	$p < .001$	$p < .001$	$p < .001$
Sex	$p < .001$		$p < .001$		$p < .001$	
Time by sex	$p < .05$		$p < .05$		$p < .05$	
$\dot{V}O_2$ at 2.5% slope						
Time	$p < .001$	$p < .001$	$p < .001$	$p < .001$	$p < .001$	$p < .001$
Sex	$p < .001$		$p < .001$		$p < .001$	
Time by sex	$p < .001$		$p < .01$		NS	
$\dot{V}O_2$ at 5% slope						
Time	$p < .001$	$p < .001$	$p < .001$	$p < .001$	$p < .001$	$p < .001$
Sex	$p < .001$		$p < .001$		$p < .001$	
Time by sex	NS		NS		NS	

Note. Treadmill speed was 8 km/h. NS = not significant.

Measures Obtained During Maximal Treadmill Testing

During the maximal treadmill test the following values were obtained: maximal slope (Fig. 4.26) and $\dot{V}O_2$max in absolute values (Fig. 4.27) and per kilogram of body mass (Fig. 4.28). As part of the standard procedure for these variables, a MANOVA for repeated measurements was carried out (Table 4.6).

Maximal slope showed a significant time effect in both males and females (Fig. 4.26). There was a significant difference between males and females with regard to maximal slope during the entire period of study, with higher values for males. The longitudinal pattern of the maximal slope for males differed significantly from that of females (Table 4.6). In males there was, during the adolescent period, a significant increase in slope, from $13.5 \pm 2.3\%$ at age 13 to $15.8 \pm 2.5\%$ by age 17; this was followed by a significant decrease, to $12.8 \pm 2.1\%$ by age 27. In females during the adolescent period a significant time effect was found, with maximal slope values varying from $10.5 \pm 2.2\%$ to $10.3 \pm 2.1\%$. However, in the light of these values these differences do not seem meaningful. By age 27 the maximal slope for females had significantly decreased to $8.3 \pm 2.4\%$.

Over the entire longitudinal period absolute $\dot{V}O_2$max in males was consistently higher than that of females (Fig. 4.27). For both sexes a significant time effect was found, and the interaction between time and sex was significant. At age 13 in males absolute $\dot{V}O_2$max was 2.7 ± 0.4 L/min. By the end of the adolescent period at age 16 it had significantly increased, to 3.7 ± 0.5 L/min. From then on a further significant increase was observed, to 3.8 ± 0.5 L/min by

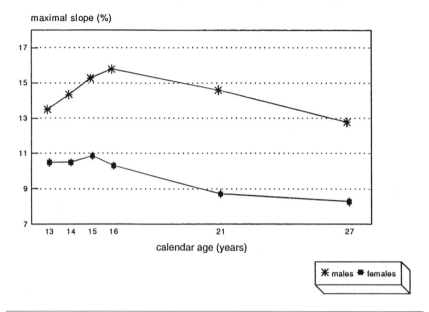

Figure 4.26   Mean and standard error of maximal slope of males and females obtained during maximal running at a speed of 8 km/h.

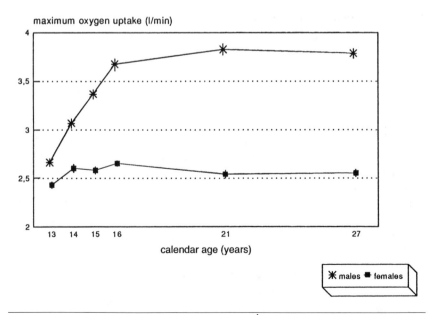

Figure 4.27   Mean and standard error of absolute $\dot{V}O_2max$ (L/min) of males and females obtained during maximal running at a speed of 8 km/h.

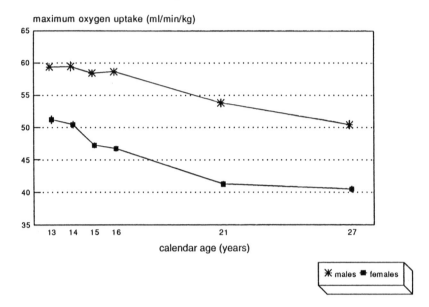

Figure 4.28   Mean and standard error of relative V̇O₂max (ml · kg⁻¹ · min⁻¹) of males and females obtained during maximal running at a speed of 8 km/h.

Table 4.6   Results of MANOVA and Subsequent Post Hoc Analysis for Maximal Slope and V̇O₂max

	1977-1991		1977-1985		1977-1979	
	Males	Females	Males	Females	Males	Females
Maximal slope						
Time	$p < .001$	$p < .001$	$p < .001$	$p < .001$	$p < .001$	$p < .001$
Sex	$p < .001$		$p < .001$		$p < .001$	
Time by sex	$p < .001$		$p < .001$		$p < .001$	
Absolute V̇O₂max						
Time	$p < .001$	$p < .001$	$p < .001$	$p < .001$	$p < .001$	$p < .001$
Sex	$p < .001$		$p < .001$		$p < .001$	
Time by sex	$p < .001$		$p < .001$		$p < .001$	
V̇O₂max relative to body weight						
Time	$p < .001$	$p < .001$	$p < .001$	$p < .001$	NS	$p < .001$
Sex	$p < .001$		$p < .001$		$p < .001$	
Time by sex	$p < .001$		$p < .001$		$p < .001$	

Note. NS = not significant.

age 27. In females during the adolescent period a significant increase was observed, from 2.4 ± 0.3 L/min to 2.7 ± 0.4 L/min; it then remained more or less stable until age 27.

$\dot{V}O_2$max relative to body weight was consistently higher in males than in females throughout the entire period of study (Fig. 4.28). However, the longitudinal pattern of males was significantly different from that of females. Both males and females showed a significant time effect, although in males there was no time effect during the adolescent period. In males during this period relative $\dot{V}O_2$max varied from 58.5 ± 4.7 ml $\cdot$ kg^{-1} $\cdot$ min^{-1} to 59.5 ± 6.3 ml $\cdot$ kg^{-1} $\cdot$ min^{-1}. By age 21 in males $\dot{V}O_2$max had significantly decreased, to 53.9 ± 5.3 ml $\cdot$ kg^{-1} $\cdot$ min^{-1}; it then further significantly decreased, to 50.5 ± 5.7 ml $\cdot$ kg^{-1} $\cdot$ min^{-1}, at age 27. In females relative $\dot{V}O_2$max gradually and significantly decreased, from 51.2 ± 6.1 ml $\cdot$ kg^{-1} $\cdot$ min^{-1} at age 13 to 41.3 ± 4.2 ml $\cdot$ kg^{-1} $\cdot$ min^{-1} at age 21; it then further, though not significantly, decreased, to 40.5 ± 5.0 ml $\cdot$ kg^{-1} $\cdot$ min^{-1} by age 27.

Tracking of Motor and Cardiovascular Fitness

IPCs, indicating the amount of tracking of motor and cardiovascular fitness in the same subject, were calculated, giving motor and cardiovascular fitness scores over 5-, 10-, and 15-year periods. Data are available for three 5-year periods (1977-1980, 1980-1985, and 1985-1991), two 10-year periods (1977-1985 and 1980-1991), and one 15-year period (1977-1991). The IPCs of the three 5-year periods and the two 10-year periods were averaged for each motor and cardiovascular fitness variable in order to obtain a single value. The interperiod correlations for 5-, 10-, and 15-year interperiods for males and females are listed in Tables 4.7a (males) and 4.7b (females).

Table 4.7a   Interperiod Correlation Coefficients for Males for Motor and Cardiovascular Fitness

Males	15-year interperiod	10-year interperiod	5-year interperiod
Plate tapping	0.65	0.72	0.79
10 × 5-m run	0.40	0.41	0.51
Sit-and-reach	0.26	0.43	0.53
Standing high jump	0.43	0.50	0.60
Arm pull relative to body weight	0.75	0.79	0.84
Bent-arm hang	0.55	0.59	0.72
Leg lifts	0.46	0.51	0.63
Absolute $\dot{V}O_2$max	0.21	0.41	0.68
$\dot{V}O_2$max relative to body weight	0.30	0.34	0.51

Note. $p < 0.05$ for all correlation coefficients.

Table 4.7b   Interperiod Correlation Coefficients for Females for Motor and Cardiovascular Fitness

Females	15-year interperiod	10-year interperiod	5-year interperiod
Plate tapping	0.46	0.58	0.65
10 × 5-m run	0.41	0.61	0.63
Sit-and-reach	0.58	0.59	0.70
Standing high jump	0.42	0.55	0.59
Arm pull relative to body weight	0.66	0.76	0.86
Bent-arm hang	0.64	0.62	0.74
Leg lifts	0.51	0.61	0.66
Absolute $\dot{V}O_2$max	0.42	0.59	0.74
$\dot{V}O_2$max relative to body weight	0.36	0.47	0.60

Note. $p < 0.05$ for all correlation coefficients.

From all motor and cardiorespiratory variables for both sexes, one can conclude that the longer the interperiod, the lower the IPC. Regardless of the length of the interperiod, males have higher IPCs compared with females for plate tapping, whereas females have higher IPCs for the 10 × 5-m run, the sit-and-reach test, the bent-arm hang, leg lifts, and $\dot{V}O_2$max (both absolute and relative). The IPCs for 15 and 5 years, but not for 10 years, for the standing high jump were higher in males. For arm pull relative to body weight, higher 15- and 10-year IPCs were found among males.

When an IPC exceeding .60 is arbitrarily used as a cutoff point for tracking, one can conclude that tracking exists

- for plate tapping in males and for arm pull relative to body weight and bent-arm hang in females over a 15-year interperiod;
- for plate tapping and arm pull relative to body weight in males and for the 10 × 5-m run, arm pull relative to body weight, bent-arm hang, and leg lifts in females over 10-year interperiods; and
- for all tests, except for the 10 × 5-m run, the sit-and-reach, and $\dot{V}O_2$max relative to body weight in males and the standing high jump in females, over 5-year interperiods.

Discussion

In the Netherlands, the last nationwide cross-sectional survey on growth in height and weight was held in 1980. In that survey, the median values for 20-year-old males was a height of 182 cm and a weight of 71 kg; for 20-year-old females, the values were 168 cm and 59 kg (Roede & van Wieringen, 1985). In our study, there was no further growth in height after age 21 among both males and females;

at age 21 the median body height for females was 170 cm and for males, 183 cm. These values match those of the earlier study. Median weight values in our study at age 27 were 74 kg in males and 63 kg in females. These values are slightly higher then those observed by Roede and Van Wieringen (1985).

As an indirect measure of body fatness, the BMI was used. Over the entire longitudinal period, no sex difference was found. Between ages 13 and 27, a gradual and significant increase in BMI was seen in the 18-22 age range, in both males and females. However, the significant interaction between time and sex showed that during adolescence, females had a higher BMI than males, whereas the reverse was seen at age 27. In population studies BMI, as an estimate of body fatness, has shown a U-shaped risk curve for total mortality in such a way that the greatest risk of death is experienced by the very lean and the very obese (Waaler, 1984; Feskens et al., 1993). In general, a BMI ranging from 20 to 25 is regarded as normal, whereas a BMI greater than 25 is classified as overweight, a BMI greater than 30 as obese, and a BMI less than 20 as underweight (Ashwell, 1992). From this perspective, the mean BMIs found in our subjects at age 27 are acceptable. Only 18% of the males and 10% of the females were found to be overweight (having a BMI between 25 and 30). No subject had a BMI greater than 30; 14% of the males and 27% of the females had a BMI less than 20.

Body fat can also be estimated from the sum of skinfolds measured at four different sites (triceps, biceps; suprailiac and subscapular sites). In our study, a steady increase in skinfolds was found in males from age 13 onward for all these locations, resulting in an average percentage of body fat of 20% at age 27. In females also, a steady increase was found until age 21, followed by a decrease, resulting in an estimated percentage of body fat of 28% at age 27. It should be noted that at age 27 the difference in percentage of body fat between males and females resulted primarily from differences in the skinfolds of the arms (biceps and triceps), since no differences were found in the skinfolds of the trunk (suprailiac and subscapular sites). If one accepts a percentage of body fat of 20% in males and 30% in females as threshold values for overweight and a risk factor for cardiovascular disease (Bell et al., 1986), then 10% of the male subjects and 15% of the female subjects should be regarded as such at age 27. In total, 39% of the males and 48% of the females had, at age 27, body fat percentages greater than 15% and 25%, respectively.

There are marked differences between individuals with regard to fat distribution. Central and peripheral fat may be distinguished. One method of assessing differences in fat distribution is by measuring the waist:hip ratio. There is accumulating evidence that an increased ratio increases the risk for disease (Ashwell, 1992; Den Tonkelaar et al., 1990; Kannel et al., 1991) in such a way that a waist:hip ratio greater than 1.0 in men and greater than 0.80 in women is regarded as a risk factor for ill health (Seidell & Deurenberg, 1985). In our study, the ratios at age 27 were 0.90 for males and 0.79 for females. These mean values were below the threshold values for increased health risk; however, further analysis of the data showed 6% of the male and 28% of the female subjects to be in excess of their respective thresholds.

At the start of the study at age 13, no difference was found between males and females with regard to resting diastolic (about 75 mmHg) and systolic (124 mmHg) blood pressure. Resting diastolic blood pressure increased significantly with age, both in males and females, to a mean value of about 80 mmHg at age 27. In males at age 27 a steadily increased resting systolic blood pressure of 135 mmHg was found. In females, during adolescence resting systolic pressure first significantly decreased to 121 mmHg and was then followed by a significant increase, to 124 mmHg at age 27. The difference between males and females in resting systolic pressure at this age was significant. Hypertension—increased resting diastolic and/or systolic blood pressure—is a commonly recognized risk factor for cardiovascular disease. The World Health Organization (WHO) defines hypertension in adults as a resting systolic blood pressure at or above 160 mmHg and/or a resting diastolic blood pressure at or above 95 mmHg. Borderline hypertension is defined as a resting systolic blood pressure less than 160 mmHg and greater than or equal to 140 mmHg and/or a resting diastolic blood pressure less than 95 mmHg and greater than or equal to 90 mmHg (World Health Organization, 1978, 1989). When comparing the mean resting diastolic and systolic blood pressure values of our subjects at age 27 to the WHO threshold values, one would tend to conclude that neither hypertension nor borderline hypertension should be regarded as a health problem in our population as a whole. However, when looking at the percentage of our population exceeding these threshold values, a borderline resting diastolic pressure was found in 12% of the males and a hypertensive diastolic pressure in an additional 12%. In females the following was found: borderline resting diastolic pressure in 11% of the subjects and hypertensive diastolic pressure in an additional 3% of the subjects. With regard to resting systolic pressure at age 27, the following percentages were found in males: borderline resting systolic pressure in 42% of the subjects and hypertensive systolic pressure in an additional 2%. In females, borderline resting systolic pressure was found in 9% of the subjects. No hypertensive systolic blood pressure was found in any of the females.

At age 13, in both males and females there were no significant differences between TC concentration, serum HDL-cholesterol concentration, and the TC:HDL-cholesterol ratio. During adolescence, on the average TC and HDL-cholesterol levels remained constant in females, then increased by age 27. In males, during adolescence a decrease was found for TC and HDL-cholesterol levels, followed by an increase in TC level and a decrease of HDL-cholesterol level by age 27. The TC:HDL-cholesterol ratio did not differ between males and females during adolescence. However, after adolescence males showed a greater ratio than females. The observed longitudinal differences between males and females in TC and HDL-cholesterol levels explain the higher TC:HDL-cholesterol ratios in males (4.0 at age 21 and 4.3 at age 27) after adolescence, compared with females (3.6 at age 21 and 3.4 at age 27).

In addition to overweight and high blood pressure, a high TC level and a high TC:HDL-cholesterol ratio are regarded as risk factors for cardiovascular disease (Binsbergen et al., 1992). The following cutoff points are often applied (Report of the National Cholesterol Education Program, 1988):

- TC > 5.2 mmol/L = moderate risk
- TC > 6.2 mmol/L = high risk
- TC:HDL-cholesterol ratio > 4.0 = moderate risk
- TC:HDL-cholesterol ratio > 5.5 = high risk

In our population, at age 27 the average TC levels in males were below the cutoff point for moderate risk (5.0 ± 0.9 mmol/L), whereas in females the value (5.3 ± 0.9 mmol/L) was just above the cutoff point. With regard to the TC:HDL-cholesterol ratio, the average value at age 27 in males (4.3 ± 1.1) just exceeded the cutoff point for moderate risk. Females (3.4 ± 0.8) at this age stayed below any cutoff point for increased risk.

However, when the percentage of the population that, at age 27, exceeded any of these cutoff points is examined, a different picture arises. Among males, 25% were found to have TC levels above the moderate-risk cutoff point and another 11% above the high-risk cutoff point. Among females, 39% of the population was found to have TC levels above the moderate-risk cutoff point and another 14% above the high-risk cutoff point. With regard to the TC:HDL-cholesterol ratio at age 27 17% of females and 44% of males were found with scores above the cutoff point for moderate increased risk. Additionally, 1% of females and 13% of males had a high increased risk.

The longitudinal development of motor fitness was monitored by means of the MOPER Fitness Test. In general, three of the seven motor fitness tests (arm pull relative to body weight, 10 × 5-m run, and 10 leg lifts) showed an increase in performance during adolescence, followed by a decrease in performance at age 21, then more or less stabilizing at age 27. In males the other four tests (plate tapping, sit-and-reach, standing high jump, and bent-arm hang) showed a relatively steep increase in performance during adolescence, followed by a small increase in performance at adult age. In females, a similar pattern was observed for the performance on the plate-tapping test and the sit-and-reach test. The performance of females on the standing high jump and the bent-arm hang did not change meaningfully over the 15-year period. Males performed significantly better with regard to the 10 × 5-m run, the standing high jump, the arm pull, and the bent-arm hang. Females showed a significantly better performance on the sit-and-reach test. No significant differences in performance between males and females were observed on the plate-tapping and the leg lift tests.

Since no other longitudinal studies covering the same length of time are described in the literature, it is impossible to make comparisons. However, there is some information available from one cross-sectional nationwide survey: the Canadian Standardized Test of Fitness (CSTF, 1986). Unfortunately, there was only one test performed in this survey that can be compared with our data: the sit-and-reach test. For reasons of practicality only the performance results of our subjects at age 27 are compared with the CSTF. At that age our male subjects had a mean score of 34 ± 10 cm, which equals the 60th percentile of the CSTF for 20- to 29-year-old Canadians. For females in our study a mean score of 40 ± 7 cm was found, equaling the 75th percentile of the CSTF for 20- to 29-year-old Canadians.

$\dot{V}O_2$ and $\dot{V}O_2$max were measured throughout the study in the same manner. This made it possible to compare submaximal oxygen uptake at the same running speed of 8 km/h at three different slopes: 0%, 2.5%, and 5%. The results showed that at all three slopes, $\dot{V}O_2$ per kilogram of body weight was similar for males and females. Over the course of time, both males and females showed a significant decrease in $\dot{V}O_2$ for each slope: about 5 ml · kg^{-1} · min^{-1} during the adolescent period and another 2 ml · kg^{-1} · min^{-1} by adult age. Males showed significantly higher $\dot{V}O_2$ values than females at all years of measurement for all three slopes (about 1-2 ml · kg^{-1} · min^{-1} greater). These findings reflect an increase in running economy with age and a higher running economy in females when compared to males at all ages. An increase in running economy with age is also found in the literature, whereas the sex difference is not (Åstrand & Rodahl, 1986).

Between ages 13 and 16 $\dot{V}O_2$max increased in both males (from 2.7 L/min to 3.7 L/min) and females (from 2.4 L/min to 2.7 L/min). In males a further increase was noted, to 3.81 L/min, by age 27. In females absolute $\dot{V}O_2$max remained constant. When this longitudinal pattern of absolute $\dot{V}O_2$ is compared with the pattern of $\dot{V}O_2$ relative to body weight, an inverse pattern is seen: In males during adolescence, stable $\dot{V}O_2$max values of about 59 ml · kg^{-1} · min^{-1} were found, followed by a decrease to about 51 ml · kg^{-1} · min^{-1} at age 27. In females between ages 13 and 27, $\dot{V}O_2$max gradually decreased, from 51 ml · kg^{-1} · min^{-1} to 41 ml · kg^{-1} · min^{-1}. However, as stated by Åstrand and Rodahl (1986), $\dot{V}O_2$max expressed per kilogram of body weight is still strongly related to body weight. Therefore, we expressed $\dot{V}O_2$max in another way: per kilogram of body weight to the two-thirds power. This enabled us to discern whether the observed changes were due to changes in the oxygen uptake system rather than to changes in body weight. This approach showed a significant increase in $\dot{V}O_2$max, from 21 ml · kg$^{-2/3}$ · min^{-1} to 23 ml · kg$^{-2/3}$ · min^{-1}, in adolescent males, followed by a significant decrease, back to 21 ml · kg$^{-2/3}$ · min^{-1} by age 27. In females between ages 13 and 17 a significant decrease in $\dot{V}O_2$max, from 19 ml · kg$^{-2/3}$ · min^{-1} to 18 ml · kg$^{-2/3}$ · min^{-1}, was found, followed by a further significant decrease, to 16 ml · kg$^{-2/3}$ · min^{-1} at age 21; this value remained constant (Fig. 4.29).

The stability of motor and cardiorespiratory fitness was assessed for three different time intervals of about 5, 10, and 15 years. In general it was found that the longer the time interval, the lower the IPC. When focusing only on the 15-year time interval, it was found that males had higher IPCs than females for plate tapping, the standing high jump, and the arm pull relative to body weight. IPCs in males for the 15-year interval varied from .75 for the arm pull relative to body weight to .21 for absolute $\dot{V}O_2$max. In females the 15-year IPCs varied from .66 for the arm pull relative to body weight to .36 for relative $\dot{V}O_2$max (kg^{-1}). Looking at the explained variance (r^2) and taking into account an arbitrary IPC cutoff value of greater than .60, one must conclude that there is moderate

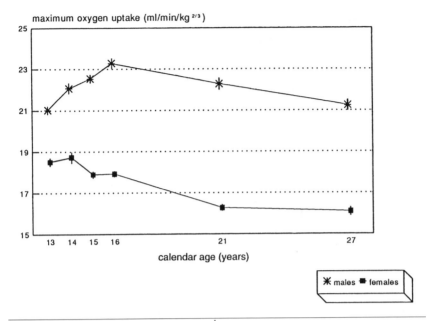

Figure 4.29 Mean and standard error of $\dot{V}O_2$max of males and females obtained during maximal running on a treadmill.

to no tracking: In males there is tracking only for the arm pull relative to body weight and for plate tapping; in females there is tracking only for the arm pull relative to body weight and for the bent-arm hang. There is only one study in the literature that has looked at tracking of motor and cardiovascular fitness in a similar manner, but only in men (Beunen et al., 1992); the following IPCs between ages 13 and 30 were found: plate tapping, .48; 10 × 5-m run, .45; sit-and-reach, .68; standing high jump, .52; arm pull (*not* relative to body weight), .33; bent-arm hang, .46; leg lifts, .68; and pulse recovery time following a standardized step test, .26. Comparing these results with ours and accepting a 10% difference in explained variance between these two studies as an acceptable measure, one can conclude that in our study a higher IPC was found for plate tapping and a lower IPC for the sit-and-reach and for leg lifts. The IPCs for the 10 × 5-m run, standing high jump, and bent-arm hang seem more or less comparable. This is also true for the IPCs of the $\dot{V}O_2$max measured in our study and the pulse recovery time measured in the Beunen et al. (1992) study. The IPCs for the arm pull are not comparable (much lower in Beunen's study). As in our study, in the Beunen et al. study IPCs increased with a decreasing interperiod.

Conclusions

For most of the observed variables discussed in this chapter marked differences were found between males and females over a 15-year time period. Moreover, for most of the variables, longitudinal changes were found.

At age 27, this population does not differ much from the standard Dutch population with regard to height and weight.

In general, in the course of time the body composition, resting diastolic and systolic blood pressures, and TC levels and the TC:HDL-cholesterol ratio of both males and females changed, from a health point of view, in an unfavorable way, although at age 27 overweight seems to be a problem in only a minority of the study population (in about 15% of the females and 10% of the males). At that age, normal diastolic blood pressures were found in 76% of the males and in 86% of the females, and normal systolic blood pressure was found in 56% of the males and 91% of the females. Of the males, 64% were found to have normal TC levels and 43% to have a normal TC:HDL-cholesterol ratio; in females, these values were 43% and 82%, respectively.

Motor fitness was measured by seven different tests. The longitudinal pattern was different for most of the tests, although some similarities were observed. For most of the tests there were sex differences; however, no longitudinal differences were found between males and females for the plate tapping and the leg lift tests.

Measurement of $\dot{V}O_2$ while running 8 km/h at three different slopes showed that running economy increased with age and that females have a higher running economy then males.

$\dot{V}O_2$max expressed per kilograms of body weight to the two-thirds power showed a significant increase in males during adolescence, followed by a significant decrease of the same magnitude by age 27. In females, from age 13 to age 21 a steady decrease was found; values then remained constant.

Finally, we may conclude that over a 15-year period only moderate tracking of arm pull relative to body weight and plate tapping in males, and of arm pull and the bent-arm hang in females, was found. There was no tracking of $\dot{V}O_2$max.

References

Ashwell M. (1992). The nature and risks of obesity. Briefing paper of the British Nutrition Foundation, 27, pp. 3-118.

Åstrand Per-O., K. Rodahl. (1986). Textbook of work physiology: Physiological bases of exercise, vol. 3. McGraw-Hill, New York.

Bell R.D., M. Macek, J. Rutenfranz, W.H.M. Saris. (1986). Health indicators and risk factors of cardio-vascular diseases during childhood and adolescence. In: J. Rutenfranz, R. Mocellin, F. Klimt (eds.), Children and exercise XII. Vol. 17 of: International series on sport sciences. Human Kinetics, Champaign, IL.

Beunen G., J. Lefevre, A.L. Claessens, R. Lysens, H. Maes, R. Renson, J. Simons, B. van den Eynde, B. van Reusel, C. van den Bossche. Age-specific correlation analysis of longitudinal physical fitness levels in men. Eur J Appl Physiol 64 (1992) 538-545.

Binsbergen J.J. van, A. Brouwer, B.B. van Drenth, A.F.M. Haverkort, A. Prins, T. van der Weijden. De NGH-standaard Cholesterol. Hart Bulletin (1992, Suppl. 23) 27-35.

Canadian Standardized Test of Fitness (CSTF) operations manual, 3. (1986). Fitness Canada.

Den Tonkelaar I., J.C. Seidell, P.A.H. Van Noord, E.A. Baanders-van Halewijn. De middel-heupomtrekverhouding bij Nederlandse vrouwen en het verband met zelf-gerapporteerde diabetes mellitus, hypertensie en cholecystectomie. Ned. Tijdschr. Geneesk. 134:39 (1990) 1900-1902.

Feskens E.J.M., W.M.M. Verschuren, M.P. Weijenberg, J.C. Seidell, D. Kromhout. Cardiovasculaire risicofactoren bij ouderen. Hart Bulletin 24 (1993) 67-72.

Kannel W.B., L.A. Cuppels, R. Ramaswami, J. Stokes III, B.E. Kreger, M. Higgens. Regional obesity and risk of cardiovascular disease: The Framingham Study. J Clin Epidemiol 44:2 (1991) 183-191.

Kemper H.C.G. The MOPER fitness test: A practical approach to standard measurement of motor performances in the field of physical education in the Netherlands (eds.) Evaluation of motor fitness. Katholieke Universiteit, Leuven (1982) 101-114.

Kemper H.C.G., R. Verschuur. Maximal aerobic power in 13- and 14-year-old teenagers in relation to biological age. Int J Sports Med 2 (1981) 97-100.

Report of national cholesterol education program expert panel on detection, evaluation and treatment of high blood cholesterol in adults. Arch Intern Med 148 (1988) 36-69.

Roede M.J., J.C. van Wieringen. Growth diagrams 1980: Netherlands third nationwide survey. Tijdschrift voor Sociale Gezondheidszorg 63 (1985, Suppl.) 1-33.

Seidell C., P. Deurenberg. Nieuwe internationale aanbevelingen voor de diagnostiek en behandeling van een riskante vetverdeling. Ned. Tijdschr. Geneesk. 129:48 (1985) 2321-2322.

Waaler H.T. Height, weight and mortality: The Norwegian experience. Acta Medica Scandinavia 215 (1984, Suppl. 679) 1-56.

Weiner, J.S., J.A. Lourie (eds.). (1968). Human biology: A guide to field methods. Blackwell, Oxford.

WHO/ISH 1989 guidelines for the management of mild hypertension: Memorandum from a WHO/ISH meeting bulletin of the World Health Organization, 1989, 67:493-498.

World Health Organization. Arterial hypertension report. Technical Report Series 628, Geneva, 1978.

Chapter 5

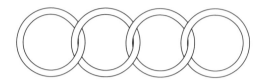

Longitudinal Development of Personality

Jan Snel, Pieter Kempe, & Willem van Mechelen

A central issue in the study of personality has been the stability and consistency of personality traits over time. *Stability* here refers to varying levels of *one* trait in time, whereas *consistency* refers to a pattern of traits and their interrelations (i.e., a profile). In general, the conclusion from experimental evidence is that the stability of personality increases with age and becomes fairly stabilized in young adulthood. This conclusion, however, must be based predominantly on cross-sectional research, since there have not been many studies following the same individuals from childhood to adulthood. Examples of the longitudinal approach are Bachman et al., 1978; Block, 1971; Kagan and Moss, 1962; and Stein et al., 1986. Consistency of personality, particularly in the period from adolescence to adulthood, was found by Bachman et al. (1978) in male subjects from age 16 to young adulthood. Block (1971) found a similar result in men and women in the period from junior high school to high school who were followed into their mid-30s. Kagan and Moss (1962) noted that long-term stability of personality traits tended to fit with sex-stereotyped behavior standards, probably induced by cultural expectations and socialization. Stein et al. (1986) collected longitudinal data on 15 personality traits at 4-year intervals in a group of males and females of ages 13 to 15 to 21 to 23. Comparing means and correlations, they found a continuity of personality traits with the greatest stability between the last two periods.

There are three points we would like to make:

1. One issue in research on stability is the longitudinal versus the cross-sectional approach. Advocates (Block, 1971; McCall, 1977) as well as opponents (Nesselroade & Baltus, 1974) of the longitudinal approach can be found. Arguments against this approach concern possible confounding with age and cohort effects, although this argument may be valid for the cross-sectional approach as well. Arguments for the longitudinal approach say that development of personality

takes place within individual lives; hence the longitudinal method is the only acceptable way to study changes in personality (Block, 1971). We subscribe to this latter view.

2. The most frequently used approach for determining stability is monitoring changes in the mean values of personality traits, whereas consistency is usually deduced from inspection of correlation coefficients. In both approaches it is not possible to estimate the consistency of the *pattern*, or profile, of personality.

3. Following changes in mean values can only be done successfully if no change of measurement instrument occurs (Backteman & Magnusson, 1981; Moss & Susman, 1980). One may wonder whether questionnaires appropriate for children as well as adults involve the same constructs. In the present study we had at our disposal both children and adult versions of two validated and reliable personality questionnaires.

Aim

The objective of this chapter is to follow the longitudinal development of the personality profile in the subjects by using two personality questionnaires. Another point we were interested in was whether and in what way personality might be related to aerobic fitness.

Methods and Subjects

The Amsterdam Health and Growth Study, conducted in 1977 to 1980, 1985, and 1991, surveyed the personality, physical fitness, lifestyle, health status, stress levels, life events, sociocultural characteristics, diet, and other characteristics of, originally, 233 subjects; 85 men and 98 women followed the whole experimental trajectory from age 12 to age 27.

Instruments

Data on personality traits were collected by using the Achievement Motivation Test (AMT) (Hermans, 1971, 1976) and the Dutch Personality Inventory (DPI) (Luteijn, 1974; Luteijn et al., 1981, 1985), two tests known for their reliability and validity. Because of the subjects' age at the time of the first four measurements (they were still in high school), from age 12 to 18, the youth versions of both inventories (AMT-y and DPI-y) were used. At ages 21 and 27 the adult versions (AMT-a and DPI-a) were administered. Details of protocol and procedures of this study are given in Part I.

Achievement Motivation Test

The following scales are found on the AMT-y and the AMT-a:

- *Achievement motivation (AM)*—the need to achieve and the will to reach achievements

- *Facilitating anxiety (FA)*—a fear of failure, leading to higher achievements, especially in unstructured task situations
- *Debilitating anxiety (DA)*—fear of failure, leading to lower achievements, especially in unstructured task situations

The reliability (KR_{20}) coefficients of the AMI-a are AM, .81; DA, .84; and FA, .85 (Hermans, 1976); those of the AMI-y are AM, .81; DA, .79; and FA, .82 (Hermans, 1983a).

Dutch Personality Inventory

The following scales are found on the DPI-y and the DPI-a:

- *Inadequacy (IN)*—vague feelings of malfunctioning, anxiety, vague physical and psychosomatic complaints, depressive mood
- *Social inadequacy (SI)*—neurotic shyness, uncomfortable feelings in social situations, avoidance of unfamiliar people or situations
- *Rigidity (RG)*—the need for regularity, having fixed habits and principles, sense of duty and a positive task appraisal, perseverance
- *Self-sufficiency* or *Recalcitrance (SS)*—mistrust, desire to solve problems alone, feelings of independence
- *Dominance (DO)*—self-reliance, trying to be or play the boss

The disattenuated correlations between the DPI-y and DPI-a versions are IN, .90; RG, .79; SI, .89; SS, .89; and DO, .71. The Cronbach's α reliability coefficients of the DPI-y are IN, .87; RG, .83; SI, .82; SS, .75; and DO, .70 (Bücking et al., 1975); those of the DPI-a are IN, .86; RG, .81; SI, .86; SS, .70; and DO, .74 (Luteijn et al., 1985).

Statistics

To answer the posed questions the following steps were taken:

- Calculation of the means of the personality traits. Means are used to describe the group with reference to norm groups.
- Calculation of the interperiod correlations (IPCs). Because the youth and adult versions of the two questionnaires assess, according to the designers of the tests, the same concepts, the AMT and DPI intercorrelations should remain similar over the course of the years. The IPCs themselves, their intercept, the slope of the regression line, and its error variance indicate the test-retest quality and the stability of each scale (see chapter 1).
- Principal components analyses (PCAs). PCAs were done to establish whether personality traits covary with one another at the points of time and to assess the consistency of the components found.
- Canonical correlation analyses. These analyses reveal as parsimoniously as possible changes in time for more than one component (set of variables or scales) simultaneously.

These analyses were performed for males and females separately.

Results

Data of the adolescent period (ages 13 to 17), young adulthood (age 21), and adulthood (age 27) were available for analysis. However, because the results of the adolescent period have been described in detail elsewhere (Kemper, 1985), for this study we analyzed the data of three points in time with 6-year intervals, at ages 15, 21, and 27.

Group Characteristics

The means seen in Table 5.1 indicate that, in general, compared with the values of reference groups (Bücking et al., 1975; Hermans, 1971, 1983a), the male subjects were characterized by a lower Achievement Motivation and Social Inadequacy; a fluctuating Debilitating Anxiety; and normal levels of Inadequacy, Rigidity, Self-Sufficiency, and Dominance. The Recalcitrance scale is found only in the DPI-y, so it is discarded from further analysis.

The female subjects, compared with the reference groups, can be described as having lower Achievement Motivation, somewhat more Debilitating Anxiety, less Inadequacy, and a lower Social Inadequacy and to be more self-critical (SS) and inclined toward dominance.

In view of the standard deviations, our conclusion is that both men and women can be described as comparable to the reference groups.

Scale Quality

IPCs were determined to establish whether comparisons between the AMT-y and AMT-a scales, on the one hand, and the DPI-y and DPI-a scales, on the other, can be made. Because the youth and adult versions of the two questionnaires should measure the same constructs, the AMT and DPI scale intercorrelations should remain similar and diminish in a linear fashion with increasing time intervals.

Consistency of personality was assessed by inspecting the IPCs (Table 5.2) between the original seven points of measurement with intervals ranging from 1 to 14 years. The expected trend of lower IPCs with increasing time intervals exhibited some exceptions. Specifically, in men the Inadequacy and Rigidity scales do not meet this criterion; to a lesser degree, this holds for the Self-Sufficiency and Dominance scales. Among women the coefficients show a non-significant linear fit for the Achievement Motivation, Facilitating Anxiety, and Self-Sufficiency scales, whereas the Self-Sufficiency and the Dominance scales reveal rather low 1-year interval correlations of .41 and .46, respectively.

Testing

The IPC trends seen in Table 5.3, in which the intercept and slope of the regression lines are determined, demonstrate a low fit for the Achievement Motivation, Inadequacy, and Rigidity scales among men. Among women the explained variance of this fit is sufficient and significant for all scales. These results are reflected

Table 5.1   Statistics for Personality Scales

| | Age (y) | | | | | | | | | | | | | |
| Scale | 15 | | | | | 21 | | | | | 27 | | | |
	Ref.	n	M	SE	SD	Ref.	n	M	SE	SD	n	M	SE	SD
Males														
Achievement Motivation	17.21	79	12.29	.63	5.63	21.32	78	16.40	.88	7.78	84	19.63	.85	7.80
Facilitating Anxiety	9.77	80	12.01	.43	3.85	11.00	78	12.95	.46	4.08	84	14.32	.44	4.07
Debilitating Anxiety	7.73	80	6.79	.40	3.56	9.38	78	8.18	.67	5.89	84	7.56	.62	5.65
Inadequacy	49.62	79	41.28	1.07	9.52	7-13	77	9.39	.87	7.64	84	7.01	.75	6.91
Rigidity	58.11	79	57.35	.92	8.16	18-25	77	20.42	.87	7.64	84	20.21	.81	7.44
Social Inadequacy	24.85	81	22.83	.68	6.08	7-12	77	8.83	.78	6.83	84	6.54	.68	6.21
Self-Sufficiency	45.80	77	43.75	.97	8.53	9-14	77	11.86	.61	5.32	84	9.58	.51	4.67
Recalcitrance						15-21	77	16.65	.77	6.75	84	14.30	.72	6.55
Dominance	26.92	80	28.90	.57	5.13	13-19	77	16.87	.73	6.37	84	18.93	.64	5.83
Females														
Achievement Motivation	17.37	90	14.30	.57	5.38	20.83	94	17.38	.72	7.00	98	19.50	.63	6.25
Facilitating Anxiety	7.99	94	9.17	.52	5.05	9.15	94	10.94	.52	5.00	98	13.02	.43	4.26
Debilitating Anxiety	9.42	96	8.86	.41	3.99	12.21	94	13.19	.61	5.92	98	11.63	.59	5.80
Inadequacy	49.62	96	43.18	.99	9.69	11-17	94	11.88	.67	6.50	98	8.43	.64	6.33
Rigidity	58.11	96	57.60	.77	7.57	18-25	94	21.29	.81	7.84	98	23.30	.76	7.48
Social Inadequacy	24.85	98	23.37	.65	6.43	10-15	94	9.33	.69	6.72	98	7.59	.61	6.04
Self-Sufficiency	45.80	96	38.43	.57	5.57	9-14	94	8.31	.42	4.08	98	8.03	.43	4.26
Recalcitrance						15-21	94	16.14	.61	5.91	98	13.13	.58	5.79
Dominance	29.92	98	27.11	.43	4.22	10-14	94	14.15	.59	5.71	98	16.06	.56	5.57

Note. Ref. = reference group values.

Table 5.2   Interperiod Correlation Coefficients of Personality Scales

							Age range (y)								
	13-14	14-15	15-16	13-15	14-16	13-16	16-21	15-21	21-27	14-21	13-21	16-27	15-27	14-27	13-27
Males															
Interval (y)	1	1	1	2	2	3	5	6	6	7	8	11	12	13	14
Achievement Motivation	62	69	74	57	62	30	49	50	82	40	28	56	57	52	32
Facilitating Anxiety	65	70	51	44	47	55	52	45	57	48	47	44	31	23	37
Debilitating Anxiety	75	70	62	65	51	55	55	49	74	44	46	50	53	35	48
Inadequacy	53	76	54	59	54	36	35	69	63	61	34	46	55	55	21
Rigidity	70	69	69	67	57	39	37	30	67	26	18	50	42	49	40
Social Inadequacy	60	76	66	57	59	42	57	44	44	40	39	34	42	37	39
Self-Sufficiency	70	71	83	51	63	43	48	39	43	34	33	34	27	14	20
Dominance	61	77	72	43	69	30	55	52	55	52	22	36	26	24	13
Females															
Interval (y)	1	1	1	2	2	3	5	6	6	7	8	11	12	13	14
Achievement Motivation	66	54	73	40	66	48	56	41	70	38	37	50	39	42	28
Facilitating Anxiety	60	67	68	57	69	69	28	38	53	43	15	26	35	37	23
Debilitating Anxiety	69	83	78	65	72	58	41	41	72	34	34	48	49	45	48
Inadequacy	68	74	78	59	71	59	53	46	68	49	37	56	43	49	37
Rigidity	63	70	83	63	63	63	31	35	74	30	19	23	25	21	17
Social Inadequacy	79	76	84	73	72	76	53	49	57	47	52	39	29	34	29
Self-Sufficiency	41	58	57	47	52	37	40	28	72	44	29	33	23	27	28
Dominance	46	55	64	40	55	31	45	48	67	35	39	32	34	33	23

Table 5.3   Regression Fit, Intercept, and the Slope of the Change in Personality Scales Over 14 Years

Scale	F-value	r²	p	Intercept	95% CI	Slope	95% CI
Males							
Achievement Motivation	2.49	.16	.14	.62	.45-.62	−.014	−.033-.005
Facilitating Anxiety	20.29	.61	.00	.60	.43-.52	−.020	−.030--.011
Debilitating Anxiety	10.55	.45	.01	.66	.50-.61	−.017	−.028--.006
Inadequacy	2.45	.16	.14	.59	.44-.59	−.013	−.030-.005
Rigidity	4.41	.25	.06	.60	.40-.57	−.019	−.039-.001
Social Inadequacy	24.29	.65	.00	.63	.45-.54	−.022	−.032--.012
Self-Sufficiency	60.22	.82	.00	.69	.40-.49	−.051	−.051--.029
Dominance	24.06	.65	.00	.67	.39-.52	−.034	−.050--.019
Females							
Achievement Motivation	9.04	.41	.01	.62	.44-.56	−.019	−.033--.005
Facilitating Anxiety	22.89	.64	.00	.66	.39-.52	−.032	−.047--.018
Debilitating Anxiety	10.06	.44	.01	.70	.49-.63	−.023	−.039--.007
Inadequacy	20.30	.61	.00	.70	.52-.61	−.022	−.033--.012
Rigidity	32.71	.72	.00	.71	.38-.52	−.059	−.059--.027
Social Inadequacy	181.41	.93	.00	.81	.54-.59	−.040	−.046--.033
Self-Sufficiency	9.97	.43	.01	.53	.35-.47	−.020	−.034--.006
Dominance	8.361	.39	.01	.54	.38-.49	−.016	−.029--.004

Note. CI = confidence interval.

further in the 95% confidence interval of the mean IPCs, ranging from .09 to .18 for men and from .05 to .14 for women.

The intercept on the x-axis estimates the immediate test-retest reliability of the scale. Whether this reliability coefficient can be interpreted as valid depends also on the reliability of the fit of the regression line (F-value). IPCs scattered narrowly around this line exhibit a high fit—a common factor has been measured. Examples of a low fit—one in which random factors influence the fit—are the Inadequacy scale in men (F-value = 2.45) and the Social Inadequacy scale in women (F-value = 181.41) (Fig. 5.1).

Another criterion for scale quality is the tangential slope of the regression line, which for a good scale must be less than 0. Table 5.3 indicates that the Achievement Motivation, Inadequacy, and Rigidity scales in men are of low psychometric quality; the 95% confidence interval of their slopes reveals positive values. We retained these scales for further analyses for three reasons: (a) lack of available data for a 15-year longitudinal study on these questionnaires; (b) ensuring comparable results for men and women; and (c) the assertion of the designers of the questionnaires that the scales assess the supposed constructs

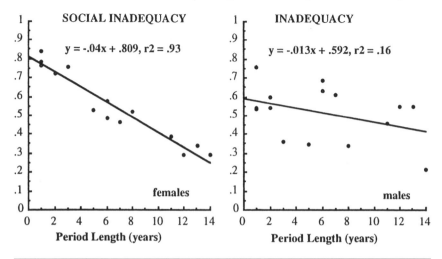

Figure 5.1   Regression lines through interperiod correlation coefficients with different time intervals for a good fit and steep slope (*left*) and bad fit and horizontal slope (*right*).

validly and reliably (Bücking et al., 1975; Hermans, 1976, 1983b; Luteijn et al., 1985).

Principal Components Analyses

Varimax rotated principal components with pairwise deletion of missing values, listwise deletion of missing values, and substitution of the mean (meansub procedure) were compared. All these showed similar results, though the determinants of the listwise covariance matrix were generally higher, and those of the meansub procedure lower. We decided to use the results of the pairwise deletion of missing values method, in order to use as much information as possible.

Large differences in number of subjects for the pairwise deletion covariance matrix were found neither between scales nor over separate years, nor was this number small. This suggests that no biased sample of the available data (men, $n = 84$; women, $n = 98$) was used. Component scores were subsequently used as input for canonical correlation analysis. The eight personality scales revealed that, in general, men and women yielded virtually identical personality factor structures through the 4 years measured during adolescence (Table 5.4; age 15). We would like to label Component 1 as Fearfulness, Component 2 as Tenacity, and Component 3 as Arrogance.

Among women, exceptions are an additional loading of $-.44$ for Social Inadequacy on component 3 at age 13; at age 14 there is an emerging Inadequacy loading of .47, which continues at age 15 and is found then for the first time in men. At age 16 this loading remains for men (.46), but is absent for women. These lower loadings may not be significant to interpretation (see Stevens [1986] for guidelines about significant loadings depending on sample size).

Table 5.4 Principal Components Analysis of the Data at Ages 15, 21, and 27

Scale	Component 1 M	Component 1 F	Component 2 M	Component 2 F	Component 3 M	Component 3 F	Commonalities M	Commonalities F
Adolescents (15 years old)								
Achievement Motivation	.82	.84					.76	.81
Debilitating Anxiety	-.80	-.72					.68	.73
Facilitating Anxiety			.87	.90			.71	.59
Dominance					.66	.70	.54	.52
Inadequacy	.62	.61			.43	.53	.63	.69
Rigidity			.85	.87			.71	.81
Social Inadequacy	.72	.76					.58	.59
Self-Sufficiency					.77	.77	.71	.61
Total $s^2\%$	31.6	29.6	20.0	20.0	15.1	17.2	66.6	66.8
Young adults (21 years old)								
Achievement Motivation			.80	.83			.67	.70
Debilitating Anxiety	.91	.89					.83	.79
Facilitating Anxiety	-.67	-.70					.47	.51
Dominance	-.51	-.42	.55	.67			.57	.65
Inadequacy	.82	.80					.68	.64
Rigidity	.83	.67				.54	.80	.73
Social Inadequacy			.84	.63		.45	.79	.80
Self-Sufficiency					.96	.89	.93	.84

	37.6	36.4	21.1	21.6	12.8	12.8	71.5	70.7
Total s²%								
Adults (27 years old)								
Achievement Motivation			.70	.73			.52	.63
Debilitating Anxiety	.88	.83					.79	.72
Facilitating Anxiety	-.83	-.72					.71	.54
Dominance			.69	.84			.58	.72
Inadequacy	.85	.85					.80	.73
Rigidity			.77			.72	.74	.67
Social Inadequacy	.41		-.46	-.62	.62	.51	.75	.73
Self-Sufficiency					.88	.82	.78	.76
Total s²%	38.5	31.3	19.1	20.3	13.3	17.1	70.9	68.7

Note. Only loadings greater than or equal to .40 and components with Eigenvalues greater than or equal to 1 are shown. M = males; F = females; Total s²% = total percentage of explained variance.

From ages 13 to 16 the personality profile is quite consistent. At young adulthood (at age 21), Components 1 and 2 remain similar to previous years, but are now enriched with moderate Dominance-loadings. For both men and women Components 1 and 2 could be named as Fearful-Insecure and Domineering Tenacity, respectively.

Component 3 for men is restricted mainly to one variable, Self-Sufficiency. For women this quality is moderated somewhat by the moderate .50 loadings of Social Inadequacy and Rigidity, and for this reason Component 3 is called Fixed Recalcitrance. As a whole, the structure is less clear-cut than 6 years before; nevertheless, the personality profiles for young adult men and women still look quite similar.

In the 27-year-old adult men Component 1 (Fearful-Insecure) is still largely intact, but, without the loading of Dominance, may be called Anxiety. This Dominance loading, which came from Component 1, strengthened Component 2 (Domineering Tenacity). The Social Inadequacy scale, fading from Component 1 (Anxiety), emerged as a negative loading in Component 2 (Domineering Tenacity) and strengthens with positive loadings in Component 3, which we labeled Fixed Recalcitrance for men as well as for women.

For the adult women, Rigidity no longer loads on Component 2, or the Hard-Driving component, but shifts to Component 3 (Fixed Recalcitrance), a change that had started between ages 16 and 21. Though for men the data indicate a similar change, that is a slight lowering of the Rigidity loading on Component 2; this change is delayed compared to women. Table 5.5 summarizes these findings.

Canonical Correlation Analysis

The number and nature of mutually independent relationships between two sets of variables or components can be determined by using canonical correlation analysis. Canonical correlation may reveal which dimension of personality is

Table 5.5   Tentative Names Ascribed to Principal Components

		Adolescence	Young adulthood	Adulthood
Males				
Component	1	Fearfulness	Fearful-Insecure	Anxiety
	2	Tenacity	Domineering Tenacity	Domineering Tenacity
	3	Arrogance	Self-Sufficiency	Recalcitrance
Females				
Component	1	Fearfulness	Fearful-Insecure	Anxiety
	2	Tenacity	Domineering Tenacity	Hard-Driving
	3	Arrogance	Fixed Recalcitrance	Fixed Recalcitrance

Note. Only unipolar titles are used.

most stable or reliable. This dimension can be interpreted by determining which loadings of the original input variables load highly on the canonical variates created. In the present analysis the input variables are the principal components found in the previous PCAs; this limits the number of variables, thus making canonical correlations more reliable (Stevens, 1986). However, because these components vary in content during the course of time, interpretation of the canonical variates may become overly abstract if the canonical dimensions consist of more than one component loading. Therefore, although we have tried to interpret all variates, some interpretations may seem somewhat farfetched. More important with respect to consistency is the total multivariate test-retest reliability of a whole set of canonical correlations. This represents the predictability of one multivariate profile (with all its intercorrelations) from another profile. This test-retest reliability is the square root of the sum of the "explained" variance proportion.

Men

Variate I of the canonical correlations shows that during men's development from adolescents to young adults Fearfulness is a stable trait (Table 5.6), with a slight coloring of the negative Tenacity component. Variate II highlights Tenacity as the main element, though Arrogance and Fearfulness have some part in this. Maybe some Arrogance is a prerequisite to sustain and profile oneself in this respect. The combination of Tenacity, Arrogance, and an element of fear is thought of as Domineering Tenacity. Variate III, called Self-Sufficiency, links Arrogance to Self-Sufficiency, a more socially withdrawn characteristic, as emphasized by the small negative Tenacity loading. The .36 association between these two sets is relatively small, however.

During the second interval, from young adult to adult, the associations are straightforward, pointing to greater stability and independence of traits in spite of the fact that the components used in time do not have exactly the same meaning. The Domineering Tenacity component has become the most important association (.80). Variate II links Fearful-Insecure to Anxiety, thus confirming the results of the PCAs, in which Anxiety differed from Fearfulness by lacking the aspect of Social Inadequacy. This last aspect (Social Inadequacy) might be linked with Recalcitrance as a defense against socially inadequate behavior. In other words the social fear aspect seems to become disconnected from Anxiety (together named Fearful-Insecure) and turned into Recalcitrance instead of Self-Sufficiency. Canonical Variate III links Self-Sufficiency to Recalcitrance; the main association with Fearfulness-Insecurity is accompanied by a small *negative* loading on Anxiety. Of relevance is that components with similar meanings seem to be associated in time during this period.

The change from a 15-year-old adolescent to a 27-year-old adult reveals two statistically significant canonical variates. Variate I, called Social-Defensiveness, predominantly links Fearfulness and Arrogance to Anxiety and Recalcitrance. Variate II, named Obstinate Tenacity, links Tenacity/Arrogance to Domineering Tenacity/Recalcitrance. Again, similar constructs are linked together, with the last (smaller) components emerging diffusely in time.

Table 5.6   Canonical Variates Over Three Age-Periods

	Age-period (y)								
	15-21			21-27			15-27		
	Canonical variate								
	I	II	III	I	II	III	I	II	III
Males									
Component 1	.88	-.32			-.99		-.85		-.50
2	-.41	-.85	-.27	-.98			.38	-.91	
3		-.47	.88			1.0	-.43	-.43	.82
Total s²%	18.6	11.7	4.1	20.8	15.9	5.5	14.3	9.9	.8
Component 1	.97	-.23			-.94	-.29	-.92		-.39
2	-.21	-.98		-.99			.21	-.94	-.26
3			.99		-.22	.96	-.28	-.30	.91
Total s²%	17.7	11.4	4.4	21.3	15.0	5.7	13.8	9.3	.9
Canonical correlation	.73*	.58*	.36*	.80*	.69*	.41*	.65*	.53*	.16
Females									
Component 1	.70	.71		-.25	-.53	.81	.97		
2	.56	-.62	-.54	.42	.68	.60	-.21	-.80	
3	.48	-.35	.81	.88	-.48			-.63	
Total s²%	13.0	7.4	.6	23.4	18.9	16.4	11.2	6.7	
Component 1	.70	.69		-.39	-.28	.87	.96	-.23	
2	.72	-.66			.89	.42	-.27	-.68	
3		-.29	.96	.91	-.29	.28		-.73	
Total s²%	12.8	7.2	.6	23.9	18.5	16.4	10.9	6.7	
Canonical correlation	.61*	.47*	.13	.84*	.77*	.70*	.58*	.44*	.08

Note. Total s²% = total percentage of explained variance.

*p < .05.

It seems that the small changes in meaning of the input components reflect general trends for this group of men—that is, correlations between components in time are restricted mainly to similar components, thus giving a picture of stability and independence of traits. Components seem to be relatively stable and unaffected by one another from ages 15 to 21 for this group of young men.

Women

From adolescence to young adulthood differences in personality development can be observed between men and women. Although, as with men, Fearfulness is the common element, Tenacity and to a lesser extent Arrogance seem to be more entangled for women than for men. Our interpretation is that women seem to change from feelings of insecurity to a more self-confident perception of themselves. The element of Arrogance involved might be interpreted similarly. However, the two first components remain fairly stable but are linked together. We like to interpret Variate I as Persistence. Variate II, labeled Helplessness, links Fearfulness and Tenacity (−.62) to Fearful/Insecure and Domineering Tenacity (−.66). The explained variance is small, however, and does not indicate a strong trait.

During the change from young adult to adult a different first canonical variate emerges for women as well as for men. The strongest association, .84, which exists between the Fixed Recalcitrance components, is interpreted as Forced Self-Assertion, also in view of the small negative Fear/Anxiety weights and the positive Domineering-Tenacity weight. Variate II, called Self-Assurance, shows primarily a Domineering/Tenacious association, whereas the Fear and Recalcitrance elements load negatively on both sets. Variate III, interpreted as Compulsively Achieving, predominantly links Components 1 and 2, Fearfulness/Insecure and Anxiety, to Components 1 and 2 of the second set, Domineering Tenacity and Hard-Driving. The three canonical correlations for the latter sets are substantial and have a considerable amount of common variance.

The 12-year period between adolescence and adulthood revealed two significant canonical variates. The variate labeled Anxiety links the long-term consistent components, Fearfulness and Anxiety. Variate II, interpreted as Social Compulsiveness, unifies the second and third components of both points in time and might reflect an attitude of controlling other people.

Discussion

The present study evaluated the consistency of personality from adolescence through adulthood. An important aspect of the study was the use of youth and adult versions of personality questionnaires. On the one hand, it might be argued that the only way to detect subjects' characteristics is the use of appropriate instruments adapted to the subjects' age. Hence, it was quite legitimate to include youth and adult versions. On the other hand, in longitudinal studies one crucial prerequisite is the use of a constant test battery. We preferred to administer the AMT and the DPI for several reasons. First, both tests are of proven reliability and validity and are thus quite frequently used in the Netherlands. Second, satisfying data are available on the scale intercorrelations of the DPI-y and DPI-a and the reliabilities of both inventories. Third, the definitions of the scales of the youth and adult versions are quite similar, except perhaps for the Self-Sufficiency scale of the DPI-y and DPI-a. Finally, at the time of the start of the Amsterdam Growth and Health Study, and at present as well, to our knowledge no personality questionnaires were or are available that were appropriate to use from young adolescence through adulthood.

The correlations between the same traits across time were all substantial, indicating a true existing continuity of each particular trait through the 15 years of the study. One interesting point was to ascertain whether the supposed Sturm und Drang period of the adolescent years is characterized by a fluctuating stability (see Table 5.2) and whether the change from adolescence to young adulthood is greater than that from young adulthood to adulthood. Indeed, during adolescence (ages 12 to 17) the IPCs with intervals ranging from 1 to 3 years demonstrate a rather unstable pattern. The canonical correlations (Table 5.5) support this observation; the period from ages 15 to 21 shows lower correlations than that from ages 21 to 27. This pattern emerges also in the IPCs of the three points of measurement with 6-year intervals.

However, restriction of range could have occurred, since the subjects continuing in our study belonged originally to a relatively homogenous sample consisting of the first classes of a high school in Amsterdam (Moss & Susman, 1980). Also, those who left the study may have increased the restriction of range, since only relatively motivated subjects may have continued their participation. The impact of this self-selection on the presented results is unknown, except for the findings that dropouts in the first year of the adolescent period showed lower Facilitating Anxiety and higher Inadequacy scores (Dekker et al., 1985) and had lower sociometric ratings from classmates than those who remained (Snel & Ritmeester, 1985). The results of this study, however, are in accordance with findings of consistency in other studies. Stein et al. (1986) found an average correlation of .52 over an 8-year period, comparable to the .59 of Nesselroade and Baltes (1974), whereas in our study for a 15-year period the average correlation in men as well as women was .48.

Although an average correlation may be important in itself, it may not always reveal concurrent changes between several traits at once. For instance, if one personality trait changes *in time*, others may change as well. Although comparing principal components can reveal some contingencies over time, there is no indication of their codependency. The advantage of using canonical correlation analysis thus lies in its ability to associate more than one variable at once, thus indicating codependency between *sets* of variables. Though interpretation of these associated sets of variables constitutes the ultimate goal of attaching meaning to the associations found and hence linking them in a theoretical framework, the choice and number of variables can limit interpretability. Thus, although in this study some variates may be interpretable and more so for men than for women, the most important indication of profile consistency is the profile test-retest reliability in time. These profile reliabilities, going from adolescent to a young adult, from young adult to adult, and from adolescent to adult, respectively, are .58, .65, and .48 for men and .45, .77, and .42 for women. These profile reliabilities indicate, first, that change occurs foremost in the adolescent to young-adult period for both men and women. Second, women change more or earlier during this period but also seem to "settle" psychologically earlier, as indicated by the higher (.77) overall correlation in the period between the young-adult to adult stages.

Some caution considering the results of canonical correlation should be expressed. Due to a small variable:subject ratio, the generalizability and the reliability of the results may be limited. Stevens (1986) considers the minimum for this ratio 1:20. Also, the change from youth to adult versions of the questionnaires used may have affected the results.

In spite of these reservations, circumstantial evidence is present in the data that supports the conclusion that women start to change *earlier*, though not necessarily in the same way. During adolescence, personality structures for men and women as a group appear to be remarkably consistent, although the components (see Table 5.4), in particular Tenacity and Arrogance, seem to become directed more to other people. During young adulthood these changes are more apparent, and previous tendencies seem to settle.

The changes predominantly are manifest in the variables Dominance, Rigidity, and Social Inadequacy and represent a striking phenomenon—namely, that men seem to lag behind women in changes in component loadings. If we take the components of the adolescent period as representative, the movements of Dominance, Rigidity, and Social Inadequacy can be represented schematically (Table 5.7). The table illustrates that changes in factors and loadings arise earlier in women than in men. What shows up from these scales is confirmed for the Inadequacy scale during the 4 years of measurement of the adolescent period. In Year 1 (age 13) the Inadequacy-loading on Component 1 changes and moves to small loadings on Components 1 and 3 in Year 2, but men follow first in Year 3. In the last year of this period and in young adulthood this Inadequacy-loading disappears from Component 3 first for women, then for men. Women seem to be more advanced than men in the development of their personality profile.

A possible methodological flaw in this study is testing, or learning, effects. This imperfection is an inherent feature of longitudinal studies. For the first 4 years of measurement we examined this point indirectly by comparing the Cronbach's α reliabilities of the longitudinal group with those of a cross-sectional control group. It was demonstrated that the yearly reliability coefficients of both groups were quite similar, around .80. Also the estimated test reliabilities from the IPC-intercepts, ranging from .65 to .85 (Dekker et al., 1985) are quite satisfactory compared with the average .64 reliability of 4-year intervals reported by Stein et al. (1986) and the .61 to .66 values presented by Conley (1984). Concerning the later points of measurement in our study, involving 6 year-intervals, retesting effects may be considered of minor importance.

An interesting question that can be answered from the data gathered in this study concerns the presumed beneficial effects of regular exercise on psychological makeup. Indeed, longitudinal studies have, after exercise training, showed improved mood and less anxiety and depression (Cramer et al., 1991; Long & Haney, 1988; MacMahon & Gross, 1988; Simons & Birkimer, 1988; and Steptoe et al., 1989). Other studies, however, did not replicate beneficial effects (de Geus, 1992; Lennox et al., 1990). The question we tried to answer was whether there was an association between personality and fitness in our subjects who had not been subjected to any exercise program at the times of measurement. To answer this question we included fitness (aerobic maximal oxygen capacity [$\dot{V}O_2max$] in milliliters per kilogram of body weight) in the PCA.

Table 5.7 Shift of Loadings Over Three Periods

Trait	Gender	Adolescence		Young adulthood				Adulthood					
		C	L	C	L	C	L	C	L	C	L	C	L
Dominance	Males	3	.66	→1	-.51	2	.55	↑		2	.69		
	Females	3	.70	→1	-.42	2	.67	↑		2	.84		
Rigidity	Males	2	.85	→2	.84	3	.45	↑		2	.77		
	Females	2	.87	→2	.63	3	.54	↑		3	.72		
Social Inadequacy	Males	1	.72	→1	.83			↑1	.41	2	-.46	3	.62
	Females	1	.76	→1	.67			↑		2	-.62	3	.51

Note. C = component; L = loading.

During adolescence in men, a component emerged consisting of a nonsignificant $\dot{V}O_2$max loading of .41 together with a .85 loading for Achievement Motivation and .82 for Rigidity. Among the adolescent women, $\dot{V}O_2$max loaded at .91, independently of other components. The total explained variance in men decreased 5%, but in women increased 4.4%. During young adulthood in men, $\dot{V}O_2$max loaded at .91 on the component Domineering Tenacity, together with a .58 loading on Facilitating Anxiety; whereas in women $\dot{V}O_2$max had a .88 loading together with Dominance (−.62) and Rigidity (.45) on Component 3. These loadings in men and women resulted in an increase in explained variance of approximately 5%.

In women, $\dot{V}O_2$max loaded at .89, together with a −.62 loading on Dominance. Since evidence indicates that psychological differences between fit and unfit individuals are primarily due to self-selection rather than any causal relationship, it may mean either that low dominant women are highly fit (non-partialed $r = -.28$) or that highly dominant women are less fit.

In adult men, $\dot{V}O_2$max loaded negatively (−.57) on the Domineering Tenacity component, which may mean a low involvement in physical activities. In adult women, loadings of $\dot{V}O_2$max were absent. In men and women the explained variance decreased 5.3% and 7.1%, respectively.

The prudent conclusion is that in this study $\dot{V}O_2$max makes neither a substantial nor a consistent contribution to the explained variance of personality components, and for that reason may be considered to have no relationship with personality (see de Geus, 1992).

Conclusions

In summary, the findings of this longitudinal study support the idea of meaningful consistency in personality profiles from adolescence through young adulthood with shifts in some traits that start earlier in women than in men. The results also indicate that the consistency of personality profiles progressively increases from adolescence through adulthood.

The use of PCAs and canonical correlation analysis appeared to be a suitable method for evaluating changes in personality traits (or profile) with time. Men and women are characterized globally by a change from Fearfulness-Insecurity to Social Assertiveness. In women this change takes place earlier and may become more firm. Aerobic capacity has neither a substantial nor a consistent association with personality.

References

Bachman J.G., P.M. O'Malley, J. Johnston (1978). Adolescence to adulthood: Change and stability in the lives of young men. Institute for Sociological Research, Ann Arbor, MI.

Backteman G., D. Magnusson. Longitudinal stability of personality characteristics. J Pers 49 (1981) 148-160.

Block, J. (1971). Lives through time. Bancroft Books, Berkeley, CA.

Bücking H., J. van Egmond, S. Elsenga, F. Haanstra. (1975). The construction of a youth version of the Dutch Personality Inventory, the DPI-y. Hermans Bulletins, Univ. of Groningen report no. HB-75-190.

Conley J.J. Longitudinal consistency of personality: Paradigmatic shift or improving the quality of research? (1984). In: D. Magnusson, N.S. Endler (eds.), Personality at the crossroads: Current issues in international psychology. Erlbaum, Hillsdale, NJ.

Cramer S.R., D.C. Nieman, J.W. Lee. The effects of moderate exercise training on psychological well-being and mood state in women. J Psychosom Res 35:4 (1991) 437-449.

Dekker H., J.-W. Ritmeester, J. Snel. (1985). Personality traits and school attitude. In: H.C.G. Kemper (ed.), Growth, health and fitness of teenagers: Longitudinal research in international perspective. Vol. 20 of: Medicine and sports. Karger, Basel.

Geus E. de (1992). The effects of fitness training on physiological stress-reactivity. Doctoral dissertation, Vrije Universiteit, Amsterdam.

Hermans H.J.M. (1971). Achievement motivation and anxiety in family and school. Swets & Zeitlinger, Amsterdam.

Hermans H.J.M. (1976). Handleiding bij de prestatie motivatietest. Swets & Zeitlinger, Lisse.

Hermans H.J.M. (1983a). Achievement Motivation Test for Children manual. Swets & Zeitlinger, Amsterdam.

Hermans H.J.M. (1983b). Achievement motivation and anxiety in family and school. Swets & Zeitlinger, Amsterdam.

Kagan J., H.A. Moss. (1962). Birth to maturity. Wiley, New York.

Kemper H.C.G. (ed.). (1985). Growth, health and fitness of teenagers: Longitudinal research in international perspective. Vol. 20 of: Medicine and sport science. Karger, Basel.

Lennox S.S., J.R. Bedell, A.A. Stone. The effects of exercise on normal mood. J Psychosom Res 34:6 (1990) 629-636.

Long B.C., C.J. Haney. Coping strategies for working women: Aerobic exercise and relaxation interventions. Behavior Therapy 9 (1988) 75-83.

Luteijn F. (1974). The construction of a personality inventory: DPI. Swets & Zeitlinger, Amsterdam.

Luteijn F., H. van Dijk, E.A.E. van der Ploeg. (1981). Dutch Personality Inventory youth version. Swets & Zeitlinger, Lisse.

Luteijn F., J. Starren, H. van Dijk. (1985). Dutch Personality Inventory manual, Revised edition. Swets & Zeitlinger, Lisse.

MacMahon J.R., R.T. Gross. Physical and psychological effects of aerobic exercise in delinquent adolescent males. American Journal of Disturbed Children 142 (1988) 1361-1366.

McCall R.B. Challenges to a science of developmental psychology. Child Development 48 (1977) 333-344.

Moss H.A., E.J. Susman. (1980). Longitudinal study of personality development. In: O.G. Brim, Jr., and J. Kagan (eds.), Constancy and change in human development. University Press, Cambridge, MA.

Nesselroade J.R., P.B. Baltes. (1974). Adolescent personality development and historical change: 1970-1972. Monographs of the Society for Research in Child Development, 39:154, pp. 1-79.

Simons C.W., J.C. Birkimer. An exploration of the factors predicting the effects of aerobic conditioning on mood state. J Psychosom Res 32:1 (1988) 63-75.

Snel J., J.-W. Ritmeester. (1985). Sociometric status. In: H.C.G. Kemper (ed.), Growth, health and fitness of teenagers: Longitudinal research in international perspective. Vol. 20 of: Medicine and sport science. Karger, Basel.

Stein J.A., M.D. Newcomb, P.M. Bentler. Stability and change in personality: A longitudinal study from early adolescence to young adulthood. J Res Personality 20 (1986) 276-291.

Steptoe A., S. Edwards, J. Moses, A. Mathews. The effect of exercise training on mood and perceived coping ability in anxious adults from the general population. J Psychosom Res 33:5 (1989) 537-547.

Stevens J. (1986). Applied multivariate statistics for the social sciences. Lawrence Erlbaum Associates, Hillsdale, NJ.

Part III

Lifestyle Changes
in Longitudinal Perspective

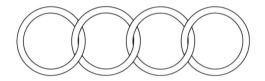

Chapter 6

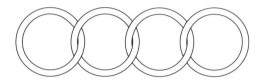

The Development of Nutritional Intake
During 15 Years of Follow-Up

G. Bertheke Post & Desiree C. Welten

In affluent societies the role of diet, or nutrient intake, in the pathogenesis of chronic diseases such as cardiovascular diseases, cancer, and diabetes has aroused much attention in research (World Health Organization, 1990; Schwerin et al., 1982). On the basis of such research, national nutrition councils establish dietary recommendations that usually reflect adequate safe levels of intake (Netherlands Nutrition Council, 1989).

During adolescence (ages 13-17) an increase in energy and nutrient intake is generally observed, especially in boys, and after the young-adult period (ages 17-21) dietary behavior eventually settles (Post, 1989). Using Dutch recommended daily allowances (DRDAs), we concluded from our five annual measurements in 200 girls and boys between ages 13 and 21 that the daily food intake of teenagers and young adults contained too few polysaccharides, but too many monosaccharides and disaccharides. Furthermore, the total daily intake of fat was too high, and the intake of polyunsaturated fatty acids too low. Another point of concern was the consumption of alcoholic beverages. At young-adult age 75% of the females and males consumed alcoholic beverages, with one drink/ day for the females and up to three drinks/day for the males. These dietary habits may be considered a threat to health on a long-term basis, especially when it is taken into account that the consumption of alcoholic beverages is spread not over the 7 weekdays but mostly concentrated on the weekend (Post & Kemper, 1985).

To verify if the nutritional value of the diet at adult age agrees with values at earlier ages, this study was extended with a sixth examination in 1991 at the mean age of 27 years.

Methods

Study Population

The study population consists of the longitudinal sample of the Amsterdam Growth and Health Study (Kemper, 1985). Of the original sample, 182 subjects (98 females and 84 males) were measured in 1991.

Dietary Intake

The method adopted for determining daily food intake was a detailed cross-check dietary history questionnaire developed for our study (Post, 1989). The measurement of food intake took place every year from January to June, to avoid seasonal bias. Study participants were asked to recall their usual food intake during the past month by reporting frequency, amounts, and methods of preparation of foods consumed. The amounts were reported in household measures or common portion sizes. A variety of visual aids (e.g., glasses, bowls, spoons, different sizes of fruits and potatoes) were used to estimate quantities. Only the food items eaten at least twice monthly were recorded. Information on foods consumed during regular meals as well as in between-meal snacks was collected separately for the 5 school/work days and for the 2 weekend days. Food items were converted to energy and macronutrient and micronutrient units using the computerized Dutch Food Composition Table (NEVO, 1989).

The reproducibility of the dietary history used in this study was assessed by means of interperiod correlations for four aspects of food consumption: energy, protein, fat, and carbohydrate (Post, 1989). The individual data of our six measurement times (1977-1991) were correlated with each other over the intervals (i.e., interperiods of 1 to 14 years) (Fig. 6.1). There were no differences between males and females with respect to carbohydrate intake (Fig. 6.1b). The slope of the regression line of energy, fat, and protein intake is steeper in females than in males (Fig. 6.1a, c, d). The interperiod correlations (IPCs) of energy, fat, and protein decreased from about .7 at 1-year intervals to .3-.1 in females and .4-.2 in males at the 14-year interval. As a measure of reproducibility of the dietary history, the zero interval was estimated with a correlation of .8 for energy, fat, and carbohydrate; the estimate was somewhat lower (.55) for protein. The results showed that the data on food consumption can be considered exact enough to indicate differences between groups of teenagers and sufficiently precise to reflect the food intake over age.

Anthropometry and Blood Characteristics

Nutritional status was characterized by anthropometric and blood serum measurements. Body weight, body height, and four skinfolds (biceps, triceps, subscapular, and suprailiacal) were measured each year to characterize the body composition of the sample population (Table 6.1), and blood serum was analyzed for total cholesterol (TC) and high-density lipoprotein (HDL) cholesterol concentrations. (Details of these measurements are described in chapter 4).

energy intake

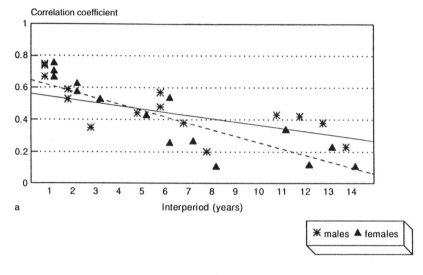

a

carbohydrate intake

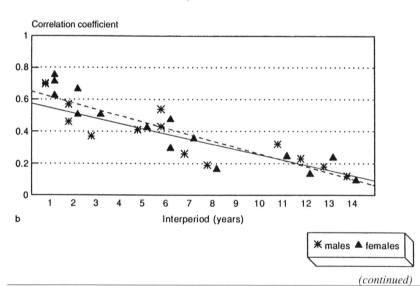

b

(continued)

Figure 6.1   The interperiod correlation coefficients of the assessment of the intake of (a) energy, (b) carbohydrate, (c) fat, and (d) protein over the six measurements.

Analyses

The data were arranged by year of measurement and gender. Differences were tested using analysis of variance (ANOVA) with repeated measurements (Dickson, 1981). ANOVA tests the effects of time of measurement (i.e., age changes),

fat intake

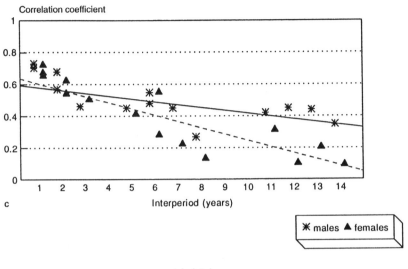

c

protein intake

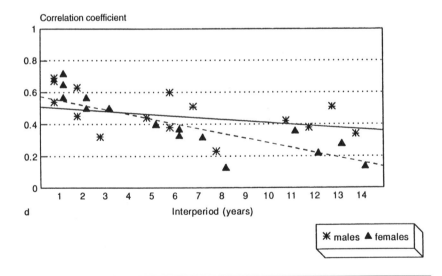

d

Figure 6.1   *(continued)*

sex effects, and the interaction between time and sex of the variable in question. Three periods were chosen: the adolescent period (ages 13-17), the period through young-adult age (ages 13-21), and the whole period from adolescence through adult age (ages 13-27). Nutrient intake variables were expressed in total grams or milligrams, as well as in percentages of the contribution to the total energy

Table 6.1   Anthropometric Data of the Longitudinal Sample

	Year of measurement					
	1977	1978	1979	1980	1985	1991
	Mean age (y)					
	13	14	15	16	21	27
Females						
Height (cm)	162.5	166.2	167.9	168.8	169.8	170.0
	(0.7)	(0.6)	(0.6)	(0.6)	(0.6)	(0.6)
Weight (kg)	48.0	51.8	55.0	56.9	61.6	63.3
	(0.8)	(0.8)	(0.8)	(0.8)	(0.8)	(0.8)
Sum four skinfolds (mm)	37.4	40.0	43.4	45.6	52.3	46.1
	(1.3)	(1.4)	(1.4)	(1.5)	(1.7)	(1.7)
Males						
Height (cm)	160.7	169.0	174.8	178.8	182.6	183.0
	(0.9)	(0.9)	(0.9)	(0.8)	(0.7)	(0.7)
Weight (kg)	44.9	52.0	57.9	62.8	71.0	75.5
	(0.8)	(0.9)	(0.9)	(0.8)	(0.8)	(0.9)
Sum four skinfolds (mm)	28.4	27.7	27.8	29.1	34.9	36.3
	(1.2)	(1.2)	(1.1)	(1.1)	(1.4)	(1.5)

Note. Values are means (and standard errors in parentheses).

intake (from protein, fat, carbohydrate, and alcohol). Alcohol was examined as the number of grams per day and also as grams per day by alcohol consumer.

Results

Anthropometry

The mean and standard error of three anthropometric variables are given in Table 6.1. Over the 15 years of follow-up, females increased in height by almost 8 cm and in weight by almost 15 kg. In males growth in height was about 22 cm, and weight increased about 30 kg. The sum of the four skinfolds (an estimation of body fat mass) increased about 40% in females during the adolescent and young-adult periods, but between the last two measurements a decrease of approximately 12% was found. The total increase in skinfold thickness over the 15 years was about 23%. The sum of four skinfolds increased for males as well, particularly during the young-adult and adult periods; the total increase was about 28%.

TC concentration (Table 6.2) in females did not change over the adolescent period (4.4 mmol/L), but over the young-adult and the adult periods an increase of almost 20% was found. In males, during adolescence TC decreased 10%,

Table 6.2   Serum Cholesterol Concentrations of the Longitudinal Sample

	Year of measurement					
	1977	1978	1979	1980	1985	1991
			Mean age (y)			
	13	14	15	16	21	27
Females						
Serum total cholesterol	4.4	4.4	4.4	4.4	4.9	5.3
(mmol/L)	(0.1)	(0.1)	(0.1)	(0.1)	(0.1)	(0.1)
HDL cholesterol	1.4	1.4	1.3	1.4	1.4	1.6
(mmol/L)	(0.03)	(0.03)	(0.03)	(0.03)	(0.03)	(0.04)
Males						
Serum total cholesterol	4.4	4.2	4.1	4	4.5	5
(mmol/L)	(0.1)	(0.1)	(0.1)	(0.1)	(0.1)	(0.1)
HDL cholesterol	1.5	1.4	1.2	1.3	1.2	1.2
(mmol/L)	(0.03)	(0.03)	(0.02)	(0.02)	(0.02)	(0.02)

Note. Values are means (and standard errors in parentheses).

whereas in the young-adult and adult periods, respectively, increases of about 10% and 20% were seen.

Serum HDL-cholesterol concentration showed hardly any change in females over the 15 years of follow-up; it was 14% higher in the adult period. In males, a 20% decrease occurred over the whole period.

Intake of Energy and Macronutrients

Table 6.3 presents the significance of the changes in nutrient intake over the three development periods. Table 6.4 presents the effects of sex and the interaction between the time of measurement and sex. In general, males show higher energy and nutrient intakes than females. Figure 6.2 shows the average intake of total *energy* over the 15 years of the study. During all three periods the daily energy intake of the females remained more or less the same, at a mean value between 9.3 and 9.9 MJ. Over the young-adult and adult periods females showed a slight, but not significant, decrease in energy intake. For males the mean energy intake increased significantly, from 11.6 MJ/day in the adolescent period to 13.8 MJ/day at the young adult period ($p < .01$). At the adult period a significant decrease, to 12.7 MJ/day, occurred.

The developmental changes of total daily *protein* intake are shown in Figure 6.3. During the adolescent period females showed a significantly decreased intake (76 g/day to 71 g/day), whereas in the young-adult period, as well as in the adult period, a significant increase appeared, 77 g/day and 79 g/day respectively. During the adolescent period males showed a significant increase, from about

Table 6.3   MANOVA Indicating Effect of Time on Nutrient Intake

	Period (ages in years)					
	Females			Males		
Variable	13-17	13-21	13-27	13-17	13-21	13-27
Energy	NS	NS	NS	++	++	+−
Energy/kg body weight	—	—	—	—	—	—
Protein	—	++	++	+	++	++
Fat	NS	NS	−	++	++	+−
Carbohydrate	−	—	—	++	++	+−
Alcohol	++	++	++	++	++	++
Cholesterol	−	++	+−	NS	++	+−
Calcium	—	++	++	NS	++	++
Iron (heme)	—	—	—	NS	++	+−
Iron (nonheme)	—	NS	NS	++	++	++
Thiamine	—	—	−+	++	++	++
Riboflavin	—	−+	−+	NS	++	++
Pyridoxine	—	−+	++	++	++	++
Ascorbic acid	NS	++	+−	NS	++	+−
Retinol	NS	NS	++	++	++	++

Note. The directions of differences are + = increase; − = decrease; +− = first period(s) increase followed by decrease; −+ = first period(s) decrease followed by increase. NS = not significant.

82 g/day to 88 g/day. Over the young-adult period the intake increased to 101 g/day and for the adult period a slight but significant decrease, to 97 g/day, was found. The contribution of protein to total daily energy intake remained 13% to 14% in females over the 15 years of the study, whereas in males 12% to 13% appeared (Fig. 6.4).

Females' total daily *fat* intake, shown in Figure 6.5, did not change during the adolescent period, but was reduced in the young-adult period; over the adult period it decreased significantly, to about 100 g/day. Males showed a significant increase during adolescence and the young-adult period, to about 150 g/day; over the adult period the amount significantly decreased, to about 130 g/day. The supply of fat to the total daily energy intake increased in females during the adolescent period from 40% to 41.5%, but decreased over both adult periods to about 39.5% (neither change was significant) (see Fig. 6.4). The change for males during adolescence was also not significant, up from 42% to 43%; they exhibited a decrease (not significant) over the young-adult and the adult periods to about 39% of energy intake.

Although cholesterol intake in females and males did not change much over the whole study period, intake levels changed significantly from adolescence to

Table 6.4   MANOVA Indicating Effect of Sex and the Interaction Between Sex and Time on Nutrient Intake

| | Period (ages in years) | | | | | |
| | Sex effects | | | Interaction effects | | |
Variable	13-17	13-21	13-27	13-17	13-21	13-27
Energy	M**	M**	M**	**	**	**
Energy/kg body weight	M**	M**	M**	NS	NS	**
Protein	M**	M**	M**	**	**	**
Fat	M**	M**	M**	**	**	**
Carbohydrate	M**	M**	M**	**	**	**
Alcohol	M*	M**	M**	*	**	**
Cholesterol	M**	M**	M**	NS	*	*
Calcium	M**	M**	M**	**	**	*
Iron (heme)	M*	M**	M**	*	**	**
Iron (nonheme)	M**	M**	M**	**	**	**
Thiamine	M**	M**	M**	**	**	**
Riboflavin	M**	M**	M**	**	**	**
Pyridoxine	M**	M**	M**	**	**	**
Ascorbic acid	NS	NS	NS	NS	*	*
Retinol	M**	M**	M**	**	*	*

M = males have higher intake; NS = not significant.
$*p < .05$; $**p < .01$.

the adult period. During adolescence the females had a cholesterol intake of about 290 mg/day; at young-adult age, 315 mg/day; and at adult age, 270 mg/day. In males no significant decrease was found during the adolescent period (about 340 mg/day), but thereafter it increased significantly over the young-adult period (to 410 mg/day) and decreased over the adult period (to 330 mg/day).

Total daily *carbohydrate* intake (Fig. 6.6) in females decreased significantly over the 15 years of the study, from 270 g/day to 245 g/day. Males showed first a significant increase, from 320 g/day at age 13 to 365 g/day at age 21, but over the adult period a significant decrease, to about 340 g/day, occurred. The energy supplied by carbohydrate was about 47% of the total energy intake in females, which decreased during the whole study period to about 44% (see Fig. 6.4). Carbohydrate intake in males contributed about 46% of the total daily energy and changed over the years to 45%. The contribution of polysaccharides (23%) and monosaccharides and disaccharides (22%) to the total daily energy intake was the same for both sexes and remained the same throughout the study.

Alcohol intake (Fig. 6.7) increased significantly in both females and males throughout the study. Males consumed twice as much alcohol as females during all periods. Because during adolescence there were naturally a number of

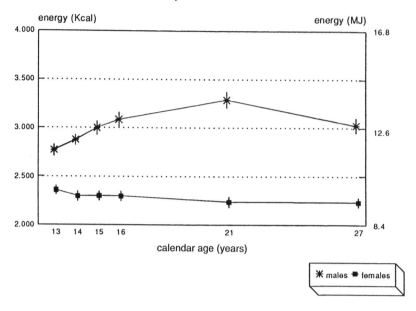

Figure 6.2   Mean energy intake by age. Standard errors are shown by vertical bars.

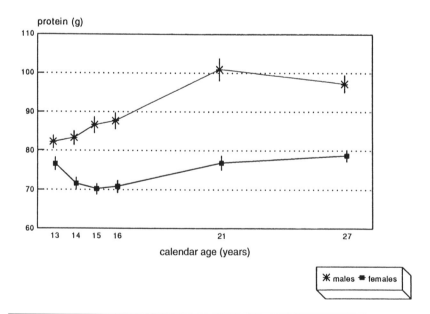

Figure 6.3   Mean and standard error of protein intake by age.

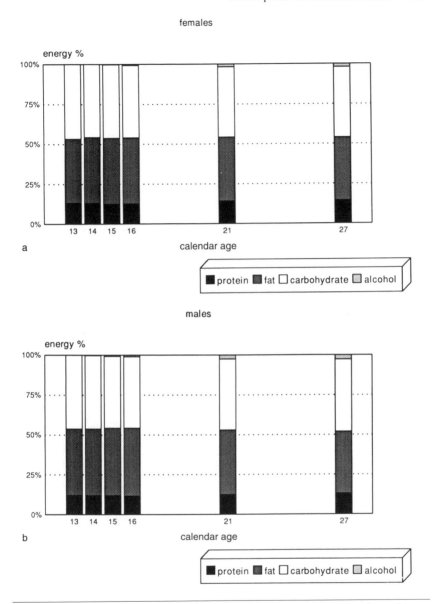

Figure 6.4   Proportions of energy supplied by macronutrients in (a) females and (b) males by age.

nondrinkers in the study, we distinguished between those who used alcoholic beverages and those who did not. The percentages of both girl and boy alcohol users increased over the adolescent period. At the young-adult period 75% of the females and 73% of the males were drinking alcoholic beverages; at the adult period 63% of the women and 87% of the men used alcohol.

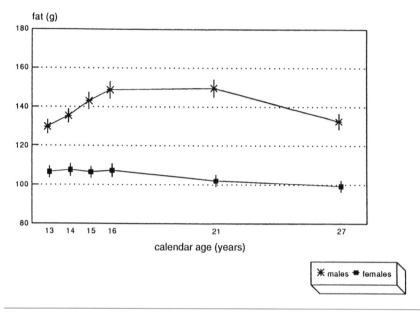

Figure 6.5   Mean and standard error of fat intake by age.

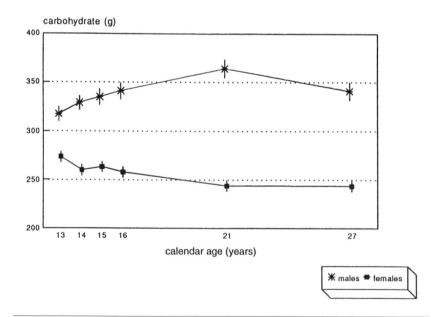

Figure 6.6   Mean and standard error of carbohydrate intake by age.

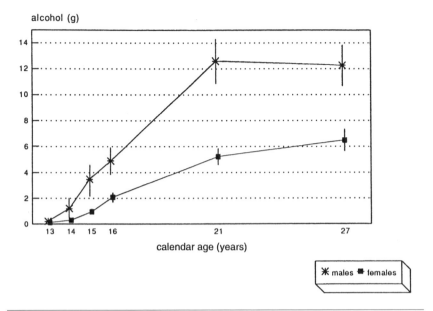

Figure 6.7   Mean and standard error of alcohol intake by age.

Micronutrients

Table 6.3 indicates the significant changes in micronutrient intake over the three developmental periods. In Table 6.4 the effects of sex and the interaction between time of measurement and sex are summarized. Figure 6.8 shows the developmental changes in total daily *calcium* intake. During adolescence contrasting development was seen for girls and boys; intake decreased (significantly) among girls and increased (not significantly) among boys. Over the young-adult and adult periods both sexes showed a significantly increased intake.

Total *iron* intake (Fig. 6.9) in females decreased significantly during adolescence (from ±12 mg/day to ±11 mg/day), remained constant over the young-adult period, and increased significantly over the adult period (to ±12.5 mg/day). Males exhibited a consistent increase over all three periods (from ±12.4 mg/day to ±14.6 mg/day). The increases were due mostly to nonheme iron.

Intake of *retinol* (Vitamin A) increased significantly in both sexes over the 15 years of the study (Fig. 6.10). Females showed no significant changes during the first two periods, but over the adult period the change was significant. In males, significant increases were seen during all three periods.

In general, changes in intake levels are the same for the three *B-vitamins* studied (Figs. 6.11-13). During adolescence, a significantly decreased intake occurred among females, after which a significant increase occurred, especially of riboflavin and pyridoxine. Among males thiamine and pyridoxine intake began increasing significantly during the adolescent period. Over the young-adult and adult periods intake of all three vitamins (thiamine, riboflavin, and pyridoxine) increased significantly.

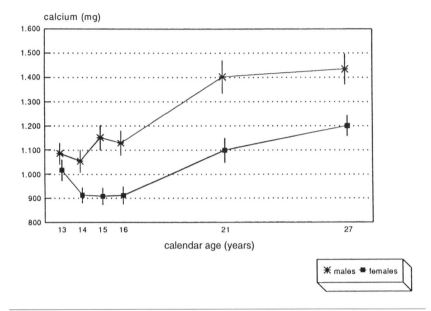

Figure 6.8   Mean and standard error of calcium intake by age.

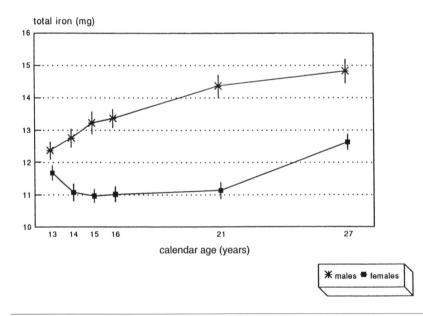

Figure 6.9   Mean and standard error of iron intake by age.

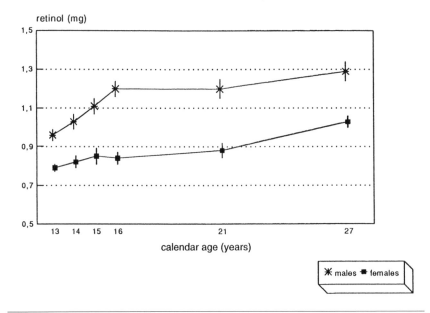

Figure 6.10   Mean and standard error of retinol intake by age.

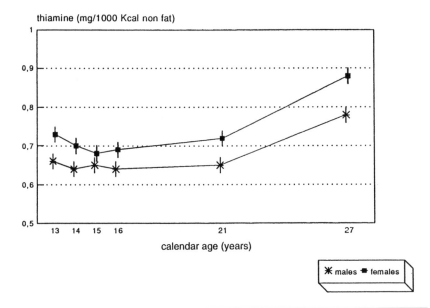

Figure 6.11   Mean and standard error of thiamine intake by age.

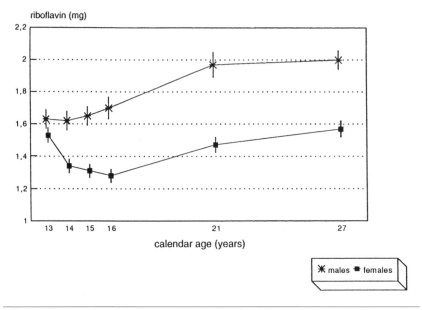

Figure 6.12   Mean and standard error of riboflavin intake by age.

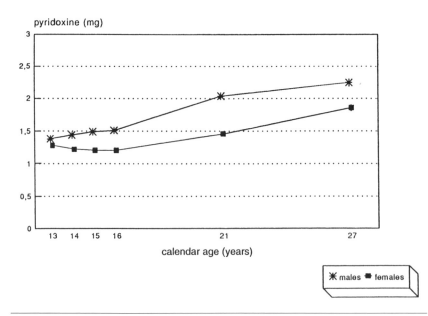

Figure 6.13   Mean and standard error of pyridoxine intake by age.

Ascorbic acid intake (Fig. 6.14) increased significantly over only the young-adult period, for both sexes, but decreased in the period thereafter to about 120 g/day among females and 115 g/day among males.

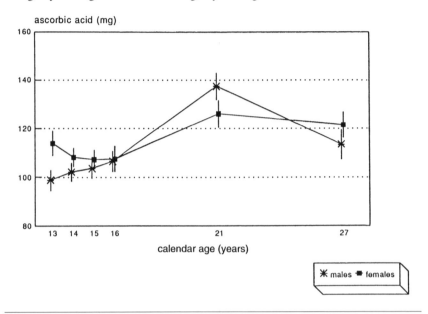

Figure 6.14   Mean and standard error of ascorbic acid intake by age.

Discussion

In the Netherlands, as well as in the United States, present guidelines for a healthy diet are based mainly on evidence for an association between diet and such chronic diseases as obesity, cardiovascular diseases, and cancer (Netherlands Nutrition Council, 1989; Food and Nutrition Board, 1989). When compared to government recommendations for a prudent diet, the consumption pattern in our study indicated in both sexes an excessive percentage of energy intake from fat and protein and an insufficient percentage of energy intake from carbohydrates, especially from polysaccharides (see Fig. 6.4). Although our study population may not have been equivalent to a sample of the Dutch population in general, compared with the general population studied by the Dutch Nutrition Surveillance system (Hulshof & van Staveren, 1991) and divided into comparable age groups, our population exhibits the same breakdown of macronutrient intake in terms of proportion of energy. However, the total daily energy intake of the women and men in our study was higher.

The mean energy intake per kilogram of body weight of the adolescent and young-adult females was equal to the recommended allowances, but during the adult period the intake was higher than recommended (Fig. 6.15). In males, the recommended energy per kilogram of body weight was lower than our findings for all periods. In observational research without explicit intervention of any kind, it is very difficult to demonstrate that significant changes in nutrition, coinciding with changes in health parameters, can be explained as cause-effect relationships. However, the strength of prospective cohort studies is that individual changes over time can be measured. Thus, we can determine the implications of the higher energy intakes over the growing years in our population. Table 6.1 indicates the development of body mass (height, weight, skinfolds). Over the whole period, only females showed an increase in the sum of skinfold thicknesses, whereas in males this phenomenon only occurred over the young-adult and adult periods. Therefore we believe that the energy recommendations, especially during adolescence, are too high for females and too low for males, at least for a population like ours. The recommendations promote obesity in girls and a marginal energy intake in boys (taking into account, of course, the daily energy output of these adolescent girls and boys) (Verschuur, 1987).

Mean daily protein intake, measured as protein per kilogram of body weight, was high over all three periods compared with the recommended intake for both sexes: 0.3 g/day higher in females and 0.4 g/day higher in males. At adult age females and males both showed a daily protein intake of 1.25 g/kg body weight.

Total daily fat intake in females was comparable to that found in the Dutch National Food Consumption Survey (DNFCS) (Hulshof & van Staveren, 1991), but in males the consumption was considerably higher, with a peak over the young-adult period. Cholesterol intake, another cardiovascular risk factor, was

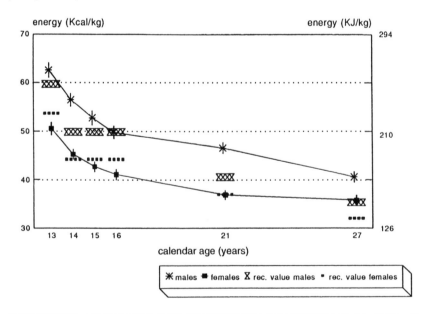

Figure 6.15   Subjects' energy intake and Dutch recommended allowances by age.

higher in both sexes in our study during the adolescent and young-adult periods. Over the adult period females as well as males had a lower cholesterol intake (Fig. 6.16). However, the consumption of dietary cholesterol did not exceed the goal of 33 mg/MJ for these age groups.

Total carbohydrate intake in the DNFCS was, over the same age period, lower than that of our study. However, the proportion of monosaccharides and disaccharides was the same, 22%. Crude-fiber intake was comparable—2.2 to 2.7 g/MJ—but was lower than the recommended value of 3 g/MJ.

In general, all the differences between the sexes (see Table 6.4) were significant over the three measurement periods, with one exception—ascorbic acid intake. Regarding time-sex interaction effects, no significant difference for the energy intake per kilogram of body weight was evident for the 13-17 and 13-21 age periods.

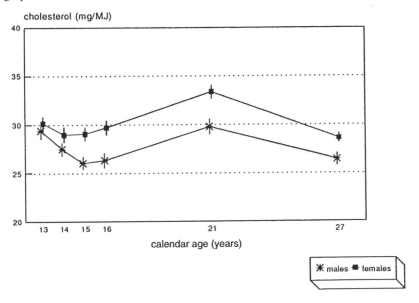

Figure 6.16   Mean and standard error of cholesterol intake by age.

Nutrient Distribution

The current longitudinal investigation sought to evaluate the relationships between changes in dietary intake over a period of 15 years and the development of several health risk factors. In order to identify nutritional factors that may influence the quality of future life, especially as concerns the development of health-threatening risks, we calculated distributions for females and males on the basis of energy supplied by fat and the cholesterol intake in mg/MJ (Table 6.5). These nutrients were adjusted to percentages of intake.

The table shows the increasing percentages of women and men who ate a rather low daily fat diet (<35 energy %), to about 20% of the total population

Table 6.5   Percentages of Subjects' Adjusted Daily Fat and Cholesterol Intake

	Fat energy %			Cholesterol mg/MJ		
	<35 (%)	35-40 (%)	>40 (%)	<30 (%)	30-35 (%)	>35 (%)
Males						
1977	7	31	62	56	15	19
1978	5	29	66	61	31	8
1979	5	26	69	71	20	9
1980	7	20	73	71	20	9
1985	13	20	67	47	33	20
1991	17	37	46	76	19	5
Females						
1977	15	29	56	47	31	22
1978	9	25	66	53	28	19
1979	12	22	65	57	22	21
1980	13	28	59	56	24	20
1985	18	22	60	26	33	41
1991	18	33	49	64	23	13

over the 15 years of follow-up; the proportion of subjects with a high daily fat intake (>40 energy %) decreased over the same period. Nevertheless, as many as 50% of the women and 46% of the men exhibited this high daily fat intake. In the DNFCS, 12% of adult women and 15% of adult men had diets with less than 35% fat energy, and 60% of the women and 52% of the men ate diets with greater than 40% fat energy (Hulshof, 1993). In comparison, our population seemed to develop a more favorable fat intake.

Dietary cholesterol intake went down over the years of our study. The proportion of the highest cholesterol intake group (>35 mg/MJ) shrank as the lowest intake group (<30 mg/MJ) increased, to 64% of the women and 76% of the men. However, at the same time, the TC concentration, after a decrease over the adolescent period (especially in men, from 4.45 mmol/L to 3.95 mmol/L), increased over the young-adult and adult periods in both sexes, in men to 4.96 mmol/L and in women to 5.28 mmol/L (see Table 6.2). The HDL-cholesterol fraction in serum went down in both sexes during adolescence until young-adult age, but at the adult period an increase was found. Several prospective studies have shown an inverse relation between HDL cholesterol and coronary heart disease (CHD). This form of cholesterol seems, however, not to play an important role in explaining differences of CHD mortality between populations, and its dietary determinants will therefore not be discussed here (World Health Organization, 1990).

In 1985 an unusual phenomenon appeared relative to cholesterol intake. In both sexes the percentages consuming more than 35 mg/MJ cholesterol/day was twice as high as the years before and as 5 years later. In this year of the study the majority of the young population started to live on their own (as students) and to manage their own households. The reason for this phenomenon might be that eating habits changed to make preparation easy—buying more fast-food snacks and easy-to-fix food, such as eggs—compared with the previous normal family food pattern.

Relation Between Energy and Fat Intake and Cardiovascular Risk Factors

To indicate possible relations between some of the nutrients and health, we made a distinction among subjects on the basis of the nutrient intake. The mean of the dietary characteristic or health factor in question over the first four measurements (the adolescent period) was calculated. The lowest and highest tertiles over that period were compared to the results of the young-adult and adult periods, separated for men and women. ANOVA was used to demonstrate the significance between the lowest and the highest tertiles. The dietary characteristics under study were daily energy intake (as energy per kilogram of body weight) and daily fat intake (as percent of energy supplied by fat). The health factors taken into account were serum cholesterol concentration and body fat mass (measured by the sum of four skinfolds).

Figure 6.17 shows the tertiles based on the energy per kilogram of body weight between 1977 and 1980 in relation to serum cholesterol concentration in both sexes over the young-adult (1985) and the adult (1991) periods. In both males and females no significant difference could be demonstrated during the

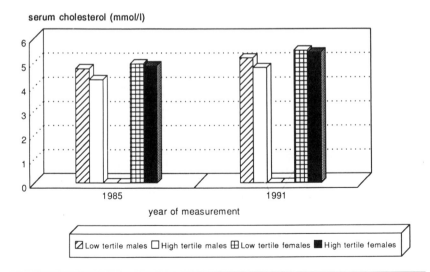

Figure 6.17   Comparison between energy intake per kilogram of body weight and serum cholesterol concentration at 1985 and 1991.

course of 15 years of the study for the serum cholesterol concentration. Figure 6.18 shows the tertiles of proportion of energy supplied by fat and the development of the serum cholesterol level; again no significant differences were found in either sex. When the tertiles of energy per kilogram of body weight were related to the development of the sum of four skinfolds (Fig. 6.19) no significant differences were discerned in men; the same was true for the proportion of energy supplied by fat (Fig. 6.20). Among females the lowest tertiles of both dietary characteristics showed a significantly higher sum of four skinfolds in both periods (Fig. 6.19 and 6.20). The lowest tertile of the energy per kilogram of body weight showed a higher sum of four skinfolds compared with the highest tertile. Thus, although the females' diet had a lower energy intake, they were fatter. As shown in earlier publications (Post, 1989), when a given population was screened on the quality of its daily diet and time spent on physical activity, total activity time and intensity of the activities were significantly lower in subjects, especially females, with the lowest energy per kilogram of body weight; these subjects also showed a higher sum of four skinfolds. The same might be the case in the tertile at issue.

Alcohol Intake

In order to study whether alcohol intake alters such health factors as body fat (as measured by the sum of four skinfolds) and serum cholesterol concentration, we calculated a distribution for both sexes by amount of alcoholic intake (Table 6.6). Considering the high percentage of nondrinkers and low-intake drinkers

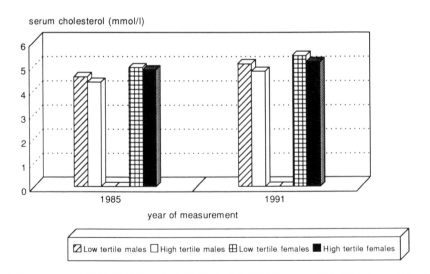

Figure 6.18   Comparison between proportion of energy supplied by fat and serum cholesterol concentration at 1985 and 1991.

Tertiles based on energy intake /kg body weight between 1977 and 1980

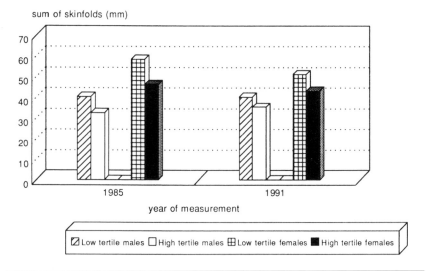

Figure 6.19   Comparison between energy intake per kilogram of body weight and sum of four skinfolds at 1985 and 1991.

Tertiles based on % energy intake by fat between 1977 and 1980

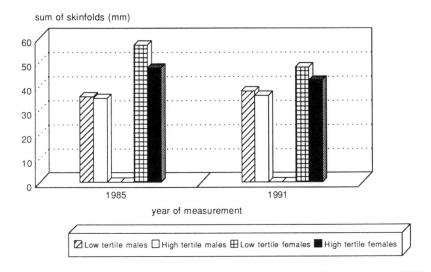

Figure 6.20   Comparison between proportion of energy supplied by fat and sum of four skinfolds at 1985 and 1991.

Table 6.6   Percentage of Subjects' Adjusted Alcohol Consumption

| | Alcohol (gram/day) | | | |
	0 (%)	0-10 (%)	10-20 (%)	>20 (%)
Males				
1977	88	12	0	0
1978	77	22	0	1
1979	67	23	6	4
1980	51	33	10	6
1985	27	27	19	26
1991	13	37	31	19
Females				
1977	87	13	0	0
1978	79	21	0	0
1979	61	38	1	0
1980	41	55	4	0
1985	25	55	17	3
1991	37	42	13	8

during the adolescent period, only the data of the young-adult (1985) and the adult (1991) periods were taken into account. This time alcohol intake was divided into three groups: those who in both periods did not drink any alcohol, those who consumed up to 10 g/day (medium-intake group), and those who consumed more than 10 g/day and less than 30 g/day (high-intake group). In our first analysis only subjects whose alcohol intake remained in the same category in both 1985 and 1991 were compared.

Figure 6.21 shows the relationship between serum cholesterol levels of men and women for the three different alcohol groups. Among females no differences were evident. Among males the nondrinkers tended to show a higher level of serum cholesterol, although this was not significant. The nondrinking men exhibited a higher increase of cholesterol at the adult period (1991).

Men and women showed an opposite development relative to the sum of four skinfolds (Fig. 6.22). In women, when the consumption of alcohol increased, the sum of skinfolds decreased; in men increase of alcohol intake occurred together with an increase in skinfold thickness.

A number of persons were excluded from our first analysis because they fell into two intake categories over the years. To extend the number of alcohol consumers in the medium- and high-intake groups, we performed additional calculations using the mean intake over the two measurement periods. As in the first analysis, the nondrinkers, especially men, still tended to show the highest levels of serum cholesterol, and skinfold thickness showed the same pattern (Fig. 6.23). It would seem that the intake of alcoholic drinks contributes to increasing body fat mass in men and a decreasing fat mass in women.

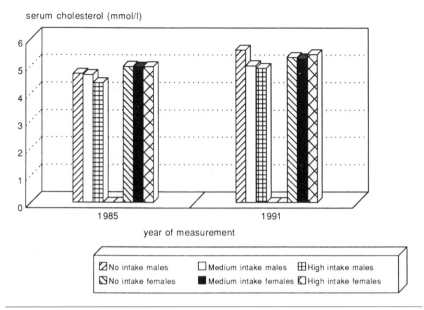

Figure 6.21   Relationship between alcohol intake (two separate measurements for three intake levels) and serum cholesterol concentration at 1985 and 1991.

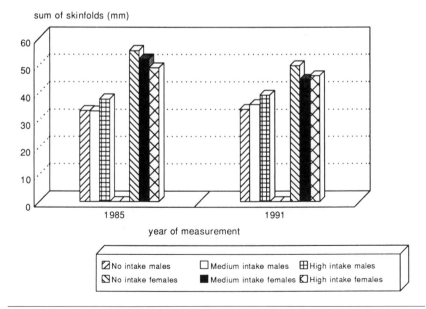

Figure 6.22   Relationship between alcohol intake (two separate measurements for three intake levels) and sum of four skinfolds at 1985 and 1991.

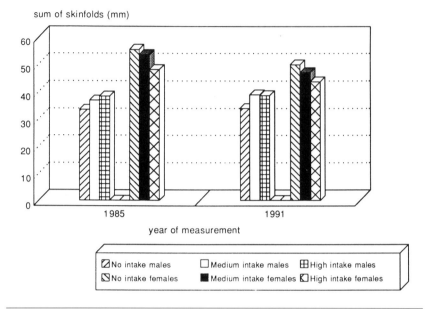

sum of skinfolds (mm)

year of measurement

☑ No intake males   ☐ Medium intake males   ⊞ High intake males
◩ No intake females   ■ Medium intake females   ▨ High intake females

Figure 6.23 Relationship between alcohol intake (mean of two measurement periods for three intake levels) and sum of four skinfolds at 1985 and 1991.

Whether alcohol energy intake contributes to obesity in the same manner as nonalcoholic energy is not yet clear (Castro & Orozco, 1990; Lands, 1991; Lieber, 1991). Gruchow et al. (1985) suggest that alcohol energy may be less efficiently utilized than nonalcohol energy. They observed that female drinkers had significantly lower body mass indexes (BMIs) than their nondrinking counterparts and that among men, BMI progressively decreased as alcohol intake increased. Thus, despite the higher energy intake, drinkers were no more obese than nondrinkers.

Colditz et al. (1991) found a total energy increase in both men and women when they consumed higher levels of alcohol. Only in women, without the contribution of energy from alcohol, was a small inverse relation found between alcohol intake and energy intake. Willet and Stampfer (1986) state that thermogenesis may compensate partly for the excess of energy.

The metabolic interaction between alcohol and other nutrients requires further analysis. The major difference in nutrient intake described in the literature is a lower carbohydrate (especially monosaccharide and disaccharide) intake in drinkers.

Conclusions

Overall, we may conclude that in a period of 15 years, from adolescence until adulthood, males showed a significantly higher energy and nutrient intake than females. Body fat mass (skinfolds) increased for both sexes after the growth period until age 27. Thus, total energy intake had an impact on this matter. Dutch recommendations for energy intake in adolescent males and females are not in agreement with our results: The recommendations suggest a growing overweight in females and marginal intakes in males.

Relationships between energy intake per kilogram of body weight or percentage energy supplied by the consumption of fat, on the one hand, and two important cardiovascular risk indicators, the sum of four skinfolds and the serum cholesterol level, on the other, could not be demonstrated in males and females. Relative to alcohol intake, the concentration of serum cholesterol showed a tendency toward higher levels only in nondrinking males. An increase in body fat (skinfolds) with increasing alcohol intake was also found only in males.

There seems to be no relation between nutrient intake and certain cardiovascular risk factors such as body fat and hypercholesterolemia among males and females aged 13 to 27. This finding can be explained partly by the fact that the level of risk factors for overweight and hypercholesterolemia were relatively low and did not approach adult risk levels. Alcohol intake was found to be a significant factor in producing overweight in males.

References

Castro JM de, S. Orozco. Moderate alcohol intake and spontaneous eating patterns of humans: Evidence of unregulated supplementation. Am J Clin Nutr 52 (1990) 246-253.

Colditz G.A., E. Giovannucci, E.B. Rimm, M.J. Tampfer, B. Rosner, F.E. Speizer, E. Gordis, W.C. Willett. Alcohol intake in relation to diet and obesity in women and men. Am J Clin Nutr 54 (1991) 49-55.

Dickson W.J. (ed). (1981). B.M.D.P. statistical software. [Computer program] University of California Press, Berkeley.

Food and Nutrition Board. (1989). Recommended dietary allowances (10th ed.). National Academy Press, Washington, D.C.

Gruchow H.W., K.A. Sobocinski, J.J. Baboriak, J.G. Scheller. Alcohol consumption, nutrient intake and relative body weight among US adults. Am J Clin Nutr 42 (1985) 289-295.

Hulshof K.F.A.M. (1993). Assessment of variety, clustering and adequacy of eating patterns: Dutch National Food Consumption Survey. Doctoral dissertation, Den Haag, Koninklijke Bibliotheek.

Hulshof K.F.A.M., W.A. van Staveren. The Dutch National Food Consumption Survey: Design, methods and first results. Food Policy 16 (1991) 257-260.

Kemper H.C.G. (ed.). (1985). Growth, health and fitness of teenagers: Longitudinal research in international perspective. Vol. 20 of: Medicine and sport science. Karger, Basel.

Lands W.E.M., S. Zakhari. The case of the missing calories. Am J Clin Nutr 54 (1991) 47-48.

Lieber C.S. Perspectives: Do alcohol calories count? Am J Clin Nutr 54 (1991) 976-982.

Netherlands Nutrition Council. (1989). Recommended dietary allowances. Voedingsraad, The Hague.

NEVO. (1989). Nederlandse Voedingsstoffen bestand [Dutch food composition table]. Stichting NEVO, Voorlichtingsbureau v.d. Voeding, The Hague.

Post G.B. (1989). Nutrition in adolescence: A longitudinal study in dietary patterns from teenager to adult. Doctoral dissertation, de Vrieseborch, Haarlem, SO 16.

Post G.B., H.C.G. Kemper. (1985). Energy and nutrient intakes: Eating and smoking practices. In: Kemper H.C.G. (ed.), Growth, health and fitness of teenagers: Longitudinal research in international perspective. Vol 20 of: Medicine and sports sciences series. Karger, Basel.

Schwerin H.S., J.L. Stanton, J.L. Smith, A.M. Riley, B.E. Brett. Food eating habits and health: A further examination of the relationship between food eating patterns and nutritional health. Am J Clin Nutr 35 (1982) 568-1325.

Verschuur R. (1987). Daily physical activity and health: Longitudinal changes during the teenage period. Thesis, Universiteit van Amsterdam, de Vrieseborch, Haarlem, SO 12.

Willett W., M.J. Stampfer. Total energy intake: implications for epidemiologic analysis. Am J Epidemiol 124 (1986) 17-27.

World Health Organization. (1990). Diet, nutrition and the prevention of chronic diseases (Technical Report Series 797). World Health Organization, Geneva.

Chapter 7

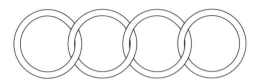

Habitual Physical Activity in Longitudinal Perspective

Willem van Mechelen & Han C.G. Kemper

The purpose of this chapter is to describe the sex-specific natural course of habitual physical activity using the results from all six of our measurements, covering a period of almost 15 years, from 1977 (when the subjects were 13 years old) to 1991 (age 27) and to describe over the full longitudinal period the stability of habitual physical activity as part of the general lifestyle pattern. Extensive descriptive information on various aspects of habitual physical activity concerning the first four measurements, covering the adolescent period from 1977 to 1980 (age 16), and the fifth measurement, in 1985, covering the young-adult period (age 21), have been reported elsewhere (Kemper, 1985; Verschuur, 1987) and will not be considered in depth here.

Subjects and Methods

At each year of measurement the subjects' habitual physical activity during the 3 months prior to the measurement were registered using a semistructured interview. The physical activity interview covered the following areas of habitual physical activity equal to or exceeding an intensity of 4 METs: (a) organized sports activities; (b) nonorganized sports and other leisure-time activities; (c) transportation to and from school, work, etc.; and (d) work-related activities. From the interview the average total weekly time in minutes was calculated. The scored activities were subsequently subdivided into three levels of intensity according to relative energy expenditure: (a) light (4-7 METs), (b) medium-heavy (7-10 METs), and (c) heavy (>10 METs). For each of the three levels the average weekly time was calculated. In order to obtain an overall measure of the amount of physical activity, containing both time and intensity, for each individual, the total amount of weekly energy expenditure above the level of

4 METs was calculated by multiplying the average weekly time (in minutes) spent per level of intensity of habitual physical activity by a fixed value (in METs per minute) for the relative energy expenditure at that level and by then summing these calculated values to a weighted activity score, as follows:

Weekly energy expenditure (METs/wk) =
(5.5 × light) + (8.5 × medium-heavy) + (11.5 × heavy)

Insight into the longitudinal pattern of the various aspects of habitual physical activity was obtained by applying a Multivariate Analysis of Variance (MANOVA) for repeated measurements, in which sex and time, as well as the interaction between those two variables, were entered. This procedure, when applicable, was always performed in the following way: First, the MANOVA was applied taking the entire period of study (1977-1991) into consideration, then the period covering 1977 to 1985, followed by the period covering 1977 to 1980. Statistical significance was accepted at the .05 level. If for the first or the second time periods either of the analyzed variables, or their interaction, proved to be not significant, then the analysis was not repeated for the next time period. This is indicated in the various tables with "NA" (not applicable). In 1991, 98 females and 84 males were measured. However not all of these subjects were measured at each year of measurement. Table 7.1 indicates the numbers of subjects measured in 1991 who were present for these measurements. The resulting small variations in numbers of subjects were accounted for when any of the statistical procedures described in this chapter were performed.

Table 7.1   Numbers of Subjects Present at the 1991 Measurements Who Were Also Present During the Preceding Years of Measurement

	1985	1980	1979	1978	1977
Males (n = 84 in 1991)	78	80	84	80	83
Females (n = 98 in 1991)	94	98	98	97	97

Results

Weekly Time Spent on Total Habitual Physical Activity

Using data from the activity interview it is possible to obtain insight into the time pattern of subjects' total habitual physical activity (Fig. 7.1) by performing a MANOVA as just described. The results of the MANOVA indicate that, in the subjects as a group, total habitual physical activity time (≥4 METs) significantly (p < .001) decreased from age 13 until age 27. Over the 15-year period the females dropped 8% in habitual physical activity time, from 9.1 h/wk to 8.4 h/wk;

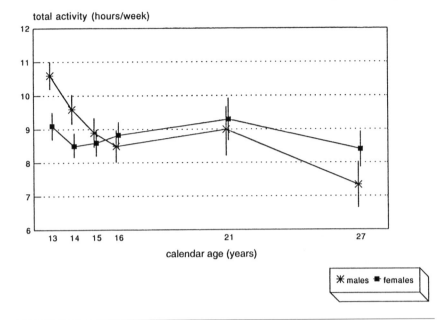

Figure 7.1   Total activity by age.

however, this time effect was not significant. Habitual physical activity time for males dropped 31%, from 10.6 h/wk to 7.3 h/wk. Specific post hoc analysis indicated there was in males a significant time effect for each period of measurement. During the adolescent period the decrease in time for females was 3%, followed by a 5% increase in their early 20s, followed by a more marked (10%) decrease in their late 20s. In males the following pattern was seen: a 20% decrease during the adolescent period, a 5% increase in their early 20s, and a 16% decrease in their late 20s.

The MANOVA indicates that over the 15-year period there were no significant differences between males and females with regard to total habitual physical activity time. Further, no significant interaction between time and sex was found, which means that both males and females showed a similar pattern for total habitual physical activity time. The results of the MANOVA and the subsequent post hoc analysis are summarized in Table 7.2.

Figures 7.2 to 7.4 show the breakdown of the total habitual physical activity time into three intensity levels: (a) light (4-7 METs), (b) medium-heavy (7-10 METs), and (c) heavy (> 10 METs). Again, for each level of intensity a MANOVA was carried out in order to evaluate the data longitudinally.

The MANOVA indicated a significant time effect ($p < .001$). For both sexes this time effect was significant for each of the three time periods. Over time there was a significant ($p < .05$) difference between males and females with regard to weekly time spent on light activities. Post hoc analysis indicated this difference to be significant for each of the three time periods. The interaction between time and sex was not significant.

Table 7.2   Results of MANOVA and Subsequent Post Hoc Analysis for Total Weekly Activity Time

	1977-1991		1977-1985		1977-1980	
	Males	Females	Males	Females	Males	Females
Time	$p < .001$	NS	$p < .05$	NA	$p < .001$	NA
Sex	NS		NA		NA	
Time by sex	NS		NA		NA	

Note. NA = not applicable; NS = not significant.

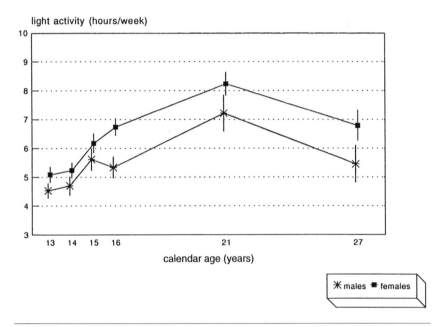

Figure 7.2   Light activity by age.

Regarding the longitudinal pattern there was, for both males and females, a gradual increase of about 60% in weekly time spent on *light* activities from the start of the adolescent period (4.7 h/wk) throughout young adulthood (age 21: 7.7 h/wk). This was followed by a 39% decrease in females (5.5 h/wk) and a 29% decrease in males (6.8 h/wk) at the adult age of 27 years. The results of the MANOVA and subsequent post hoc analysis are summarized in Table 7.3.

For weekly time spent on *medium-heavy* activities, the MANOVA showed a significant ($p < .001$) time effect for each of the three periods. No significant differences between males and females were indicated by the MANOVA. Also,

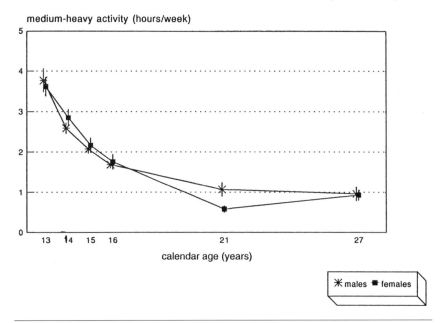

Figure 7.3   Medium-heavy activity by age.

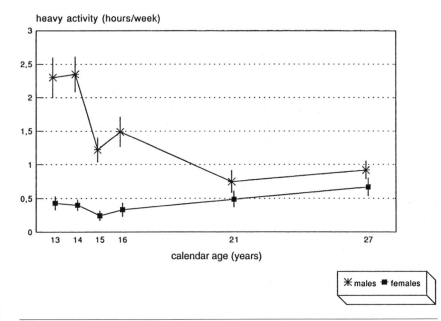

Figure 7.4   Heavy activity by age.

Table 7.3   Results of MANOVA and Subsequent Post Hoc Analysis for Total Weekly Light (4-7-MET) Activity Time

	1977-1991		1977-1985		1977-1980	
	Males	Females	Males	Females	Males	Females
Time	$p < .001$	$p < .001$	$p < .001$	$p < .001$	$p < .01$	$p < .001$
Sex		$p < .05$		$p < .05$		$p < .05$
Time by sex		NS		NA		NA

Note. NA = not applicable; NS = not significant.

Table 7.4   Results of MANOVA and Subsequent Post Hoc Analysis for Medium-Heavy (7-10-MET) Activity Time

	1977-1991		1977-1985		1977-1980	
	Males	Females	Males	Females	Males	Females
Time	$p < .001$	$p < .001$	$p < .001$	$p < .001$	$p < .001$	$p < .001$
Sex		NS		NA		NA
Time by sex		NS		NA		NA

Note. NA = not applicable; NS = not significant.

no significant interaction between time and sex was found. The results of the MANOVA and the subsequent post hoc analysis are summarized in Table 7.4.

The weekly time spent on medium-heavy activities showed, in a longitudinal perspective, a similar pattern in both males and females: a gradual decrease of 84% in females and of 72% in males from the age of the start of the adolescent period (3.7 h/wk) throughout the young-adult period (0.6 h/wk in females and 1.1 h/wk in males), followed by an increase of 16% in females and a further decrease of 3% in males at adult age.

Finally, the MANOVA of the weekly time spent on *heavy* activities showed that males spent significantly ($p < .001$) more time on this level of intensity than females throughout the whole longitudinal period, that there was a significant ($p < .001$) time effect, and that there was a significant ($p < .001$) interaction between sex and time, the latter indicating that the development of the pattern of heavy physical activity was significantly different for males and females. For these observed findings subsequent post hoc analysis was carried out, and the results are summarized in Table 7.5.

From the start of the adolescent period (2.3 h/wk) through the young-adult period, time that males spent on heavy activities shrunk about 68%; this was

Table 7.5   Results of MANOVA and Subsequent Post Hoc Analysis for Heavy (> 10-MET) Weekly Activity Time

	1977-1991		1977-1985		1977-1980	
	Males	Females	Males	Females	Males	Females
Time	$p < .001$	$p < .01$	$p < .001$	NS	$p < .001$	NA
Sex	$p < .05$		$p < .001$		$p < .001$	
Time by sex	$p < .01$		$p < .001$		$p < .001$	

Note. NA = not applicable; NS = not significant.

followed by a 7% increase at adult age. Females showed a 23% decrease during the adolescent period (0.4 h/wk), followed by a gradual 80% increase at adult age.

To summarize, no significant differences were found between males and females in overall weekly time spent on habitual physical activity, as well as in weekly time spent on light and medium-heavy activities. Males spent significantly more time on heavy activities than females over the full period. No significant differences were found between the pattern of males and females in overall weekly time spent on habitual physical activity and in time spent on light and medium-heavy activities. From the start of the adolescent period until adult age, females showed a gradual decrease of 8% in overall time spent on habitual physical activity, males a 31% decrease. From the start of the adolescent period until the young-adult period, both males and females showed a gradual increase of about 60% in time spent on light activities; this was followed by a 39% decrease in females and a 29% decrease in males during the adult period. From the start of the adolescent period until the young-adult period there was a gradual decrease (84% in females, 72% in males) in time spent on medium-heavy activities, followed by an increase of 16% in females and a further decrease of 3% in males until adult age.

Over time, males spent significantly more time on heavy activities than females. In males a gradual decrease of 68% was seen from the start of the adolescent period until the young-adult period, followed by a 7% increase during the adult period. Females exhibited a gradual increase of 57% in time spent on heavy activities from the start of the adolescent period until adult age. When the data from our last two measurement times (1985 and 1991) are compared, one may conclude that in males and females the overall weekly time spent on activities exceeding 4 METs/min declined, indicating an increasingly inactive lifestyle. This decrease is due mainly to a decrease in time spent on light activities. However, one should bear in mind that at the penultimate measurement, the time spent on medium-heavy and heavy activities had already reached such low levels that a further reduction by the last measurement would seem quite impossible.

Weekly Energy Expenditure in Relation to Habitual Physical Activity

In order to obtain an overall measure of the amount of physical activity containing both time and intensity, for each individual the total amount of weekly energy expenditure above the 4-MET level was calculated by multiplying the average weekly time in minutes spent per level of intensity of habitual physical activity by a fixed value (in METs per minute) for the relative energy expenditure at that level and then summing these calculated values to a weighted activity score (Fig. 7.5). Again a longitudinal analysis was done using a MANOVA for repeated measurements, in which sex and time as well as the interaction between these two variables were entered. The MANOVA revealed that in the course of time males showed a significantly ($p < .05$) greater amount of METs per week than did females. The MANOVA also showed that there was a significant time effect ($p < .001$) and that the evaluation of the pattern of the amount of weekly physical activity differed significantly ($p < .01$) between males and females. The results of the post hoc analysis are given in Table 7.6.

From the start of the adolescent period until adulthood (age 27) there was a significant decrease in total average weekly energy expenditure of 42% in males and 17% in females. For males, the decrease was most marked during the adolescent period; from the end of the adolescent period until adulthood (age 27) the decrease was only 15% in males and 5% in females. Our post hoc analysis indicates a significant difference only between the two sexes, but does not give information about the direction of observed differences. Bearing this in mind, one will note that in 1991, at adult age, compared with all previous years of

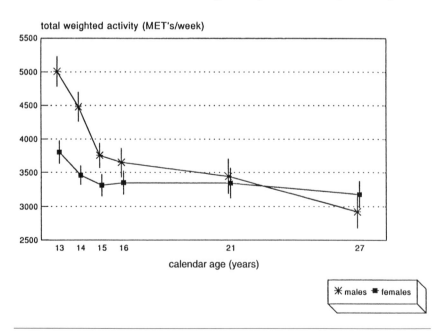

Figure 7.5   Total weighted activity by age.

Table 7.6   Results of MANOVA and Subsequent Post Hoc Analysis for Weighted Total Weekly Activity (METs)

	1977-1991		1977-1985		1977-1980	
	Males	Females	Males	Females	Males	Females
Time	$p < .001$	$p < .05$	$p < .001$	NS	$p < .001$	NA
Sex		$p < .05$		$p < .01$		$p < .001$
Time by sex		$p < .01$		$p < .01$		$p < .01$

Note. NA = not applicable; NS = not significant.

measurements the females as a group exhibited a trend toward a higher total weekly energy expenditure than did the males.

Weekly Time and Energy Expenditure in Relation to Organized Sports Activities

Time that subjects spent as a member of a club performing organized sports activities, both training and games, was also noted during the physical activity interview. Figure 7.6 shows data on overall weekly time spent in organized sports activities. A MANOVA indicated no significant differences between males and females throughout the whole period of study, although beginning at the age of

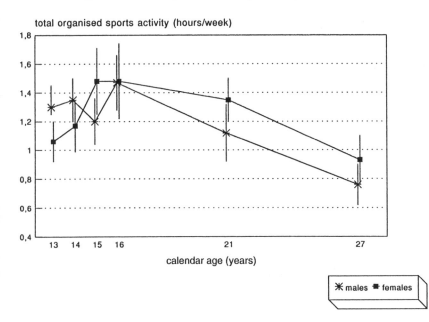

Figure 7.6   Total time spent on organized sports activities by age.

14 or 15 years, males tended to spend more time on organized sports activities than females. The MANOVA indicated a significant ($p < .01$) time effect. The interaction between time and sex was not significant, meaning that there was no difference between males and females in the evaluation of the longitudinal pattern of the overall weekly time spent in organized sports activities. The results of the post hoc analysis are summarized in Table 7.7.

In males there was at first a slight increase in weekly time spent in sports activities, from 78 min/wk to 90 min/wk during the adolescent period; this was followed by a decrease to 46 min/wk at adult age. For females there was over the same period first an increase from 64 min/wk to 89 min/wk, followed by a decrease to 55 min/wk.

Figures 7.7, 7.8, and 7.9 show the average time spent on organized light, medium-heavy, and heavy sports activities. A MANOVA for repeated measurements and subsequent post hoc analysis was applied to these data. The MANOVA and subsequent post hoc analysis revealed that for each of the three periods females spent significantly more time on organized sports of a light level of intensity than did males (Table 7.8). The analysis indicated a significant ($p < .001$) time effect, which was due completely to the time effect within females. The interaction between time and sex was not significant.

Table 7.7   Results of MANOVA and Subsequent Post Hoc Analysis for Total Weekly Time Spent on Organized Sports Activities

	1977-1991		1977-1985		1977-1980	
	Males	Females	Males	Females	Males	Females
Time	$p < .01$	$p < .05$	NS	NS	NA	NA
Sex	NS		NA		NA	
Time by sex	NS		NA		NA	

Note. NA = not applicable; NS = not significant.

Table 7.8   Results of MANOVA and Subsequent Post Hoc Analysis for Time Spent on Light (4-7-MET) Organized Sports Activities

	1977-1991		1977-1985		1977-1980	
	Males	Females	Males	Females	Males	Females
Time	NS	$p < .001$	NA	$p < .001$	NA	$p < .001$
Sex	$p < .01$		$p < .05$		$p < .05$	
Time by sex	NS		NA		NA	

Note. NA = not applicable; NS = not significant.

Figure 7.7 shows that for males there was an increase in average time spent on *light* organized sports activities from 13 min/wk at age 13 to 28 min/wk at age 16, followed by a decrease to 6 min/wk at adult age. For females over the same period of time the following was found: first an increase from 19 min/wk to 54 min/wk, followed by a decrease to 13 min/wk.

With regard to *medium-heavy* organized sports activities, the MANOVA showed that females spent significantly ($p < .05$) more time on these kind of activities than did males throughout the entire period (Table 7.9), but not for the two shorter periods of measurement. For both males and females the time effect was not significant.

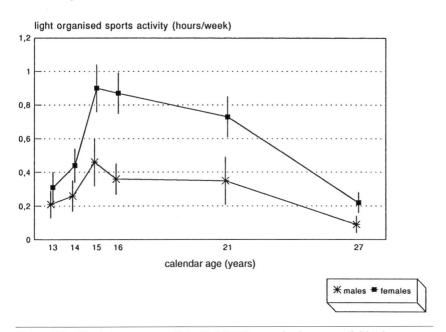

Figure 7.7   Total time spent on light (4-7-MET) organized sports activities by age.

Table 7.9   Results of MANOVA and Subsequent Post Hoc Analysis for Time Spent on Heavy-Medium (7-10-MET) Organized Sports Activities

	1977-1991		1977-1985		1977-1980	
	Males	Females	Males	Females	Males	Females
Time	NS	NS	NA	NA	NA	NA
Sex	$p < .05$		NS		NA	
Time by sex	NS		NA		NA	

Note. NA = not applicable; NS = not significant.

From Figure 7.8 it can be seen that males and females show a somewhat opposite, though not significantly different, longitudinal pattern: In females there was a decrease in time spent on medium-heavy sports activities from 26 min/ wk at the start of the adolescent period to 12 min/wk at age 21, followed by a slight increase to 17 min/wk at adult age. In males during the adolescent period a stable pattern was seen, with an average weekly time spent on medium-heavy sports activities of about 2 min/wk, followed by an increase to 11 min/wk during the young-adult period, in turn followed by a decrease to 7 min/wk at adult age.

The MANOVA for the longitudinal pattern of time spent on *heavy* organized sports activities showed that males spent significantly more time in such activities than females for each of the three periods of time (Table 7.10). The analysis also indicated a significant ($p < .05$) time effect, which was for each of the three periods due entirely to the significant time effect within males. Females did not show a time effect. Finally, the longitudinal pattern for males and females proved to be significantly different throughout the whole period of study, as well as for the period covering both the adolescent and young-adult periods.

Figure 7.9 shows that during the entire period of study there was a slight increase in average weekly time spent on heavy organized sports activities, from 19 min/wk at the start of the adolescent period to 26 min/wk at adult age for females. Among males the average weekly time spent on heavy organized sports activities during the adolescent period was about 64 min/wk, with a dip to 42 min/wk at the age of 15. During the young-adult period this figure gradually decreased to about 35 min/wk by adult age.

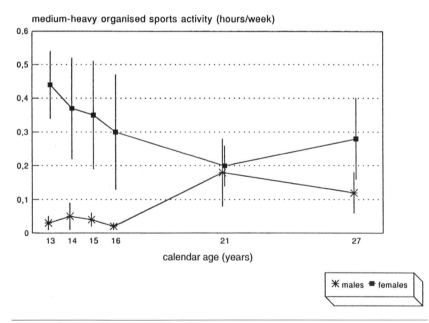

Figure 7.8   Total time spent on medium-heavy (7-10-MET) organized sports activities by age.

Table 7.10   Results of MANOVA and Subsequent Post Hoc Analysis for Time Spent on Heavy (> 10-MET) Organized Sports Activities

	1977-1991		1977-1985		1977-1980	
	Males	Females	Males	Females	Males	Females
Time	$p < .001$	NS	$p < .01$	NA	$p < .05$	NA
Sex	$p < .001$		$p < .001$		$p < .001$	
Time by sex	$p < .001$		$p < .01$		NS	

Note. NA = not applicable; NS = not significant.

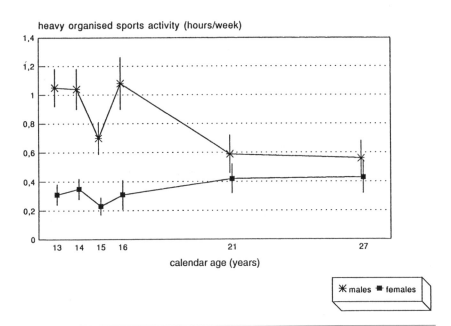

heavy organised sports activity (hours/week)

calendar age (years)

✳ males   ▪ females

Figure 7.9   Total time spent on heavy (>10-MET) organized sports activities by age.

In order to obtain an overall weighted measure of the amount of organized sports activities containing both time and intensity, the equation on page 136 was applied (Fig. 7.10). Upon applying a MANOVA to this weighted measure of the amount of organized sports activities, no significant differences between males and females were found, nor was there a significant interaction between time and sex, meaning that there was no significant difference between males and females in the longitudinal pattern of this variable (Table 7.11). The MANOVA did indicate a significant time effect, which was, for both males and females, only significant ($p < .05$) for the entire period of study.

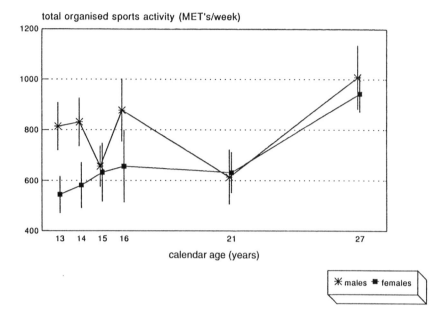

Figure 7.10   Total weighted organized sports activities by age.

Table 7.11   Results of MANOVA and Subsequent Post Hoc Analysis for Weighted Total Weekly Energy Expenditure Relative to Organized Sports Activities (METs)

	1977-1991		1977-1985		1977-1980	
	Males	Females	Males	Females	Males	Females
Time	$p < .05$	$p < .05$	NS	NS	NA	NA
Sex		NS		NA		NA
Time by sex		NS		NA		NA

Note. NA = not applicable; NS = not significant.

Figure 7.10 shows that over the whole period of study females exhibited a gradual increase, from 555 METs/wk to 933 METs/wk at adult age. In males the average weekly energy expenditure as a result of organized sports activities throughout the adolescent period was about 850 METs/wk, with a dip to 671 METs/wk at the age of 15. During the young-adult period this figure decreased to 614 METs/wk, followed by an increase to 1,009 METs/wk at adult age.

To summarize, we found that the longitudinal pattern of overall time spent on organized sports activities (game and training), as well as the weighted measure expressed as METs per week, did not differ significantly between males and females. For both measures a significant time effect was found over the entire longitudinal period: Between the end of the adolescent period until adulthood (age 27) there was a gradual decrease in overall time spent on sports activities from about 90 min/wk to 46 min/wk for males and to 56 min/wk for females, whereas over the same period of time there was among males a gradual increase in the weighted measure for organized sports activities from 850 METs/wk to 1,009 METs/wk and among females from 555 METs/wk to 933 METs/wk. This perhaps contradictory finding can be explained by the fact that in a longitudinal perspective there were marked differences between males and females for time spent on different intensity levels of the organized sports activities. Compared with males, females spent significantly more weekly time on light and medium-heavy organized sports activities, whereas males spent significantly more weekly time on heavy organized sports activities than females. Significant time effects were found for time spent on light and heavy organized sports activities, and a pattern of decline similar to that for overall time spent on organized sports activities was found. No time effect was found for medium-heavy organized sports activities.

When the average weekly energy expenditure as a result of organized sports activities was evaluated longitudinally, no significant differences were found between males and females, despite the effects, just mentioned, in time spent on organized sports activities at the three levels of intensity. One must conclude that the significant differences between males and females at the three levels of intensity were compensated for when calculating a weighted average.

Over the entire period of study, no significant time effect was found for the weighted weekly energy expenditure, nor was there a significant interaction between sex and time.

Weekly Time and Weekly Energy Expenditure in Relation to the Use of Transportation

As part of the physical activity interview, we asked throughout the longitudinal period what means of transportation subjects used to get to and from all regular daily activities (school, work, sports, other leisure-time activities); e.g., walking, bicycling, public transport, moped, or car. Only physically active means—walking and cycling—were scored for transportation time. Walking and cycling were both considered activities of light intensity (4-7 METs); therefore, no distinction was made between them in terms of weekly transportation time and energy expenditure expressed by a weighted average. Again, the data were analyzed in a longitudinal perspective by applying a MANOVA for repeated measurements, followed by the standard post hoc analysis (Table 7.12).

No significant differences were found between males and females. The MANOVA demonstrated for both males and females a significant ($p < .001$) time effect over the entire longitudinal period. The time effect was also present in females between 1977 and 1985. The interaction between time and sex was significant for none of the distinguished periods.

In terms of the longitudinal pattern, females showed a more or less stable pattern during the adolescent period. During this period about 2.5 h/wk were

Table 7.12   Results of MANOVA and Subsequent Post Hoc Analysis for Weekly Time (Hours) Spent on Active Transportation to and From Work, School, Leisure-Time Activities, Etc.

	1977-1991		1977-1985		1977-1980	
	Males	Females	Males	Females	Males	Females
Time	$p < .001$	$p < .001$	NS	$p < .001$	NA	NS
Sex	NS		NA		NA	
Time by sex	NS		NA		NA	

Note. NA = not applicable; NS = not significant.

spent walking and cycling as means of transport. During the young-adult period this figure dropped to about 1.8 h/wk, followed by a further decrease to 1.1 h/wk at adult age. In males the pattern was the same, with the exception that the decrease in weekly time spent on walking and cycling as means of transport had already started at the end of the adolescent period, at the age of 17: During the first 4 years of the adolescent period, active transportation time was about 2.3 h/wk, and at ages 17 to 21 it was about 1.9 h/wk; this was followed by a drop to 1.3 h/wk at age 27 (Fig. 7.11). One may conclude that between ages 21 and 27 our subjects had, in general, adopted less active means of transportation

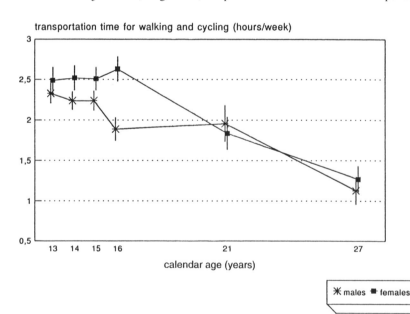

Figure 7.11   Total transportation time for walking and cycling by age.

to and from school, work, and leisure-time activities. This was probably caused by an increased use of public transport and private cars.

Tracking of Habitual Physical Activity

Interperiod correlation coefficients (IPCs), indicating the amount of tracking of habitual physical activity in the same subject, were calculated to relate average levels of the 1977-1980 weighted measure of physical activity with those of both 1985 and 1991, in order to gain insight into the constancy of the amount of habitual physical activity within the subjects. Subsequently, IPCs were calculated relating 1977 with 1980, 1985, and 1991; relating 1980 with 1985 and 1991; and relating 1985 with 1991. Also, the values of 1977 through 1980 were averaged and then correlated with the values obtained during the following years. These IPCs are listed in Table 7.13.

The IPCs indicate that among both male and female subjects habitual physical activity tracked neither over the entire period of study (15 years) nor over the shorter time period of 10 years. For time periods of about 5 years there seems to be a certain amount of tracking, as indicated by the significant correlation coefficients. However, one should realize that these IPCs explain only 6% to 34% of the total variance.

Tracking was also analyzed for weekly energy expenditure related to organized sports activities and for active weekly transportation time (Tables 7.14 and 7.15). Over the entire period of study there was no tracking of weekly energy expenditure related to organized sports activities, nor for active weekly transportation time. For shorter periods of time (between 1977 and 1985 and between 1977 and 1980), there was in males a certain amount of tracking of weekly energy expenditure related to organized sports activities over the periods 1977 to 1980 and 1980 to 1985, as indicated by the IPCs of .53 and .54, respectively, and in

Table 7.13   Interperiod Correlation Coefficients Indicating the Amount of Tracking of Total Weekly Habitual Physical Activity Within Subjects

Interperiod	Interperiod correlation, males	Interperiod correlation, females
'77/'80-1985	.27*	.24*
'77/'80-1991	.10	.21
1977-1980	.44***	.58***
1977-1985	.20	.18
1977-1991	.05	.17
1980-1985	.37***	.25**
1980-1991	.09	.16
1985-1991	.32**	.36***

$*p < .05; **p < .01; ***p < .001.$

Table 7.14   Interperiod Correlation Coefficients Indicating the Amount of Tracking Within Subjects of Weekly Energy Expenditure Due to Organized Sports Activities

Interperiod	Interperiod correlation, males	Interperiod correlation, females
'77/'80-1985	.40**	.32
'77/'80-1991	.17	.14
1977-1980	.53**	.59**
1977-1985	.19	.33**
1977-1991	.09	.11
1980-1985	.54**	.25*
1980-1991	.16	.13
1985-1991	.22	.34**

$*p < .05; **p < .01.$

Table 7.15   Interperiod Correlation Coefficients Indicating the Amount of Tracking Within Subjects of Weekly Energy Expenditure Due to Active Transportation

Interperiod	Interperiod correlation, males	Interperiod correlation, females
'77/'80-1985	.17	−.12
'77/'80-1991	.04	−.11
1977-1980	.53*	.75*
1977-1985	.15	−.17
1977-1991	−.08	−.09
1980-1985	.21	−.09
1980-1991	.10	−.11
1985-1991	0	.36*

$*p < .01.$

females over the period 1977 to 1980 (IPC = .59). Tracking of weekly energy expenditure due to active transportation time was found in both males and females only with regard to the 1977-1980 IPCs (males, .53; females, .75).

From the various IPC analyses it can be concluded that within subjects habitual physical activity does not track over longer periods of time, regardless of the nature of the activity.

An alternative method of studying the amount of tracking of habitual physical activity is by looking at the constancy of appearance of subjects in either the upper (P_{75}) or the lower (P_{25}) quartile at each point of measurement throughout the whole period of study (Table 7.16a). Again, values for 1977 through 1980 were also averaged in order to obtain a more or less stable baseline value (Table 7.16b).

From Table 7.16a it can be seen that in 1980 9 of the 21 1977 upper-quartile male subjects were found among the 1980 upper quartile. In 1985 and 1991 only 4 and then 1 remained a member of the upper quartile. For lower-quartile males, the following was observed: 1977, 21 subjects; 1980, 12 subjects; 1985, 5 subjects; and 1991, 2 subjects. For females a similar pattern was found. When the mean values over the first 4 years are taken as baseline, one can conclude that both for the relatively active and inactive males and females there is, over the entire period of study (1977/1980-1991), some sort of tracking: About 30% of the males and females remain active, and 35% inactive.

Again, one is led to conclude that there is no tracking of habitual physical activity in subjects showing relatively low levels of habitual physical activity, and little tracking in subjects showing relatively high levels of physical activity.

Table 7.16a   Constancy of Appearance of Subjects According to Total Weekly Energy Expenditure in the Upper (P_{75}) and the Lower (P_{25}) Quartiles During the Entire Period of Study

		1977 (n)	1980 (n)	1985 (n)	1991 (n)
Males	P_{75} (1977)	21	9	4	1
Males	P_{25} (1977)	21	12	5	2
Females	P_{75} (1977)	26	15	6	2
Females	P_{25} (1977)	24	11	3	1

Note. The 1977 values served as baseline values.

Table 7.16b   Constancy of Appearance of Subjects According to Total Weekly Energy Expenditure in the Upper (P_{75}) and the Lower (P_{25}) Quartiles During the Entire Period of Study

		1980 (n)	1985 (n)	1991 (n)
Males	P_{75} ('77/'80)	21	7	8
Males	P_{25} ('77/'80)	21	6	5
Females	P_{75} ('77/'80)	24	7	7
Females	P_{25} ('77/'80)	24	7	10

Note. The average of the values of 1977 through 1980 served as baseline values.

Given the low IPCs for active transportation time and the weighted measure of organized sports activities, no further attempt was made to discern the constancy of appearance of subjects in quartile groups for these two subcategories of habitual physical activity.

It is noteworthy not only to see whether there is tracking of subcategories of habitual physical activity but also to see for each year of measurement whether there are shifts in the relative contribution (share) of the various subcategories of activity to the total amount of habitual physical activity. Among males there is not much variation in the relative contribution of the three subcategories of activity to the total amount of weekly energy expenditure until the fifth point of measurement. At the last (sixth) point of measurement, in contrast to the other points, a decrease in the relative contribution to the total amount of weekly energy expenditure of active transport, an increase in the share of organized sports activities, and a decrease in the share of other activities were noted. In females at the young-adult age a slight decrease was seen in the relative contribution to the total amount of weekly energy expenditure of active transport, as well as a slight increase in the share of organized sports activities. These observed shifts in females in the relative contributions to the total weekly energy expenditure continued toward the last point of measurement.

Discussion

The follow-up of the same individuals over a long period of time is a major strength of our study and enables useful observations on trends in time. However, as indicated by Lamb and Brodie (1990), our method has not been used in other studies, which hampers the comparison of our results with those of others. Furthermore, one needs to realize that the method as such has not been extensively validated. An attempt to validate the method was made by Kemper (1992). Mean daily heart rate measurements and mean pedometer scores obtained during the first 4 years of the study (1977-1980) were related to the mean results of the habitual physical activity interview by calculating Pearson correlation coefficients; none of the calculated coefficients exceeded .20. Kemper concluded that the various methods for assessing physical activity should be considered to measure different aspects of physical activity; thus they would naturally show low intercorrelation coefficients. As stated by other physical activity epidemiologists, such as Paffenbarger et al. (1993), measures similar to the ones used in our study should be seen as indicators of physical activity rather than as absolute measures. Bearing this in mind, some remarks with concern to our results can be made.

In our longitudinal study, at each year of measurement only those activities exceeding a baseline value of 4 METs were taken into consideration, without relating the level of energy expenditure of each scored activity to the individual's aerobic capacity. This method has a drawback in that it does not reveal differences between subjects with regard to the amount of aerobic strain placed on them as they perform a similar task, nor for a given person does it account for the effect of the decline in aerobic capacity at subsequent years of measurement.

In our study a gradual decrease was observed in the total weekly time spent on physical activities exceeding 4 METs. The same was found for the total amount of physical activity expressed in METs per week. This decline in habitual physical activity with age is in accordance with the report of Haskell (1985). There is no literature available that covers an age group similar to that of our study with which to compare our results. With regard to older age groups it should be noted that Lee et al. (1992), in a prospective study of 6,092 Harvard College alumni, reported stable median levels of energy expenditure from physical activity in men from age 30 (in the early 1960s) onward until age 70.

Concerning specific subcategories of activity, a decrease was found in the amount of weekly energy and time spent on active transportation and in the weekly time spent on organized sports activities, but not for the total amount of physical activity related to organized sports. This means that in the course of time organized sports activities played an increasingly important role in total weekly energy expenditure, both in males and females. These findings are in line with those of the study of Lee et al. (1992), who reported an increase in the median duration of time spent per week in playing sports from 1 hour in the early 1960s to 2.5 hours in 1988. From the standpoint of public health, regular physical activity is important in the prevention of disease. Less active people sustain a greater risk of mortality due to a variety of diseases (Blair et al., 1989; Haskell et al., 1992; Leon & Connet, 1991; McGinnis, 1992; Paffenbarger et al., 1986, 1993). For instance, Paffenbarger et al. (1986) showed in men a consistent trend toward a lower all-cause death rate as physical activity increased from less than 500 kcal/wk to 2,000 kcal/wk or more. In this study the age-adjusted relative risk for all-cause mortality for men with a physical activity index greater than 2,000 kcal/wk was .72 ($p < .0001$). At our last measurement (1991) the average weekly energy expenditure was found to be 2,925 METs/wk for males (average body weight in 1991 = 75.5 kg) and 3,179 METs/wk for females (average body weight in 1991 = 63.3 kg). Assuming that 1 MET is equivalent to 3.5 ml oxygen uptake · kg^{-1} body weight · min^{-1} and that the caloric equivalent of 1 L of oxygen is 4.85 kcal, the average number of kilocalories spent per week by our subjects was 3,813 for males and 3,416 for females. These values are well above the all-cause mortality threshold value of 2,000 kcal/wk mentioned by Paffenbarger et al. (1986). However, one should bear in mind that there are marked differences in the assessment of the amount of habitual physical activity between our study and the Paffenbarger et al. (1986) study. In the latter, walking blocks, stair climbing, and weekly sports participation were performed, whereas in our study active transportation time and leisure-time activities, as well as sports, were registered.

A second example of the health benefits of regular habitual physical activity comes from Leon and Connet (1991) who, in a 10.5-year follow-up study on 12,866 men with a mean age of 46.4 years at baseline, found a significant excess age-adjusted all-cause mortality rate of 15% in the least active tertile (0-29 min/ day of leisure-time physical activity; average = 15.2 min/day) of their population, when compared with the other tertiles. The average weekly energy expenditure of the subjects in the least active tertile was 500 kcal/wk, whereas subjects in the middle tertile spent an average of 1,500 kcal/wk on leisure-time physical activity (Leon et al., 1987).

If a certain level of habitual physical activity is advantageous in the prevention of disease, it then becomes interesting to know whether or not the pattern of physical activity remains constant over time. Our study indicated—by the low and not significant correlation coefficients—that there was no tracking of habitual physical activity over the entire longitudinal period. This finding is supported by the findings of Lee et al. (1992) and Ballard-Barbash et al. (1990), who both reported low habitual physical activity IPCs. Lee et al. (1992) found in their study on 4,238 male Harvard College alumni IPCs between collegiate sports activities and alumni physical activity (one to seven decades later) ranging from .05 to .17. Ballard-Barbash et al. (1990) reported IPCs of .17-.29 between two assessments of physical activity 16 years apart.

In terms of a policy emphasizing the preventive benefits of regular physical activity, the lack of constancy of the habitual physical activity pattern is an important finding because it implies that constant efforts have to be directed toward keeping people active and consequently toward "reactivating" those who have for some reason or other gone from an active lifestyle to a more sedentary one. This change from a sedentary to an active lifestyle is effective because it is known from the study of Paffenbarger et al. (1993) that among Harvard College alumni, even those in their fourth decade or later, a change from a sedentary lifestyle (e.g., <2,000 kcal/wk) to a more active one (e.g., ≥2,000 kcal/wk) significantly lowered the age-adjusted all-cause mortality risk, especially when they also quit smoking, maintained normal blood pressure, and avoided obesity.

Conclusions

In males but not in females there was a significant decrease in weekly time spent on habitual physical activity between ages 13 and 27. No significant differences were found in total weekly time spent on habitual physical activities between males and females.

Looking more specifically at the intensity of the various activities, we may conclude the following:

• Both in males and females a significant increase was found in time spent on light activities. Females spent significantly more time on activities at this level of intensity than males.

• Both in males and females a significant decrease was found in time spent on medium-heavy activities. There was no difference between males and females with regard to the time spent at this level of intensity.

- In males a significant decrease was found in time spent on heavy activities, whereas in females a significant increase was found in time spent at this level of activity.

In order to account for the observed differences between males and females according to the level of intensity, a weighted total amount of weekly energy expenditure was calculated. Based on this measure, between ages 13 and 27 a significant decrease was found for both males and females. This decrease was significantly greater for males (42%) than for females (17%). The difference in results for males and females between total weekly time and the weighted measure for physical activity clearly demonstrates the necessity of applying a weighted score on the basis of energy expenditure when assessing levels of habitual physical activity.

Over the entire longitudinal period, no tracking of the weighted measure of habitual physical activity was observed, for either males or females. With relatively shorter periods of time (about 4-5 years), however, there was some tracking, as indicated by IPCs varying from .32 to .44 in males and from .25 to .58 in females.

With regard to more specific activities, the following interesting findings may be reported:

- Between the ages of 21 and 27, organized sports activities became relatively more important contributors to both weekly habitual activity time and weekly energy expenditure, for both males and females.
- Between the ages of 13 and 27, a marked decrease in active transportation time was observed, both in males and females, reflecting an increasingly sedentary lifestyle.

References

Ballard-Barbash R., A. Schatzkin, D. Albanes, M.H. Schiffman, B.E. Kreger, W.B. Kannel, K.M. Anderson, W.E. Helsel. Physical activity and the risk of large bowel cancer in the Framingham Study. Cancer Res 50 (1990) 3610-3613.

Blair S.N., H.W. Kohl III, R.S. Paffenbarger, D.G. Clark, K.H. Cooper, L.W. Gibbons. Physical fitness and all-cause mortality: A prospective study of healthy men and women. JAMA 262:17 (1989) 2395-2401.

Haskell, W.L. Physical activity and health: Need to define the required stimulus. Am J Cardiol 55 (1985) 4D-9D.

Haskell W.L., A.S. Leon, C.J. Caspersen, V.F. Froelicher, J.M. Hagberg, W. Harlan, J.O. Holloszy, J.G. Regensteiner, P.D. Thompson, R.A. Washburn, P.W.F. Wilson. Cardiovascular benefits and assessment of physical activity and physical fitness in adults. Med Sci Sports Exerc 23:6 (1992) S201-S220.

Kemper H.C.G. (ed.). (1985). Growth, health and fitness of teenagers: Longitudinal research in international perspective. Vol. 20 of: Medicine and sport science. Karger, Basel.

Kemper H.C.G. (1992). Physical development and childhood activity. In: N.C. Norgan (ed.), Physical activity and health symposium, vol. 34 SSHB (pp. 84-101). Cambridge University Press.

Lamb K.L., D.A. Brodie. The assessment of physical activity by leisure-time physical activity questionnaires. Sports Med 10:3 (1990) 159-176.

Lee A., R.S. Paffenbarger, C. Hsieh. Time trends in physical activity among college alumni, 1962-1988. Am J Epidem 135:8 (1992) 915-925.

Leon A.S., J. Connet. Physical activity and 10.5-year mortality in the Multiple Risk Factor Intervention Trial (MRFIT). Int J Epidem 20:3 (1991) 690-697.

Leon A.S., J. Connet, D.R. Jacobs, R. Rauramaa. Leisure-time physical activity levels and risk of coronary heart disease and death: The Multiple Risk Factor Intervention Trial. JAMA 258:17 (1987) 2388-2395.

McGinnis J. The public health burden of a sedentary lifestyle. Med Sci Sports Exerc 24:6 (1992) S196-S200.

Paffenbarger R.S., R.T. Hyde, A.L. Wing, I.M. Lee, D.L. Jung, J.B. Kampert. The association of changes in physical-activity level and other lifestyle characteristics with mortality among men. N Engl J Med 328:8 (1993) 538-545.

Paffenbarger R.S. Jr., R.T. Hyde, A.L. Wing, C.C. Hsieh. Physical activity, all-cause mortality and longevity of college alumni. N Engl J Med 314:10 (1986) 605-613.

Verschuur R. (1987). Daily physical activity and health: Longitudinal changes during the teenage period. Thesis, Universiteit van Amsterdam, de Vrieseborch, Haarlem SO 12.

Chapter 8

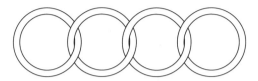

Lifestyle and Health From Young Adulthood to Adulthood

Jan Snel & Willem van Mechelen

Much effort and money have been invested in attempts to disentangle the factors involved in the relationships among stress, coping style, and health. In particular, the association between stressors and illness has been ascertained for life events and daily hassles that are appraised as undesirable (Fondacaro & Moos, 1989; Lu, 1991; Suls & Mullen, 1981) and uncontrollable (Antoni, 1985). Apparently, the effort of coping with life events and daily hassles is psychologically and physiologically stressful—and even more so the longer they last. Another factor involved in the way people react to and cope with stressors is their behavioral style. Schmitz (1992) noted that the occurrence of psychosomatic complaints is related to personality, coping style, and health behavior. In particular, the so-called coronary-prone behavior pattern, more commonly known as the Type A behavior pattern, characterized by high levels of competitive achievement striving, time urgency, and hard driving, comes into focus. Keltikangas-Jarvinen et al. (1991) found that hard driving was most strongly related to cardiovascular disease risk factors levels in young adulthood, when subjects felt that they could not cope with life. This finding suggests that Type A behavior is a coping mechanism. Support for this was given by Dorreboom & Snel (1988) and Snel & Gosselink (1989), who found that highly Type A men are characterized by rigidity in their behavior and practice a one-sided problem-focused coping style. Moreover, these men were less healthy than highly Type A women, who were reported to practice a more flexible coping style. Physiologically, Type A's show intensified cardiovascular and neuroendocrine reactivity (Abbott & Sutherland, 1990; Dembroski et al., 1977; Matthews et al., 1986), especially in tasks that favor low or no arousal (Gastorf, 1981); for these reasons it is not surprising to find that Type A's have at least twice the likelihood of heart disease as people with the Type B behavior pattern (Friedman & Rosenman, 1974). Referring to more specific health disorders, Appels et al. (1987b) found that sleep problems, notably the feeling of exhaustion and fatigue after rising, were long-term determinants of myocardial infarction, in particular among Type A's.

The risk of physical and psychological illness tends to increase in proportion to life change (Rabkin & Struening, 1976). This tendency is even more explicit where negative life events are concerned (Williams & Deffenbacher, 1983). Evidence also indicates that Type A's tend toward more self-induced life change (Strube et al., 1985) and seek more challenges than Type B's (Ortega & Pipal, 1984). In conclusion, the assumption is plausible that Type A's who have an inadequate coping style run a higher risk of worse health than non–Type A's with an appropriate coping style.

Thus, the first question we would like to answer is whether the impact of stressors on health complaints has to do with the techniques or strategies people use to cope with stressors and what role Type A behavior has in this. Another topic we would like to look at is whether there is some stability in the interrelationship of stress, coping style, Type A behavior, and reported health symptoms. In the present study we were able to do this by comparing the data on two points of measurement with a 6-year interval.

Objectives

The aim of our study was twofold. One goal was to examine whether in men and women health is related to the incidence of stressors, while taking into account coping style and the coronary-prone (Type A) behavior pattern. The other goal was to ascertain whether there is persistence or stability in the reporting of stressors, behavioral style, and health-related symptoms over a period of 6 years.

Subjects

The longitudinal Amsterdam Growth and Health Study (Kemper, 1985) was conducted on 85 men and 98 women when they were 21 and 27 (±0.6) years old. The subjects came to the lab in a large hospital for 1 day from 9 a.m. to 5 p.m. Besides other measurements, the subjects filled out questionnaires on their experience with stressors, on behavior style, and on mild health discomforts. Using the scores on these questionnaires, the objectives of the present study were answered.

Instruments

Stressors

• *Life events.* The Life Event List (LEL), a translated version of the Life Events Survey of Sarason et al. (1978) has 89 life events in five domains of life. These domains are health (8 events), work (14), home/family (38), personal/

social relations (23), and finances (6). Each event can be scored on the intensities of impact. The subject is asked to indicate only those events that have been experienced during the past year and to assess them in terms of negative or positive impact. For the present study, the incidence of scores was used.

• *Daily hassles.* These were ascertained using the Everyday Problem Checklist (EPCL) (Vingerhoets et al., 1989). Each of the 114 items with four alternatives can be scored from 0 (''Doesn't mind at all'') to 3 (''Do mind very much''). The score used in the present study is the sum of daily hassles that occurred during the past 2 months.

Behavior Style

• *Coronary-prone behavior pattern (Type A behavior pattern).* This was measured with the Dutch version of the Jenkins Activity Survey (JAS) (Appels et al., 1979). The 36 items with three to five response alternatives and scores of 1 to 5 result in a scoring range of 36 to 180.

• *Coping style.* This was evaluated with the Dutch version of the Ways of Coping Checklist (WCC) (Vingerhoets & Flohr, 1984). This list is based on the WCC of Folkman and Lazarus (1980). The list counts 67 dichotomous items; 24 refer to problem-focused coping and 40 to emotion-focused coping. Both scores are found by summation.

Health Complaints

• *Mild health complaints.* The Checklist on Experienced Health (CLEH) (Dirken, 1967) is an index of long-term health or physical malaise. Jansen and Sikkel (1981) have shown that the scale is responsive to situational stress. The 13 dichotomous items each have a weighing factor. The mean score for 15- to 22-year-old men is 2.44 and for women, 3.25.

• *Sleep-wake problems.* These were assessed with the SWEL, the Sleep Wake Experience List (van Diest et al., 1989). The scale contains 14 items, asking for problems in falling asleep, staying asleep, waking too early, waking in the morning, and functioning during the day. The answers, based on the past 3 months, are summed.

• *Vital exhaustion.* This is defined as feelings of depression, malfunctioning, apathy, and anxiety; it was measured with the Maastricht Questionnaire (MQ) (Appels et al., 1987a). The 21 items have a score range of 0 to 42 and load on one factor, that is, vital exhaustion. The reliability (Cronbach's α) is .89.

• *Inadequacy.* The Inadequacy scale of the Dutch Personality Inventory (DPI) (Luteijn et al., 1985) contains 21 items with three response alternatives; scoring ranges from 0 to 63. The Inadequacy scale asks for vague physical complaints, depressed mood, and vague feelings of anxiety and malfunctioning. The reference value for men is 7 to 13 and for women, 11 to 17.

Statistics

The method of Principal Components Analyses (PCA) (Stevens, 1986) was applied to investigate whether stressors, behavior style, and health complaints interact. This was done with the data collected at adult age, because then all scales had been administered. The second hypothesis, on persistence in reporting, was verified by checking the scale intercorrelation matrices of both points of measurement separately and the matrix of retest or interperiod correlations.

Results

During the subjects' young adulthood, at age 21, we measured the following parameters: Life Events, coping style, Type A Behavior pattern, Mild Health Complaints, and Inadequacy. During adulthood, at age 27, these and the following additional parameters were measured: Daily Hassles, Vital Exhaustion, and Sleep Complaints (Table 8.1). There were no large differences between the means of

Table 8.1   Statistical Data From Questionnaires on Stressors, Behavioral Style, and Health Complaints

Scale	Age 21 (young adulthood)					Age 27 (adulthood)				
	n	M	SD	Min	Max	n	M	SD	Min	Max
Males										
Life events	78	16.58	9.45	0	42	82	17.67	12.88	3	84
Daily hassles						84	22.35	16.37	3	114
Emotion-focused coping	78	16.94	5.54	6	78	83	18.58	5.70	5	31
Problem-focused coping	78	16.08	3.34	8	22	82	16.15	3.32	5	21
Type A behavior	78	99.63	15.06	61	142	84	111.05	16.84	73	154
Vital exhaustion						82	5.85	7.46	0	39
Sleep complaints						84	.42	.75	0	3
Mild health complaints	78	2.39	2.56	0	10.2	84	2.26	2.73	0	11.5
Inadequacy	77	9.39	7.64	0	34	84	7.01	6.91	0	37
Females										
Life events	94	15.98	9.49	0	46	97	16.73	11.68	2	78
Daily hassles						98	18.51	13.30	0	71
Emotion-focused coping	94	18.79	4.62	7	30	96	20.03	4.82	8	35
Problem-focused coping	94	15.80	3.46	3	22	95	16.22	2.74	7	22
Type A behavior	94	110.35	14.89	73	147	97	113.56	17.95	70	156
Vital exhaustion						98	7.37	8.37	0	40
Sleep complaints						98	.57	1.04	0	4
Mild health complaints	94	4.01	3.69	0	14.6	98	2.89	3.03	0	13.9
Inadequacy	94	11.88	6.50	0	31	98	8.43	6.33	0	29

the scores of any of the parameters measured at ages 21 and 27. In adulthood, however, the women scored below the reference values (Luteijn et al., 1985) for Mild Health Complaints ($t = 2.29$; $p < .05$) and Inadequacy ($t = 3.72$; $p < .01$), indicating a tendency to report less physical and psychosomatic symptoms and to have fewer feelings of diminished anxiety and malfunctioning. A comparison of the data for men and women indicates that they are quite similar, except for the higher incidence of Mild Health Complaints and higher Inadequacy scores in women.

Principal Components Analyses

Varimax-rotated PCA (Stevens, 1986) on the data collected at age 27 was performed with Eigenvalues of 1 or greater (Table 8.2). The results reveal that in general men and women yielded a very similar component structure with a substantial percentage of explained variance. The scales fit into three distinct components that may be called a Stressor component, a Coping Style component, and a Health component. An interesting exception concerns the Type A behavior pattern. In men, this behavioral dimension loads rather substantially (.61) on the Stressor component and is apparently perceived as a stress-inducing factor rather than as a behavioral style, whereas in women this aspect of behavior is evaluated more as a health-related component.

A PCA with Eigenvalues of .80 or greater (Table 8.3) produces a four-factor solution, which keeps globally intact the three-component structure. It

Table 8.2   Principal Components Analysis

	Factor loadings of a three-factor solution							
	Factor 1		Factor 2		Factor 3		Commonalities	
Scale	M	F	M	F	M	F	M	F
Life events			.86	.77			.62	.63
Daily hassles			.78	.73			.72	.54
Emotion-focused coping					.60	.86	.54	.75
Problem-focused coping					.87	.63	.78	.48
Type A behavior		.69	.61				.48	.71
Vital exhaustion	.86	.85					.75	.73
Sleep complaints	.79	.72					.70	.65
Mild health complaints	.83	.83					.76	.74
Inadequacy	.81	.79					.69	.66
% explained variance							67.0	65.3

Note. Only loadings of .40 or greater components (from pattern matrix) and components with Eigenvalues of 1 or greater are mentioned. M = males; F = females.

Table 8.3 Principal Components Analysis With Eigenvalues of .80 or More

									Commonalities	
	Factor 1		Factor 2		Factor 3		Factor 4			
Scale	M	F	M	F	M	F	M	F	M	F
Life events			.87	.80					.83	.76
Daily hassles			.53	.79					.74	.63
Emotion-focused coping					.64	.86	.56		.72	.84
Problem-focused coping					.84			.96	.79	.95
Type A behavior		.60				-.58	.82		.74	.74
Vital exhaustion	.88	.82							.82	.75
Sleep complaints	.81	.77							.77	.69
Mild health complaints	.82	.85							.76	.75
Inadequacy	.79	.81							.74	.67
% explained variance									76.7	74.4

Note. Only loadings of .40 or greater components are mentioned. M = males; F = females.

supports the impression that arose from the three-component solution, namely, that the Type A behavior pattern is seen as a stressorlike variable in men and as a health-related behavioral dimension in women.

An interesting phenomenon concerns coping style. In men, problem-focused coping and emotion-focused coping appear to belong to one factor. In women, however, problem-focused coping becomes an isolated factor with an impressive 95% explained variance, whereas emotion-focused coping goes together with a negative loading of Type A behavior; hence, this combination could be interpreted as representing a strong emotional component of behavior.

The second aim of the study concerned the stability or persistence of scale scores. As mentioned previously, there were no statistical differences in the parameters between the two points in time, except in women for mild health complaints and inadequacy. Since stability is not only characterized by differences in absolute means but also by stable scale intercorrelations, or interperiod correlation coefficients (IPCs), we inspected these in more detail (Table 8.4).

In men all IPCs on the diagonal are significant at the 1% level, with one of the highest coefficients (.58) for the Type A behavior pattern. Previous evidence (Dorreboom & Snel, 1988) pointed out that men who have this pattern to an extreme extent are also rigid in their general behavior and practice predominantly a problem-focused style of coping. That Type A behavior measured 6 years apart still results in an IPC of .58 indicates that it is justifiable to speak of a very

Table 8.4 Two-Tailed Correlation Coefficients Between Scale Scores Gathered at Ages 21 and 27

Scale	Life events	E-coping	P-coping	Type A	Complaints	Inadequacy
Males (n = 77)						
Life events incidence	**.34**	.16	.18	.22	.08	.12
Emotion-focused coping	−.03	**.49**	.06	.13	.07	**.23**
Problem-focused coping	−.04	.06	**.31**	.11	−.12	−.15
Type A behavior	.10	.12	**.25**	**.58**	−.03	−.12
Mild health complaints	.06	**.31**	.01	−.02	**.35**	**.44**
Inadequacy	.13	**.29**	.07	.08	**.44**	**.65**
Females (n = 94)						
Life events incidence	**.31**	.04	.00	.16	.16	.16
Emotion-focused coping	−.06	**.46**	.06	−.08	.13	.16
Problem-focused coping	−.14	−.05	.19	−.04	−.08	−.12
Type A behavior	−.05	−.07	.18	**.55**	.13	**.27**
Mild health complaints	.16	.15	−.07	**.38**	**.56**	**.58**
Inadequacy	**.25**	**.26**	.00	.17	**.43**	**.70**

Note. Coefficients in bold are significant at $p < .01$, except when $r < .29$, $p < .05$.

stable behavior dimension. A similar result is found for inadequacy (.65), which reflects a behavioral disposition that does not change much over 6 years, from young adulthood to adulthood.

Women, to the contrary, seem to be involved rather emotionally, and persistently, as seen in the 6-year retest reliability of .46 for emotion-focused coping and the other IPCs, which show a substantial stability in reporting mild health complaints ($r = .56$) and inadequacy ($r = .70$). It is remarkable that in women Type A behavior correlates .38 ($p < .01$) with mild health complaints, while in men this association is of no significance.

Discussion

So far, the findings show two points. First, the parameters used belong to three independent components: stressors, behavior style, and health. Second, there is substantial stability in the height of the scores on the relevant parameters at ages 21 and 27, although this stability is stronger for men than for women. The pattern in Table 8.4 shows that all IPCs are significant in men and thus reflect stability. In women the exception is Problem-Focused Coping.

Inspection of the scale intercorrelations reveals differences between men and women that are worth commenting on. Arguments can be found from the literature that suggest for our data a common neurotic or neurosomatic element underlying the health component. Luteijn et al. (1985) found a correlation of .72-.83 between inadequacy and neuroticism and neurosomatism as assessed with the Dutch version of the Eysenck Personality Inventory. Jansen and Sikkel (1981) reported that mild health complaints as determined using the CLEH correlates at .65 with Inadequacy as assessed using the DPI in student nurses and psychiatric patients. In our subjects this correlation is .52 and .62 for males at ages 21 and 27, respectively, and .62 and .53 for females (see Table 8.5). Zonderman et al. (1986) also found this relationship. To develop our point further it is relevant to refer to the close correspondence in definition of the inadequacy concept and the syndromes of vital exhaustion and depression as measured with the MQ (Appels, 1988; Appels et al., 1987b). If our guess of a neurotic element in the reported health symptoms has some validity, the correlations found should change when partialing out inadequacy.

In order to verify this hypothesis, the intercorrelations of the parameters of the health component were partialed for inadequacy separately for ages 21 and 27. By doing so, a judgment could be made on the stability of the partialed correlation coefficients for young adulthood and adulthood. Because life events, daily hassles, and coping style did not load on the health component, for the sake of brevity their correlations are not given.

Table 8.5 shows that the partial correlation coefficients of Type A behavior with daily stressors, life events, and the parameters belonging to the behavioral style component did not change substantially. The conclusion is that in men these patterns were stable over years and that inadequacy did not play a role in them.

Table 8.5 Unpartialed (u) and Partialed (p) Correlation Coefficients Between Scales Belonging to the Health Component at Young Adulthood and Adulthood

Component	Scale	Young adulthood				Adulthood							
		Type A behavior		Health complaints		Type A behavior		Health complaints		Vital exhaustion		Sleep complaints	
		u	p	u	p	u	p	u	p	u	p	u	p
Males													
	Correlations												
Stressors	Life events	.26	.25	.05	.03	**.27**	.26	**.28**	.15	.05	-.17	.04	-.09
	Daily hassles					**.30**	**.29**	**.37**	**.30**	.16	.03	.23	.15
Behavior style	Emotion-focused coping	.20	.19	**.36**	**.28**	.15	.12	**.34**	.14	.24	-.02	**.38**	.25
	Problem-focused coping	**.30**	**.31**	-.07	-.03	.26	.26	.03	.06	.06	.11	.24	**.29**
	Type-A behavior	—	—	.02	-.03			.11	.07	.17	.16	.13	.10
Health complaints	Vital exhaustion	.02	.02			.17	.16	**.62**	**.36**	—	—	**.66**	**.54**
	Sleep complaints					.13	.10	**.61**	**.47**	**.66**	**.54**	—	—
	Health complaints			—	—	.11	.07	—	—	**.62**	**.36**	**.61**	**.47**
	Inadequacy	.09		**.52**		.09		**.62**		**.66**		**.46**	
Females													
Stressors	Life events	.02	-.03	.19	.10	-.01	-.12	.22	.12	.09	-.06	**.27**	.19
	Daily hassles					.00	-.06	.15	.10	.15	.09	.14	.09
Behavior style	Emotion-focused coping	-.07	-.16	.18	.03	-.15	**-.30**	.14	.00	.08	-.11	.13	-.00
	Problem-focused coping	-.07	-.02	-.22	-.14	-.01	-.02	.03	.02	.13	.15	-.02	-.03
	Type A behavior	—	—	**.28**	.13			**.39**	.21	**.48**	**.30**	.25	.04
Health complaints	Vital exhaustion					**.48**	**.30**	**.66**	**.50**	—	—	**.49**	.25
	Sleep complaints					.25	.04	**.70**	**.58**	**.49**	.25	—	—
	Health complaints	**.28**	.13	—	—	**.39**	.21	—	—	**.66**	**.50**	**.70**	**.58**
	Inadequacy	**.29**		**.62**		**.42**		**.53**		**.62**		**.51**	

Note. Significant correlation coefficients are in bold. When r ≥ .27, p < .05; when r ≥ .35, p < .01.

A different picture arose for the mutual intercorrelations of those parameters that belong to the health component. Partialing inadequacy illustrates that, in men, inadequacy is an "explaining" factor in the mutual correlations of the health-related parameters and between emotion-focused coping and mild health complaints. It illustrates the presence of a "neurotic," or more cautiously, a "complaining" element.

In women, the unpartialed and partial correlation coefficients show, as in men, that for both points in time the patterns found for scale intercorrelations were and remained similar; hence it might be said that the pattern of scale interrelationships is basically relatively stable. When evaluating the role of inadequacy in women, however, there are two findings that deviate from those of men. First, in women there is an increased negatively significant partial correlation of Type A behavior with emotion-focused-coping, while in men this correlation did not change. The second finding is that in women, the partial correlations of Type A behavior and mild health complaints become nonsignificant, while in men they remain similar. This indicates that for women Type A behavior tends to have a neuroticizing or somatizing characteristic instead of the stressor-related characteristic found in men.

Other interpretations may be given. For example, Yuen and Kuiper (1992) found that a main underlying characteristic of the Type A behavior pattern are negative self-evaluations. Dorreboom and Snel (1988) pointed to the prominent role of debilitating anxiety in 21-year-old Type A men and women. A similar finding was reported by Nay and Wagner (1990), who pointed out that Type A children (ages 1-12) and adolescents (ages 13-17) had higher anxiety levels than non-Type A's. Although these findings are important and invite more study, a more practical question concerns the significance of our findings for future health. Appels (1988) demonstrated that in middle-aged myocardial infarction (MI) patients and controls, vital exhaustion appeared to be predictive of coronary heart disease. Also, significant associations between coronary heart disease, the Type A behavior pattern, and neuroticism have been reported by van Doornen (1988), Lundberg (1980), and Lovallo and Pishkin (1980), but predominantly in MI and high-risk controls or in extreme Type A's compared to Type B's. The present study, however, was done in normal, healthy young adults, so the question is whether the association between neuroticism and physical problems may lead eventually to more dramatic health problems. Because neuroticism, or inadequacy, as we measured it is a personality trait, it may predispose one to worse health, but also it may potentially contribute to the identification of high-risk groups.

A last point we would like to comment on is that in this study we did not cover the role of social support as a moderator of stress symptomatology. Indeed, Solomon et al. (1990) found in soldiers who suffered from combat stress that social resources were related to somatization, and Holahan and Moos (1991) found that under high stress, personal and social resources were related to physiological health through more adaptive coping strategies. The picture is not that simple, however, for Aldwin and Revenson (1987) showed that under high stress, those in poorer mental health used less adaptive coping strategies. The point is that ascertaining the role of social support could have been done in our findings on partial social adequacy relative to the association between stressors, behavioral style, and health-related parameters. Because social adequacy in our subjects increased from youth to adulthood (see chapter 14), one might assume more adaptive coping with increasing social skill. Future analysis should clarify this point.

Conclusions

In conclusion, the present study shows that from young adulthood to adulthood there is a stable pattern of intercorrelations among those parameters that load on three components: Stressors, Coping Style, and Health. Type A behavior in men belongs to the stress component, while in women it belongs to the health component. The correlations partialed for inadequacy show that both in men and women the health-related parameters comprise a neurotic element. Whether this finding is of clinical significance for future health is unknown at this time. The continued follow-up of our subjects should clarify this.

References

Abbott J., C. Sutherland. Cognitive, cardiovascular and haematological responses of Type A and Type B individuals prior to and following examinations. Journal of Social Behavior and Personality 5:1 (1990) 343-368.

Aldwin C.M., T.A. Revenson. Does coping help? A reexamination of the relation between coping and mental health. J Pers Soc Psychol 53:2 (1987) 337-348.

Antoni M.H. Temporal relationship between life events and two illness measures: A cross-lagged panel analysis. Journal of Human Stress 10:1 (1985) 21-26.

Appels A. (1988). Vital exhaustion as a precursor of myocardial infarction. In: S. Maes, C.D. Spielberger, P.B. Defares, I.G. Sarason (eds.), Topics in health psychology. Wiley, Chichester.

Appels A., W. de Haes, J. Schuurman. Een test ter meting van het "coronary prone behaviour pattern" Type A. Nederlands Tijdschrift voor de Psychologie 34 (1979) 181-188.

Appels A., P. Höppner, P. Mulder. A questionnaire to assess premonitory symptoms of myocardial infarction. Int J Cardiol 14 (1987a) 15-24.

Appels A., Y. de Vos, R. van Diest, P. Höppner, P. Mulder, J. de Groen. Are sleep complaints predictive of future myocardial infarction? Activitas Nervosa Superior 29 (1987b) 147-151.

Dembroski T.M., J.M. MacDougall, J.L. Shields. Physiologic reaction to social challenge in persons evidencing the Type A coronary prone behavior pattern. Journal of Human Stress 3:3 (1977) 2-11.

Diest R. van, H. Milius, R. Markusse, J. Snel. De Slaap-Waak Ervaring Lijst. Tijdschrift voor Sociale Geneeskunde 10 (1989) 343-347.

Dirken, J.M. (1967). Arbeid en stress. Wolters-Noordhoff, Groningen.

Doornen L.J.P. van. (1988). Physiological stress reactivity: Its relationship to behavioral style, mood, sex and aerobic fitness. Doctoral dissertation, Vrije Universiteit, Amsterdam.

Dorreboom G., J. Snel. Type A/B behaviour and its relationship to personality, coping style and life events in young men and women. Gedrag & Gezondheid 16:2 (1988) 68-76.

Folkman S., R.S. Lazarus. An analysis of coping in a middle-aged community sample. J Health Soc Behav 21 (1980) 219-239.

Fondacaro M.R., R.H. Moos. Life stressors and coping: A longitudinal analysis among depressed and nondepressed adults. Journal of Community Psychology 17:4 (1989) 330-340.

Friedman M., R.H. Rosenman. (1974). Type A Behavior and your heart. Knopf, New York.

Gastorf J.W. Physiologic reaction of type A's to objective and subjective challenge. Journal of Human Stress 6:1 (1981) 16-20.

Holahan C.J., R.H. Moos. Life stressors, personal and social resources, and depression: A 4-year structural model. J Abnorm Psychol 100:1 (1991) 31-38.

Jansen M.E., D. Sikkel. Verkorte versie van de voegschaal. Gedrag & Samenleving 2 (1981) 78-82.

Keltikangas-Järvinen L., K. Raikkonen, P. Keskivaara, M. Pietikäinen, J. Viikari, E.A. Kaprio, H.K. Akerblom. Predictive validity of preadolescent Type A determinants for Type A dimensions in young adulthood: A 6-year follow-up. Ann Medi 23:1 (1991) 81-84.

Kemper H.C.G. (ed.). (1985). Growth, health and fitness of teenagers: Longitudinal research in international perspective. Vol. 20 of: Medicine and Sport Science. Karger, Basel.

Lovallo W.R., V. Pishkin. A psychophysiological comparison of Type A and B men exposed to failure and uncontrollable noise. Psychophysiology 17 (1980) 29-36.

Lu L. Daily hassles and mental health: A longitudinal study. Br J Psychol 82:4 (1991) 441-447.

Lundberg U. Type A behaviour and its relation to personality variables in Swedish male and female university students. Scand J Psychol 21 (1980) 133-138.

Luteijn F., J. Starren, H. van Dijk. (1985). Nederlandse Persoonlijkheids Vragenlijst. Handleiding, Herziene uitgave. Swets & Zeitlinger, Lisse.

Matthews K.A., S.M. Weiss, T. Detre, T.M. Dembroski, B. Falkner, S.B. Manuck, R.B. William (eds.). (1986). Handbook of stress, reactivity, and cardiovascular disease. Wiley, New York.

Nay R.E., M.K. Wagner. Behavioral and psychological correlates of Type A behavior in children and adolescents: An overview. Psychology and Health 4:2 (1990) 147-157.

Ortega D.F., J.E. Pipal. Challenge seeking and the type A coronary-prone behavior pattern. J Pers Soc Psychol 46 (1984) 1328-1334.

Rabkin J.G., E.L. Struening. Life events, stress, and illness. Science 194 (1976) 1013-1020.

Sarason I.G., J.H. Johnson, J.M. Siegel. Asessing the impact of life changes: Development of the Life Experience Survey. J Consult Clin Psychol 46 (1978) 932-946.

Schmitz P.G. Personality, stress-reactions and disease. Personality and Individual Differences 13:6 (1992) 683-691.

Snel J., H. Gosselink. Health, personality and physiological variables as discriminators of the type A behavior pattern in young adults. Journal of Psychophysiology 3 (1989) 291-299.

Solomon Z., M. Mikulincer, N. Habershaim. Life-events, coping strategies, social resources, and somatic complaints among combat stress reaction casualties. Br J Med Psychol 63:2 (1990) 137-148.

Stevens J. (1986). Applied multivariate statistics for the social sciences. Lawrence Erlbaum Associates, Hillsdale, NJ.

Strube M.J., J.M. Berry, B.K. Goza, D. Fennimore. Type A behavior, age and psychological well-being. J Pers Soc Psychol 49 (1985) 203-218.

Suls J., B. Mullen. Life event, perceived control and illness: The role of uncertainty. Journal of Human Stress 7:2 (1981) 30-34.

Vingerhoets A.J.J.M., P.J.M. Flohr. Type A behavior and self-reports of coping preferences. Br J Med Psychol 57 (1984) 15-21.

Vingerhoets A.J.J.M., A.J. Jeninga, L.J. Menges. The measurement of daily hassles and chronic stressors: The development of the Everyday Problem Checklist (EPCL) II. Gedrag & Gezondheid 17:1 (1989) 10-17.

Williams N.A., J.L. Deffenbacher. Life stress and chronic yeast infections. Journal of Human Stress 9:1 (1983) 26-31.

Yuen S.A., N.A. Kuiper. Type A and self-evaluations: A social comparison perspective. Personality and Individual Differences 13:5 (1992) 549-562.

Zonderman A.B., V.L. Leu, P.T. Costa. Effects of age, hypertension history, and neuroticism on health perceptions. Exp Gerontol 21 (1986) 449-458.

Part IV

Relationships Between Lifestyle and Health

Chapter 9

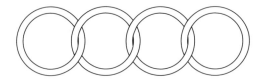

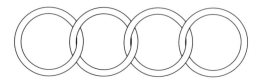

Physical Fitness and the Relationship to Physical Activity

Han C.G. Kemper & Willem van Mechelen

Hypoactivity is thought to be a direct or indirect cause of many pediatric diseases (Bar-Or, 1983). Hypoactivity is inherent to arthritis, cerebral palsy, cystic fibrosis, severe cyanotic heart disease, obesity, and scoliosis. Children with bronchial asthma, diabetes mellitus, epilepsy, noncyanotic heart diseases, and hemophilia can be active, but often they are not. Restrictions reflect overprotection by the parents or an uneducated attitude of teachers and health practitioners, or both. Physical inactivity is also an important direct and indirect risk factor for adult diseases, such as cardiovascular diseases, cancer, and other chronic diseases. Powell et al. (1987) and Berlin et al. (1990) have summarized the epidemiological evidence for an indirect or direct causal relationship between physical activity and morbidity and mortality of coronary heart disease (CHD). On World Health Day (7 April 1992), the International Society and Federation of Cardiology published a position statement for the World Health Organization (Bijnen et al., 1994).

Many industrialized countries have adopted prevention policies designed to reduce the prevalence of the three prime risk factors: high serum cholesterol, smoking, and high blood pressure. However, physical inactivity should be added as a fourth important undeniable risk factor for CHD. Several large-scale epidemiological studies have indicated that physical inactivity results in CHD indirectly through various physiologic mechanisms, which relate partly to beneficial effects of physical activities on blood pressure and serum lipoprotein profiles. Furthermore, most studies that have statistically adjusted for the confounding effects of traditional risk factors indicate that physical activity seems also to be an independent and direct risk factor for CHD (Powell et al., 1987) and all-cause mortality (Blair et al., 1989). Technological progress in industrialized countries has led to decreasing physical activity in most jobs; therefore, public-health attention is often focused on leisure-time physical activity. The high prevalence of physical inactivity compared to the other three traditional risk factors in the United States is striking. Caspersen (1989), for example, estimated that 59% of the population fails to perform regular leisure-time physical activity. These prevalences are much higher than the 10% of the population with high blood pressure, the 10% with hypercholesterolemia, and the 18% who smoke cigarettes.

The burden of physical inactivity on public health can be estimated as relative risks for the four selected risk factors. This "population attributable risk" (PAR) offers a balanced view of the need to act on stronger risk factors that affect fewer people versus the need to act on weaker risk factors that are far more prevalent. In 43 studies reviewed by Paffenbarger et al. (1986), the PAR for physical activity on all-cause mortality and mortality due to CHD seems greater than the effect of hypertension, hypercholesterolemia, and smoking, mainly because of the large number of physically inactive people. The increase in relative risk (RR) for each of these four CHD risk factors is of similar magnitude; the RR varies between 1.9 (physical inactivity) and 2.5 (cigarette smoking). With the prevalences of the three other CHD risk factors being small compared to the prevalence of those failing to perform regular exercise, the PAR of physical inactivity is the highest. Therefore, physical activity appears to be a more important concern for its population impact than the other three CHD risk factors (Caspersen, 1989). Physical inactivity can thus be assumed to be an important risk factor for CHD. Atherosclerosis starts soon after birth (Montoye, 1985). It is often suggested that a sufficient amount and intensity of regular physical activity could decelerate this process. However, an epidemiological prospective study comparing a large number of physically active children with a randomized group of less active children over a long period so that differences in incidence rate of CHD risk factors and/or mortality rate can be tested has never yet been conducted and apparently cannot be carried out. There is, unfortunately, no possibility of a double-blind study in which physical activity can be measured over such a long period (Kemper, 1990).

One way out of this dilemma is to measure habitual physical activity on a longitudinal basis and to group individuals according to different activity patterns (Mirwald et al., 1981; Rutenfranz et al., 1974, 1975; Sprynarova, 1974). Another possibility is an experimental longitudinal study such as that conducted in the Trois Rivières region of Canada (Shephard et al., 1980), which measured the effects of additional physical education in primary school children.

In this chapter we analyze the longitudinal physical fitness data of males and females by regrouping the two sexes with respect to relative active and inactive patterns of habitual physical activity during the 15 years of follow-up, during which time the subjects ranged from ages 13 to 27.

Methods

Physical fitness was measured using seven motor performance test items from the Motor Performance (MOPER) Fitness Test (Bovend'eerdt et al., 1980) and a maximal-running treadmill test. The MOPER test battery includes four strength tests, two speed tests, and one flexibility test. Because all the MOPER tests except the arm pull test result in scores that are inherently body weight–dependent, the arm pull test was made weight-dependent by dividing the absolute strength score in kilograms by the body weight. This procedure does not imply that these tests have statistical correlations with body weight (Kemper et al., 1983).

Maximal aerobic endurance was measured by a direct method—a standard running test on a treadmill with a constant speed of 8 km/h. We used a two-step procedure: First, subjects engaged in submaximal running 2 minutes each at three successive slopes of 0%, 2.5%, and 5%. Second, after a 10- to 15-minute period of recovery, they ran again, with the slope increasing by 2.5% or 5.0% every 2 minutes until complete exhaustion.

Oxygen uptake ($\dot{V}O_2$) and ventilation ($\dot{V}_E$) were measured continuously by analyzing the volume and content of exhaled air. $\dot{V}O_2$ and $\dot{V}_E$ were measured at the end of each submaximal exercise as the mean value of the last minute. Heart rate was measured at rest. The 15-beat value during the last 20 seconds of the period was converted into a heart rate frequency (in beats per minute). The maximal amount of oxygen used per minute was used as the maximal oxygen uptake ($\dot{V}O_2$max). The maximal slope (slope$_{max}$) that could be reached during running on the treadmill was used as the maximal running performance (Kemper & Verschuur, 1981). $\dot{V}O_2$max was measured in absolute values (liters per minute) and expressed relative to body weight to the two-thirds power.

Physical Activity Grouping Procedure

Habitual physical activity was measured six times over a period of almost 15 years. The method applied was a standardized activity interview based on a questionnaire (Verschuur et al., 1987); the interview took place between January and June of each year of measurement and was retrospective over the previous 3 months. All activities with an energy expenditure of more than 4 METs came under review and were classified in one of three intensity levels. The total habitual physical activity score was the result of the amount of minutes per week multiplied by the mean MET score of that activity. This weighted activity score (MET score) was calculated for each subject during each year of measurement.

To compare (relatively) highly active subjects with (relatively) less active subjects, for each sex the bottom tertile ($<P_{33}$) and the top tertile ($>P_{67}$) were compared. The tertile division was based on the following procedure: The MET scores of each subject over the first four measurements in the adolescent period (ages 13-17) were averaged and totaled with the MET scores at the young-adult age (21 years) and adult age (27 years). These overall MET scores were ranked for each sex, and then the tertile ranking was completed.

From the 84 males and 98 females that were measured during the 15 years of follow-up, active groups and inactive groups amounted to 22 to 33 subjects/ activity group depending on sex and the physical fitness parameter that was measured. Differences between activity groups were analyzed by multivariate analysis of variance (MANOVA) over the whole period, taking into account interaction effects between age and activity. A level of significance of $p < .05$ was used.

Results

In Table 9.1 the results of the MANOVA identifying the effects of habitual physical activity over the whole period of investigation are summarized. Comparison of males and females with different activity levels shows that in both sexes the highly active groups had significantly better endurance performances than the less active groups (Figs. 9.1, 9.2). In females the "activity effect" is apparent in absolute $\dot{V}O_2$max ($p < .01$), $\dot{V}O_2$max relative to body weight to the two-thirds power ($p < .01$), and slope$_{max}$ ($p < .01$). In males the differences between activity groups are significant in $\dot{V}O_2$max relative to body weight to the two-thirds power ($p < .05$) and slope$_{max}$ ($p < .05$). Active males also demonstrated a significantly better ($p < .01$) flexed-arm hang performance (Fig. 9.3) than their inactive counterparts.

Significant interaction effects between age and activity can also be demonstrated. Of both sexes the high-activity groups raised their absolute $\dot{V}O_2$max over time significantly more ($p < .01$) than the inactive groups (Fig. 9.4). This interaction effect was also true in females with respect to $\dot{V}O_2$max and slope$_{max}$. Although no "activity effects" could be proved in standing high jump performance, a significant interaction was present in males ($p < .01$). In the females the same was seen in the sit-and-reach test ($p < .05$).

Table 9.1   MANOVA Results of the Effects of Habitual Activity Divided Into Tertiles

	Activity effect (13-27 years)		Interaction: age × activity	
	Males	Females	Males	Females
Flexed-arm hang	**	NS	NS	NS
Arm pull	NS	NS	NS	NS
10 leg lifts	NS	NS	NS	NS
Standing high jump	NS	NS	*	*
Sit-and-reach	NS	NS	NS	*
Plate tapping	NS	NS	NS	NS
10 × 5-m sprint	NS	NS	NS	NS
$\dot{V}O_2$max (absolute)	NS	**	**	**
$\dot{V}O_2$max (relative to BW$^{2/3}$)	*	**	NS	**
Slope$_{max}$	*	**	NS	**

Note. * or ** means significantly better performances of highly active subjects ($>P_{67}$) compared to less active ones ($<P_{33}$). BW = body weight; NS = not significant.

$*p < .05$; $**p < .01$.

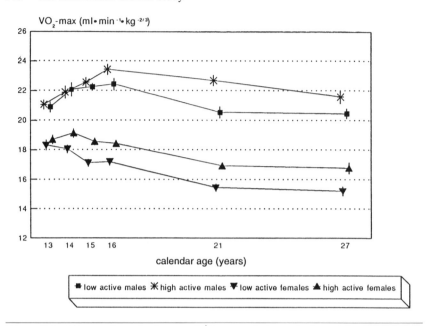

Figure 9.1   Mean and standard error of $\dot{V}O_2$max relative to body weight divided into high-activity (top tertile, $>P_{67}$) and low-activity (bottom tertile, $<P_{33}$) groups.

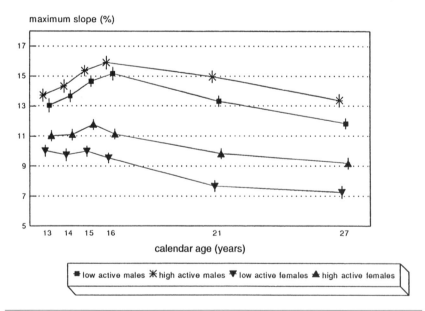

Figure 9.2   Mean and standard error of maximal slope reached during treadmill running at a speed of 8 km/h divided into high-activity (top tertile, $>P_{67}$) and low-activity (bottom tertile, $<P_{33}$) groups.

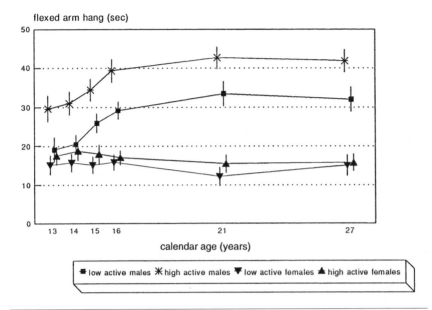

Figure 9.3 Mean and standard error of flexed-arm hang divided into high-activity (top tertile, >P_{67}) and low-activity (bottom tertile, <P_{33}) groups.

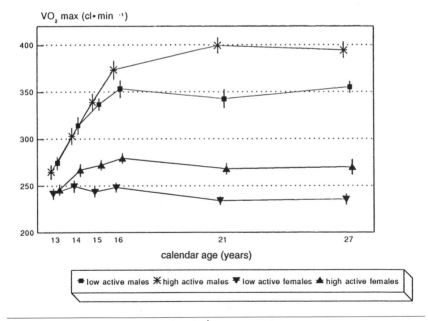

Figure 9.4 Mean and standard error of $\dot{V}O_2$max divided into high-activity (top tertile, >P_{67}) and low-activity (bottom tertile, <P_{33}) groups.

All other physical fitness parameters measured during rest (i.e., heart rate) and during the three levels of submaximal treadmill exercise showed significant differences between activity groups.

Discussion

Comparing groups with relatively high and low physical-activity patterns over a relatively long period of observation assumes that there is a certain amount of tracking present in these subjects. However, tracking over the period of 15 years appeared relatively low in both males and females (see chapter 7).

We chose to divide subjects by tertiles. This division combines a relatively high contrast in activity (not taking into account the middle third of the population) and enough subjects in each subgroup. The activity level of each subject was a weighted score constructed as the sum of the average of the four adolescent measurements, the young-adult measurement, and the adult measurement. In that way each of the three 5-year periods was weighted equally.

Table 9.2 is an overview of the mean weighted activity scores of the top and bottom tertiles in both sexes. The mean activity scores between the two tertiles do show large differences: The mean values of active males and females are more than twice the mean values of the inactive groups, and the ranges do not overlap. The high contrast in physical activity level cannot explain why most fitness performances are not significantly different between activity groups (arm pull, 10 leg lifts, sit-and-reach, plate tapping, and 10×5-m sprint).

The results show further that the differences between the activity groups are only significant in maximal performances and not in resting performance (heart rate) or submaximal performances ($\dot{V}O_2$, $\dot{V}_E$, and heart rate). Moreover, the aerobic endurance performances—absolute $\dot{V}O_2max$, $\dot{V}O_2max$ relative to body weight to the two-thirds power, and slope$_{max}$—are significantly related to the level of physical activity in both sexes. The flexed-arm hang was the only physical fitness test in which there were significantly better scores among active males compared with inactive males. This was not the case in females; also, no inter-action effect was present.

Most physical performance parameters that showed significantly higher values in active groups compared with relatively inactive groups also showed

Table 9.2   Statistics of the Weighted Physical Activity Scores in the Top and Bottom Tertiles Over the 15-Year Period of Follow-Up

Weighted activity score (METs/week)	Top tertile($>P_{67}$)			Bottom tertile ($<P_{33}$)		
	M	SD	Range	M	SD	Range
Males ($n = 28$)	4,988	1,228	3,768-7,580	1,925	477	760-2,650
Females ($n = 33$)	4,742	975	3,700-8,290	1,846	461	704-2,365

interaction effects, apparently indicating that the effects of habitual physical activity became greater in the course of the longitudinal study. This effect was present in females for absolute $\dot{V}O_2$max, $\dot{V}O_2$max relative to body weight to the two-thirds power, and slope$_{max}$ ($p < .01$). Furthermore, three items that were not significantly different between activity groups showed significant interaction effects: the standing high jump in both sexes (Fig. 9.5), the sit-and-reach in females (Fig. 9.6), and $\dot{V}O_2$max in males. All these interaction effects are in favor of the high-activity groups. Although the arm pull did not reach a level of significance between activity groups in both sexes over the whole period of observation, significant differences ($p < .05$) were found after the adolescent period (Fig. 9.7).

The interaction effects between age and activity are new and important observations; Verschuur et al. (1987) analyzed the longitudinal data for age 13 to age 21 of the same population. When both sexes were contrasted on their sports participation, no positive effects of physical activity could be demonstrated. The interesting finding from the present study is that the effects of different levels of physical activity seem to be more important after the adolescent and young-adult period. In these periods we observed in both males and females a drastic reduction in the amount and intensity of physical activity (see chapter 7). The same decrease in physical activity has also been shown by Rowland (1990).

Further analyses of the effects of activity concentrating on the young-adult and adult periods confirm the importance of physical activity at later ages, although the effects of physical activity are considerably less than during youth.

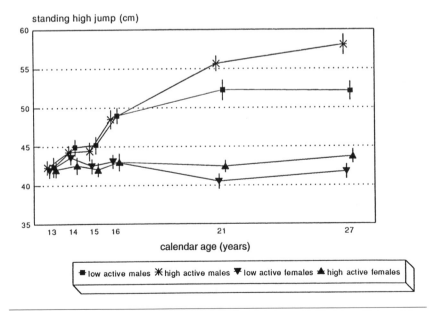

Figure 9.5   Mean and standard error of standing high jump divided into high-activity (top tertile, >P$_{67}$) and low-activity (bottom tertile, <P$_{33}$) groups.

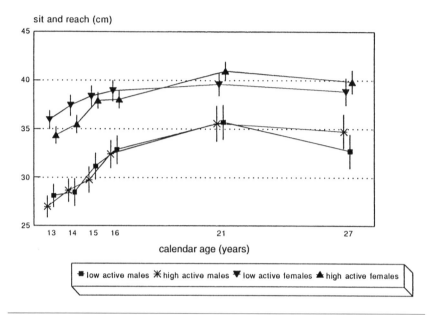

Figure 9.6   Mean and standard error of sit-and-reach divided into high-activity (top tertile, $>P_{67}$) and low-activity (bottom tertile, $<P_{33}$) groups.

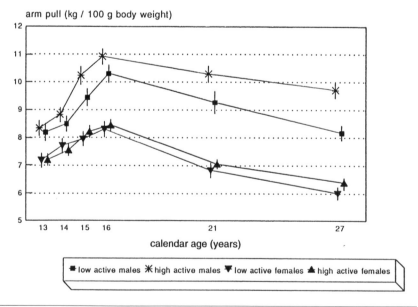

Figure 9.7   Mean and standard error of arm pull relative to body weight divided into high-activity (top tertile, $>P_{67}$) and low-activity (bottom tertile, $<P_{33}$) groups.

In young-adult males, the arm pull relative to body weight and in young-adult females the flexed-arm hang (see Fig. 9.3) are significantly better in the active groups compared with the inactive groups.

Because most of the performance measures used in this analysis are body weight–dependent (jumping, hanging, running) or were mathematically transformed to relative body weight parameters ($\dot{V}O_2$max, arm pull), the possibility remains that differences in body dimensions can account for differences between activity groups. Therefore, we compared the top and bottom tertiles of both sexes on height, body weight, and sum of four skinfolds. Height was not significantly different in the high- and low-activity groups for the 15-year period of follow-up (Fig. 9.8). Body weight, likewise, reflected no differences in either sex, but there were interaction effects between age and activity. During the young-adult period high-activity groups had a higher body weight than did inactive groups (Fig. 9.9). The significantly higher body weight in active groups cannot be explained by a higher percentage of body fat: Although the sum of four skinfolds is not significantly different between activity groups (Fig. 9.10), inactive males tended to have slightly more fat than active males throughout the study. In females this trend is true only at ages 21 and 27. A higher fat-free mass in the active group possibly contributes to the higher body weight.

In general, the results show significant differences between physical activity groups with respect to aerobic endurance performance ($\dot{V}O_2$max, slope$_{max}$, flexed-arm hang), but not in other physical performances, such as running speed, flexibility, and explosive muscle strength. This can be explained by the questionnaire/

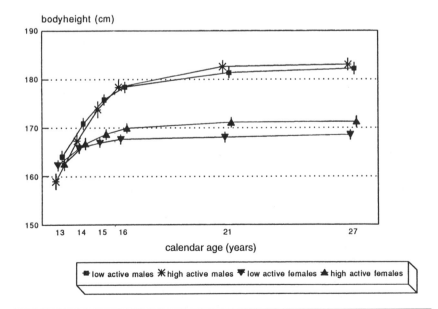

Figure 9.8   Mean and standard error of height divided into high-activity (top tertile, >P_{67}) and low-activity (bottom tertile, <P_{33}) groups.

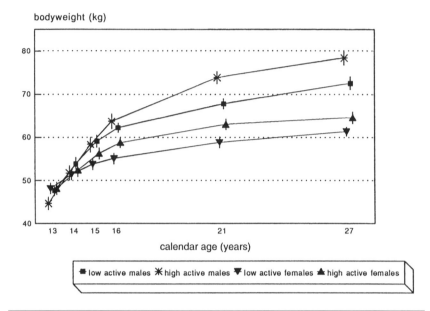

Figure 9.9   Mean and standard error of body weight divided into high-activity (top tertile, $>P_{67}$) and low-activity (bottom tertile, $<P_{33}$) groups.

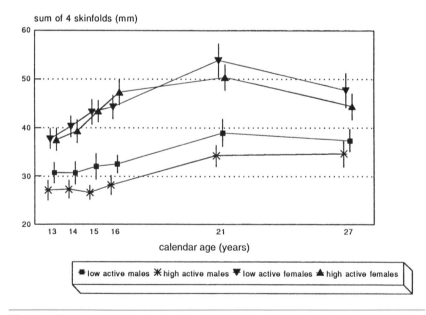

Figure 9.10   Mean and standard error of sum of four skinfolds divided into high-activity (top tertile, $>P_{67}$) and low-activity (bottom tertile, $<P_{33}$) groups.

interview method of measuring habitual physical activity. The activities were categorized into intensity levels favoring activities with high intensity (>5 METs) and did not take into account short bursts of activities (activities with a duration of less than 5 minutes were ignored). Therefore, performances that are dependent on the energy expenditure such as $\dot{V}O_2$max and slope$_{max}$ turn out to be influenced by differences in activity levels. Verschuur et al. (1987) also demonstrated a positive relationship between daily physical activity, sports participation, and physical fitness for aerobic endurance only in the adolescent years of this population. Because the difference does not increase systematically over the adolescent years despite differences in activity level, Verschuur et al. concluded that the higher aerobic endurance in the high-activity groups cannot just be attributed to the differences in activity but to the result of childhood activities and/or self-selection of natural endowment.

The important fact in the follow-up of our subjects at ages 21 and 27 is that the differences in aerobic endurance performance between active and inactive males and females increased and became more prominent after the adolescent period. These interaction effects are limited not only to aerobic endurance performance but also to isometric armforce (arm pull), flexibility (sit-and-reach), explosive leg strength (standing high jump), and arm endurance (flexed-arm hang). Only a small portion of the activity effects can be attributed to differences in body composition. No differences were found in height. The higher body weight at young-adult age in the high-activity groups cannot be explained by differences in percentage of body fat.

Two major types of longitudinal training studies are found in the literature: *observational* studies, with contrasting high- and low-activity children in a retrospective analysis, and *intervention* studies, with changes initiated in the activity levels in experimental groups with respect to control groups. In general, observational studies show that active children demonstrate higher physical fitness than less active children. However, these results are not conclusive about the effects of physical activity: Because the children themselves made the decision to be active or not, self-selection may have influenced the results. Furthermore, the results of Kemper (1986) show that aerobic power in adolescent boys and girls is significantly higher in active ones, but the differences became no higher from 12 to 18 years of age, as would be expected as a result of higher training stimuli over the years. From this the author concluded that differences in $\dot{V}O_2$max are caused not only by training but also by genetics: Active adolescents are more active because they have a higher aerobic power at their disposal.

Intervention studies, which utilize the school environment by adding physical education lessons, in general do not show effects on physical fitness before puberty (Kemper et al., 1976). The main reasons for this are (a) the high training status of pubertal children, (b) low intensity and small number of physical education classes, (c) nonhomogeneity of maturation between children, and (d) low specificity of the training stimulus for aerobic power in physical education programs. Specific aerobic training programs reviewed by Sady (1986), Pate and Ward (1990), and Vaccaro et al. (1987) prove to be effective both before and after puberty. However, the degree of trainability seems to depend on motivation and pretraining levels. Although it is possible that a critical age (e.g., before the age of peak height velocity) exists before which a child is less trainable (Kobayashi et al., 1978; Mirwald et al., 1985), other authors cast considerable doubt on this hypothesis (Cunningham et al., 1981; Froberg et al., 1991; Weber et al., 1976).

In the present study we found higher physical fitness scores in highly active subjects compared to less active subjects during adolescence (ages 13-21), but no interaction effects were present. At adult age (27 years), however, in both sexes the highly active subjects showed more of an increase in physical fitness level than the less active subjects. Although the absolute levels of physical activity decrease considerably in both sexes, the relative differences seem to be very important to the development of physical fitness level at adult age.

Conclusions

A regrouping of males and females on a percentile ranking in habitual physical activity level over a period of 15 years showed that subjects in the top tertile, with the highest activity pattern, became significantly more fit than those of the bottom tertile, with relatively low activity. Although no significant differences were found in either sex during the adolescent period, the difference increased by young-adult age (21 years) and was even more pronounced at age 27.

The interaction effects are predominantly present in aerobic endurance, measured as $\dot{V}O_2$max in both absolute and relative (to body weight to the two-thirds power) terms and slope$_{max}$, but both were also found in other physical fitness parameters, such as muscle force, flexibility, and speed, at young-adult age.

These results make clear that, although the absolute differences between active and inactive subjects are small, the habitual physical activity level after the adolescent period is of utmost importance to physical fitness levels in both sexes. Because most activity effects tend to increase with age, this suggests that the differences between the high- and low-activity groups is caused by the activity pattern itself and not by self-selection.

References

Bar-Or O. (1983). Pediatric sports medicine for the practitioner. Springer, New York.

Berlin J.A., G.A. Colditz. A meta-analysis of physical activity in the prevention of coronary heart disease. Am J Epidemiol 132:4 (1990) 612-620.

Bijnen F.C.H., C.J. Caspersen, W.L. Mosterd. Physical inactivity as a risk factor for coronary heart disease: A WHO and International Society and Federation of Cardiology position statement. Bulletin of the World Health Organization 72:1 (1994) 1-4.

Blair S.N., H.W. Kohl III, R.S. Paffenbarger, D.G. Clark, K.H. Cooper, L.W. Gibbons. Physical fitness and all-cause mortality: A prospective study of healthy men and women. JAMA 262:17 (1989) 2395-2401.

Bovend'eerdt J.H.F., H.C.G. Kemper, R. Verschuur. (1980). The MOPER Fitness Test: User's guide and norm scales. De Vrieseborch, Haarlem.

Caspersen C.J. Physical activity epidemiology concepts, methods and applications to exercise science. Exerc Sport Sci Rev 17 (1989) 423-473.

Cunningham D.A., J.J. Stapleton, I.C. MacDonald, D.H. Paterson. Daily expenditure of young boys as related to maximal aerobic power. Canadian Journal of Applied Sports Science 6 (1981) 207-211.

Froberg, K., B. Andersen, O. Lammert. (1991). Maximal oxygen uptake and respiratory functions during puberty in boy groups of different physical activity. In: R. Frenkl, I. Szmodis (eds.), Children and exercise, pediatric work physiology, XV. National Institute for Health Promotion, Budapest.

Kemper H.C.G. Longitudinal studies on the development of health and fitness and the interaction with physical activity of teenagers. Pediatrician 13 (1986) 52-59.

Kemper H.C.G. (1990). Exercise and training in childhood and adolescence. In: R.J. Shephard (ed.), Current therapy in sports medicine 2. Decker, Toronto.

Kemper H.C.G., R.A. Verschuur. Maximal aerobic power in 13- and 14-year-old teenagers in relation to biological age. Int J Sports Med 2 (1981) 97-100.

Kemper H.C.G., R. Verschuur, P. Dok, J.W. van Ritmeester. (1983). Influence of age, body height and body mass upon the MOPER fitness test results of 12-18 year old boys and girls. In: T. Ishiko (ed.), Physical fitness research. Baseball Magazine Sha, Tokyo.

Kemper H.C.G., R. Verschuur, J.G.A. Ras, J. Snel, P.G. Splinter, L.W.C. Tavecchio. Effect of 5 versus 3 lessons a week physical education program upon the physical development of 12 and 14 year old schoolboys. J Sports Med Phys Fitness 16 (1976) 319-326.

Kobayashi K., K. Kitamure, M. Miura, H. Sodeyama, Y. Murase, M. Miyashita, H. Matsui. Aerobic power as related to body growth and training in Japanese boys: A longitudinal study. J Appl Physiol 44 (1978) 666-672.

Mirwald R.L., D.A. Bailey, N. Cameron, P.L. Rasmussen. Longitudinal comparison of aerobic power in active and inactive boys aged 7.0 to 17.0 years. Ann Hum Biol 8 (1981) 405-414.

Mirwald R.L., D.A. Bailey, N. Cameron, P.L. Rasmussen. (1985). Longitudinal analysis of maximal aerobic power in boys and girls by chronological age, maturity and physical activity. Saskatoon University of Saskatchewan.

Montoye H.J. (1985). Risk indicators for cardiovascular disease in relation to physical activity in youth. In: Binkhorst, Kemper, Saris (eds.), Children and exercise, XI. Vol. 15 of: International series on sport sciences. Human Kinetics, Champaign, IL.

Paffenbarger R.S. Jr., R.T. Hyde, A.L. Wing, C.C. Hsieh. Physical activity, all-cause mortality and longevity of college alumni. N Engl J Med 314 (1986) 605-613.

Pate R.R., D.S. Ward. (1990). Endurance exercise trainability in children and youth. In: Grano, Lombardo, Sharkey, Stone (eds.), Advances in sports medicine and fitness, vol. 3. Year Book Medical, Chicago.

Powell R.E., P.D. Thompson, C.S. Caspersen, J.S. Kendrick. Physical activity and the incidence of coronary heart disease. Annu Rev Public Health 8 (1987) 253-287.

Rowland T.W. (1990). Exercise and children's health. Human Kinetics, Champaign, IL.

Rutenfranz J., I. Berndt, P. Knauth. Daily physical activity, investigated by time budget studies and physical performance capacity of schoolboys. Acta Paediatrica Belg. 28 (1974, Suppl.) 79-86.

Rutenfranz J., V. Seliger, K.L. Andersen. (1975). Differences in maximal aerobic power related to the daily physical activity in childhood. In: G. Borg (ed.), Physical work and effort. Pergamon, London.

Sady S.P. Cardiorespiratory exercise training in children. Clin Sports Med 5:3 (1986) 493-514.

Shephard R.J., H. Lavalleé, J. Jéquier, M. Rajic, R. Labarre. (1980). Additional physical education in the primary school. In: Ostijn, Bennen, Simons (eds.), Kinanthropometry II. University Park Press, Baltimore.

Sprynarova S. Longitudinal study of the influence of different physical activity programs on functional capacity of boys from 11-18 years. Acta Paediatrica Belg. 28 (1974, Suppl.) 204-213.

Vaccaro P., A. Mahon. Cardiorespiratory response to endurance training in children. Sports Medi 4 (1987) 352-303.

Verschuur R., A. van Zundert, H.C.G. Kemper. (1987). Longitudinal participation in sports in girls and boys in relation to physical fitness in their late teens and early twenties. In: H. Ruskin, A. Simkin (eds.), Physical fitness and the ages of men. Academon Press, Jerusalem.

Weber G., W. Kartodihardjo, V. Klissouras. Growth and physical training with reference to heredity. J Appl Physiol 40:2 (1976) 211-215.

Chapter 10

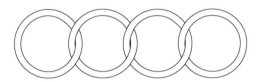

Are Physical Fitness and Physiological and Psychosocial Indices Related to Sports Injuries?

Willem van Mechelen, Han C.G. Kemper, Jos Twisk, & Jan Snel

The health benefits of regular physical activity and sports participation are well documented (Bouchard et al., 1993) and need no further justification. However, there are drawbacks to physical activity, such as the risk of sustaining a sports injury. In the Netherlands, a recent nationwide representative telephone survey with a 6-week recall period was carried out. Based on the data of this survey, of a total population of about 15 million, an absolute number of 2.7 million sports injuries/year was calculated, of which 1.7 million were supposedly treated medically (van Galen & Diederiks, 1990). It should be noted that in this study a broad definition of sports injuries was used: "any self-reported injury sustained while performing sports." Similar figures have been reported in studies abroad. Sandelin et al. (1987) estimated that in the adult population in Finland about 1.5 million acute medically treated injuries occurred in 1980. Work-related injuries made up 17%, sports injuries 14%, and traffic injuries 12%. De Loës (1990) found in a municipality study in Sweden that acute work-related injuries made up 26% of all acute-injury visits; acute home injuries, 19%; and acute sports injuries, 17%.

Based on the findings of these surveys one may conclude that the sports injury problem is substantial and calls for preventive action. Prevention can only be effective if it is based on knowledge of the etiological factors that influence potentially dangerous sports behavior. Thus, before any preventive action can take place these etiological factors must first be identified. Van Mechelen et al. (1992) distinguished six main categories of etiological factors that enhance the chances of sustaining an injury. One category is athlete-related risk factors, such as the level of physical fitness, psychological and psychosocial variables, anthropometric variables, and health-related variables.

The identification of risk factors should preferably be done with the help of epidemiological research. Many attempts have been made and many potential risk factors for sports injuries have been identified. However, the majority of the risk factors indicated in the literature are derived from studies that applied improper study designs; they lack, for instance, the use of control groups, uniform and unambiguous definitions of sports injuries and sports participation, or a multivariate analysis of results. Identifications of risk factors seem to be based on common sense or, even worse, on faith. So in fact still little is known about the significance of potential risk factors with respect to the etiology of sports injuries. In the Amsterdam Growth and Health Study so-called athlete-related risk factors for sports injuries, such as psychological, psychosocial, and physical fitness variables, have been measured as a part of the standard routine of the study.

Given the extent of the sports injury problem and the lack of knowledge of etiology, we decided to investigate the significance of the athlete-related variables just mentioned, measuring them at age 21 as potential risk factors for sports injuries six years later at age 27.

Design

In 1991 our subjects (mean age = 27 years) were asked to complete a questionnaire on their history of sports injury over the preceding 12 months. It should be emphasized that the sports injury data were gathered retrospectively in this way. By relating the results of this questionnaire to the information on physiological, psychosocial, and physical fitness variables of the subjects gathered 6 years earlier (at age 21) it is possible to study prospectively the influence of these factors on the risk of sustaining a sports injury.

Subjects

At the age of 27 years, 84 males and 98 females completed our sports injury questionnaire. Of these subjects, 78 males and 94 females had also been measured 6 years earlier, at age 21. Subjects not participating at both occasions in either organized or leisure-time sports activities at a level of intensity exceeding 4 METs (as assessed by the habitual physical activity interview described in chapter 4) were excluded from the analysis; data on 7 males and 4 females were thus discarded. The analysis described in this chapter therefore concerns 161 males and females, about whom descriptive anthropometrical information at age 27 is given in Table 10.1.

Methods

Sports Injuries and Sports Injury Incidence

Information on the sports injuries sustained by our subjects was gathered by means of a questionnaire. This sports injury questionnaire was an adapted version

Table 10.1   Mean and Standard Deviation of Height and Weight of the Subjects Included in the Sports Injury Analysis, Measured at Age 27

	Height (cm)	Weight (kg)
Males (n = 71)	183.0 ± 6.5	75.5 ± 8.4
Females (n = 90)	170.5 ± 6.1	63.3 ± 7.9

of one used in previous studies (van Mechelen et al., 1993; Schlattmann et al., 1987). As noted previously, our questionnaire asked for the occurrence of sports injuries in the preceding 12 months. A sports injury was defined as "any self-reported injury that occurred in the 12 months prior to the completion of the questionnaire as a result of sports participation and that caused one or more of the following: The subject has to stop playing sports and/or cannot fully participate in sports at the next occasion and/or cannot go to work the next day and/or needs (para)medical attention." Any injury that met this definition was then further questioned for more specific details on the severity of the injury, taking criteria for severity into account, including location and medical diagnosis, as described by van Mechelen et al. (1992).

In sports injury research it is preferable to calculate an incidence rate rather than a cumulative incidence, thereby taking exposure time (i.e., actual time at risk) into account (van Mechelen et al., 1992). Given the retrospective nature of the questionnaire and the lack of information on the real time at risk before the injuries did occur, it is not possible to calculate an injury incidence rate that takes exposure into account. However, from the data, a 1-year retrospective cumulative injury incidence could be calculated.

Potential Risk Factors for Sports Injuries

Figure 10.1 indicates the potential risk factors for sports injuries that we take into consideration in this analysis.

Maximum Oxygen Uptake

Maximum oxygen uptake ($\dot{V}O_2$max) was measured by means of a treadmill protocol consisting of a submaximal test and a maximal test (Kemper & Verschuur, 1980). The running speed was 8 km/h for both tests. The slope of the treadmill increased every second minute by 2.5% for the submaximal test and by 2.5% or 5% (depending on the heart rate) for the maximal test. The subject's electrocardiogram (ECG) was monitored telemetrically throughout the test. Oxygen uptake ($\dot{V}O_2$) was measured directly each minute using an Ergo-analyser. $\dot{V}O_2$max was expressed as milliliters of oxygen uptake per kilogram to the two-thirds power per minute.

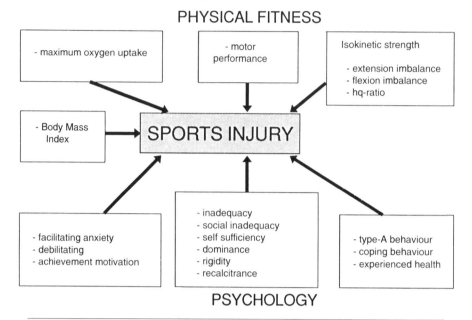

Figure 10.1   Potential athlete-related risk factors for sports injuries taken into consideration in the analysis described in this chapter.

Motor Performance

Motor performance was assessed by means of the Motor Performance (MOPER) Fitness Test (Kemper & Verschuur, 1985); the standardized measuring protocol is described in chapter 3. The test measures the following seven motor fitness variables:

• *Arm speed*, expressed in seconds, was measured by the best time needed to alternately tap two plates, whose midpoints lie 75 cm apart, at the umbilical level as fast as possible using the hand of preference for 25 complete cycles

• *Explosive leg strength*, expressed in centimeters, was measured by vertical jump height.

• *Running speed*, expressed in seconds, was the time needed for a 10 × 5-m run.

• *Static arm strength*, expressed in kilograms of pulling force, was measured with an arm-pull test in which the subject was asked to pull a calibrated dynamometer with the preferred arm. The dynamometer was fixed to the wall in such a way that its handgrip was in the plane of the stretched supporting arm, which was held horizontally against the wall. The score was divided by body weight.

• *Flexibility of the trunk*, expressed in centimeters, was measured using the sit-and-reach test. Reaching the toes with straight legs gave a score of 25 centimeters.

• *Trunk/leg strength*, expressed in seconds, was measured as the time scored on a leg lift test in which the subject was asked to lift the legs as quickly as possible 10 times from the horizontal to the vertical with extended knees.

• *Endurance strength of the arms*, expressed in seconds, was measured by the maximal time that the subject was able to keep the eyes above a horizontal bar in a bent-arm hang position.

In order to obtain an overall measure for motor performance fitness, the following procedure was applied. First, for all tests the individual scores of all subjects were ranked according to performance in such a way that the best performance was ranked 1; the next best 2; and so on. Then, for each subject, his or her ranking on all tests was summed. Because not all subjects performed all seven motor fitness tests, each subject's total score was divided by the number of tests that he or she actually performed. All subjects participated in at least five motor fitness tests.

Isokinetic Strength of Hamstrings and Quadriceps Muscles

In addition to the measures of physical fitness just described, the strength of the hamstrings and quadriceps muscles was measured on a Cybex II according to the protocol described by van Velzen and Kemper (1988); the peak torque of the two muscles was measured isokinetically at speeds of 30°/sec, 60°/sec, 180°/sec, and 300°/sec. One hamstrings-to-quadriceps peak torque ratio (H:Q ratio) was obtained by averaging the scores at these four different speeds.

Besides an average H:Q ratio, the left and right leg extensor and flexor muscle strength disbalance indicators were assessed according to the following procedure: for each speed of measurement the absolute value of the torque difference between the left and right leg was calculated for the hamstrings and quadriceps muscles separately and then expressed as a percentage of the maximal torque of the stronger leg at that specific speed. Then for all subjects for each speed of measurement these percentages were ranked as percentiles. Arbitrarily, subjects were considered to have extreme flexor disbalance if for at least three of the four speeds of measurement their percentile ranking exceeded the median score, and to have moderate flexor disbalance if for one or two of the four speeds of measurement their percentile ranking exceeded the median score. Extensor disbalance was assessed in a similar way.

Body Mass Index

Body Mass Index (BMI) was expressed as body weight per body height squared (i.e., kilograms per meter squared).

Psychological and Psychosocial Variables

Psychological and psychosocial variables were assessed by means of standardized questionnaires, listed next.

Achievement Motivation Test

The scales on the Achievement Motivation Test (AMT) (Hermans, 1976) are Achievement Motivation (the need to achieve and the will to reach achievements), Facilitating Anxiety (a fear of failure leading to higher achievements, especially in unstructured task situations), and Debilitating Anxiety (a fear of failure leading to lower achievements, especially in unstructured task situations).

Dutch Personality Inventory

The Dutch Personality Inventory (DPI) (Luteijn et al., 1985) has the following scales: Inadequacy (vague feelings of malfunctioning, anxiety, vague physical and psychosomatic complaints, and depressive mood), Social Inadequacy (neurotic shyness, uncomfortable feelings in social situations, and the avoidance of unfamiliar people and situations), Self-Sufficiency (feelings of being satisfied with oneself, reluctance to be interested in another person or his or her problems), Recalcitrance (mistrust, desire to solve problems alone, feelings of independence), Dominance (self-reliance, trying to be or play the boss), and Rigidity (the need for a regular life, fixed habits, sense of duty, and being persevering).

Jenkins Activity Survey

The Jenkins Activity Survey (JAS) (Appels et al., 1979) measures Type A/B personality, which is considered to reflect coronary-prone behavior.

Ways of Coping Checklist

The Dutch version of the Ways of Coping Checklist (WCC) (Vingerhoets & Flohr, 1984) assesses problem-focused coping and emotion-focused coping.

Experienced Health Questionnaire

The Experienced Health Questionnaire (EHQ) (Jansen & Sikkel, 1981) contains questions on physical symptoms and sensations relative to general well-being and responsiveness to situational stress.

Data Analysis

To investigate the relationship between physical fitness, psychological and psychosocial variables, and the occurrence of sports injuries a stepwise multiple logistic regression (MLR) analysis (Hosmer & Lemeshow, 1989) was applied according to the following procedure. First, all continuous physical fitness, psychological, and psychosocial variables were related to the occurrence of sports injuries in univariate analyses by comparing results of injured and noninjured subjects (for males and females separately) using a two-tail Student t-test. Differences between injured and noninjured with respect to flexor and extensor disbalance status were tested by means of a two-tail χ^2 test. Then only those variables that in the univariate analyses showed a level of significance of $p < .25$ for the observed difference were entered into the stepwise MLR model.

Earlier research (van Mechelen, 1992; van Mechelen et al., 1993) showed that the obvious risk factor for sports injuries is the time spent in sports. Therefore, the exposure time (i.e., time at risk) before the occurrence of the injury should be considered when studying the etiological role of potential risk factors. However, owing to the design of the Amsterdam Growth and Health Study this was not possible, since no information on sports exposure time was collected between ages 21 and 27, nor was the occurrence of sports injuries assessed prospectively. At age 21, however, as in all years of measurements, a habitual physical activity interview was conducted. This interview addressed all organized and leisure-time sports activities exceeding a level of 4 METs. From these data the total weekly time spent on organized and leisure-time sports activities was calculated. This variable was entered as a covariate into the MLR model as an approximation of exposure time. Lastly, sex was entered into the model as a covariate.

To determine the goodness of fit of the final models, the Hosmer and Lemeshow C statistic was calculated. The higher the p-value and the lower the C-value, the better the goodness of fit (Hosmer & Lemeshow, 1989). All data were processed using the personal computer version of the statistical package for the social sciences (SPSS-X).

Results

Our questionnaire revealed 47 injuries sustained during the preceding 12 months: 13 injuries in females and 34 injuries in males; 3 male subjects sustained 2 injuries and 1 male subject 3. The 1-year person cumulative incidence of injury for males was 42.3% (30/71 × 100%) and for females, 14.4% (13/90 × 100%). Given the small number of injuries sustained by females no attempt was made to present descriptive injury data for males and females separately. Table 10.2 lists the criteria for reporting an event as an injury.

The questionnaire showed that 25 injuries were sustained during contact sports—15 of them during soccer; 18 injuries were sustained during indoor sports. Regarding site of injury, 6 were to the upper extremity, 3 to the head and torso, 4 to the upper leg (including the groin and the hip), 9 to the knee, 7 to the lower

Table 10.2   Criteria for Reporting an Event as an Injury

Injury criterion	Number of injuries meeting the injury criterion
Subject had to stop playing sports	25
No (full) participation in sports at the next occasion	22
Absence at work or study the next day	13
Need for (para)medical attention	29

Note. Because the questionnaire allowed the indication of more than one injury criterion, the total of the last column exceeds the total of 47 injuries.

leg, 10 to the ankle, and 4 to the foot. Due to insufficient information the exact localization could not be established for four injuries.

Regarding medical diagnosis, 29 of the injuries concerned a problem of a joint, 10 injuries were related to damage to a muscle, and 6 injuries were located in a tendon. There was 1 injury to the skin, and 1 injury remained unidentified.

In Table 10.3 means and standard deviations are listed for all potential risk factors, for males and females. The significance of the difference in numbers of injured and noninjured subjects classified as either having no disbalance or disbalance (either moderate or extreme) was tested by means of a χ^2 test (α = .25). In males a difference was found at the indicated level of significance in extension disbalance, indicating a tendency for moderate or extreme disbalance in injured subjects when compared with noninjured subjects. No such difference was found for flexion disbalance, both in males and females. Based on the results of the t-tests presented in Table 10.3 and the χ^2 test, only the variables showing a difference between injured and noninjured subjects at $p < .25$ were entered into the MLR model. These variables were recalcitrance, facilitating anxiety, emotion-focused coping, type A/B behavior, self sufficiency, and extension disbalance. Sport-playing time and sex were entered as covariates.

The results of the stepwise MLR analysis are summarized in Table 10.4. The results show a significant model with a goodness of fit of $p = .10$ and $C = 13.3$ for the combined variables of recalcitrance, emotion-focused coping, and extension disbalance. However, only for recalcitrance was a significant odds ratio found: a 5-point higher score equals an odds ratio of 0.71 (95% confidence interval = 0.50-0.99). None of the other potential risk factors mentioned in Table 10.3 were found to be significantly related to sports injuries.

Discussion

The results of this study showed a 1-year person cumulative sports injury incidence of 42% for males and 14% for females; together, these data represent a 1-year cumulative sports injury incidence of 27%. Although in general it is not possible to compare sports injury incidence figures accurately due to differences in methodology and definitions, the observed incidence does not deviate from what is found in the literature (van Mechelen et al., 1992). Also the injury localization—i.e., predominantly lower extremity injuries, with a preference for the knee and ankle—as well as the nature of the sustained injuries, is in line with what is found in the literature (van Mechelen et al., 1987; van Galen & Diederiks, 1990).

The purpose of this study was to investigate the potential role of physiological, physical-fitness, and psychosocial variables as risk factors for sports injuries. In the univariate analyses, using a very conservative level of significance (α = 0.25), the following variables were found to differ between injured and noninjured sportspersons, in either males or females: Self-Sufficiency, Recalcitrance, Facilitating Anxiety, Emotion-Focused Coping, and Extension Disbalance. The MLR analysis in which these variables, as well as sports-playing time and sex, were

Table 10.3   Means and Standard Deviations at Age 21 of Scores of Potential Risk Factors for Injured and Noninjured Males and Females at Age 27

Potential risk factor	Males		Females	
	Noninjured ($n = 44$)	Injured ($n = 27$)	Noninjured ($n = 76$)	Injured ($n = 13$)
$\dot{V}O_2$max (ml · kg$^{-2/3}$ · min^{-1})	22.3 ± 2.4	22.8 ± 2.1	16.2 ± 1.6	16.9 ± 1.6
Motor Performance Fitness score	41.8 ± 13.6	41.5 ± 13.1	43.5 ± 16.2	40.3 ± 11.8
H:Q ratio (%)	73.8 ± 8.8	75.6 ± 5.3	71.6 ± 7.2	73.2 ± 7.0
Body Mass Index (kg/m^2)	21.3 ± 1.8	21.5 ± 1.7	21.2 ± 2.7	21.7 ± 1.8
Inadequacy (score)	10.0 ± 8.0	8.2 ± 7.0	11.9 ± 6.5	11.7 ± 6.0
Social inadequacy (score)	8.9 ± 6.7	8.0 ± 6.8	9.3 ± 7.1	9.5 ± 5.3
Self-sufficiency (score)	11.8 ± 5.1	11.7 ± 5.4	8.6 ± 4.2*	6.1 ± 2.7
Rigidity (score)	21.3 ± 7.7	20.3 ± 7.2	21.1 ± 8.1	22.8 ± 6.6
Recalcitrance (score)	17.6 ± 5.7*	15.3 ± 8.1	16.3 ± 6.2	15.2 ± 5.2
Dominance (score)	17.3 ± 7.0	16.9 ± 5.4	14.3 ± 5.9	14.0 ± 4.6
Facilitating anxiety (score)	12.5 ± 4.4*	14.0 ± 3.6	10.3 ± 5.1	11.3 ± 4.4
Debilitating anxiety (score)	7.8 ± 6.1	8.3 ± 6.0	13.1 ± 6.0	14.1 ± 4.7
Achievement motivation (score)	17.0 ± 7.1	15.3 ± 8.1	17.4 ± 7.0	19.2 ± 7.2
Type A/B (score)	100.6 ± 15.9	101.1 ± 12.3	109.8 ± 15.3*	116.5 ± 7.9
Problem-focused coping (score)	16.0 ± 5.1	16.7 ± 2.9	15.7 ± 3.6	16.2 ± 2.6
Emotion-focused coping (score)	16.2 ± 5.1*	18.3 ± 5.8	19.0 ± 4.7	17.8 ± 4.3
Experienced health (score)	2.2 ± 2.5	2.7 ± 2.3	3.9 ± 3.7	4.2 ± 3.7
Sports time (1985; min/wk^{-1})	107.6 ± 124.1	119.9 ± 136.9	94.0 ± 95.2	125.0 ± 96.6

Note. H:Q ratio = hamstrings-to-quadriceps peak torque ratio.

*$p < .25$ (two-tail Student t-test).

entered resulted in a final model containing the variables Recalcitrance, Emotion-Focused Coping, and Extension Disbalance. From these variables only Recalcitrance showed an independent significant relation with sports injuries.

Recalcitrance

The Recalcitrance scale of the DPI assesses "mistrust, the desire to solve problems alone and feelings of independence." For this variable a significant odds ratio of 0.71 (95% confidence interval = 0.50-0.99) was found, indicating that a 5-point higher score on the Recalcitrance scale results in a 0.71 smaller chance of sustaining a sports injury. In other words, the higher the recalcitrance score, the lower the chance of sustaining a sports injury. There are no other studies that

Table 10.4   Stepwise Multiple Logistic Regression Analysis for All Injuries

Variable	Odds ratio	95% confidence interval
Recalcitrance	0.71	0.50-0.99*
Emotion-focused coping	1.58	0.99-2.52
No extension disbalance	Reference	NA
Moderate extension disbalance (males)	0.97	0.24-3.94
Moderate extension disbalance (females)	0.18	0.02-1.53
Extreme extension disbalance (males)	2.90	0.88-9.55
Extreme extension disbalance (females)	0.13	0.02-1.12

Note. $n = 47$; NA = not applicable.
*$p < .05$; goodness of fit: $p = .10$, $C = 13.3$.

have used the DPI in sports injury research, so it is not possible to compare this finding straightforwardly with the literature. However, in a study by Jackson et al. (1978), Catell's Sixteen Personality Factor Inventory was used to study prospectively the relation between personality traits and American football injuries in high school athletes. Tender-minded, dependent, overprotected, sensitive players (measured by a single factor) were more likely to be injured than tough-minded, self-reliant, no-nonsense individuals. Applying the same inventory, Vaillant (1981) also found the same factor (tender-minded, dependent, over-protected, sensitive) in runners to be related to running injuries. These results are in line with ours.

With regard to the underlying mechanism, one may speculate that independent-minded sports players go their own way, not taking into account the opinions of others, such as teammates and the trainer, involved in the sport. If this is also true when the first signals of a sports injury appear, such an independent-minded sportsperson may obey "the language of his or her body" and stop playing rather than carrying on in order to satisfy the coach or teammates. In other words, such behavior may lower the risk of sustaining a sports injury.

Emotion-Focused Coping

A high emotion-focused coping score is indicative of an emotional style of coping with stressors. In general, this style of coping with problems of everyday life is regarded as inadequate. The results of the MLR analysis showed that a higher emotion-focused coping score contributed to the final model in such a way that it enhanced the risk of sports injuries. This finding is in line with the prospective study of Hanson et al. (1992), who found that in a multivariate analysis in college athletes a lack of adequate coping resources significantly distinguished injured from noninjured athletes.

To explain the mechanism, one may speculate that sportspersons character-ized by an emotion-focused coping style neglect "body language" or are inclined to run a higher risk to achieve their preset goals and thus obtain feelings of satisfaction, but also thereby enhance the risk of sustaining a sports injury.

Extension Disbalance

Extension disbalance of the quadriceps muscle was the third variable that contributed to the final logistic regression model. The analytical results indicated an interaction with sex: In males increasing disbalance seems associated with increased injury risk, whereas in females the opposite trend was found. However, as an independent factor, extension disbalance was not found to be of significant importance. In interpreting these findings, one should bear in mind that 13 of the 47 registered injuries did not concern the lower extremity. Therefore, the MLR analysis was repeated for lower-extremity injuries only. The result of this analysis is given in Table 10.5 and strengthens the previous result.

This model shows a much better goodness of fit ($p = .78$, $C = 4.80$) than the final model for all injuries regardless of their localization ($p = .10$, $C = 13.3$). Recalcitrance proved to be an even stronger independent and significant risk factor for lower-extremity injuries, with an odds ratio of 0.58 (95% confidence interval = 0.40-0.85). Also, extension disbalance contributed again to the final model. In males, extreme extension disbalance was found to be a significant independent risk factor for lower-extremity injuries, with an odds ratio of 3.80 (95% confidence interval = 1.07-13.72). This finding seems in line with the literature; according to many authors, muscle strength imbalance between ipsilateral antagonists and between identical bilateral muscle groups is thought to facilitate the occurrence of various musculoskeletal injuries of the lower extremity (Agre, 1985; Grace, 1985). It should, however, be stressed that these assumptions are not at all well supported by evidence from sound epidemiological studies (van Mechelen et al., in press). However, the outcome of our multiple regression analysis for extension disbalance in males seems to verify the hypothesis that

Table 10.5   Stepwise Multiple Logistic Regression Analysis for Lower-Extremity Injuries

Variable	Odds ratio	95% confidence interval
Recalcitrance	0.58*	0.40-0.85
Debilitating anxiety	1.47	0.94-2.30
No extension disbalance	Reference	NA
Moderate extension disbalance (males)	1.32	0.31-5.54
Moderate extension disbalance (females)	0.19	0.04-1.63
Extreme extension disbalance (males)	3.80*	1.07-13.72
Extreme extension disbalance (females)	0.18	0.02-1.58

Note. $n = 34$; NA = not applicable.

*$p < .05$; goodness of fit: $p = .78$, $C = 4.8$.

this factor plays an important role in the etiology of lower-extremity sports injuries. Flexion disbalance and the H:Q ratio were not confirmed as risk factors by the results of our study.

One last remark needs to be made with regard to results of the MLR analyses of lower-extremity injuries. Instead of emotion-focused coping, which contributed to the final model for all injuries, debilitating anxiety contributed to the lower-extremity model. Debilitating anxiety is defined as "a fear of failure, leading to lower achievements, especially in unstructured task situations." On the basis of our results it seems that higher levels of debilitating anxiety not only lead to lower achievement but also enhance the risk of sustaining a lower-extremity injury. There are no other studies on sports injuries that have investigated the role of debilitating anxiety as risk factor. However, in the previously cited study by Hanson et al. (1992) competitive trait anxiety—the tendency to perceive competitive situations as threatening—was found to contribute independently to maximizing the differences between groups of injured sportspersons according to the severity of injury (but not according to the frequency of injury).

Most of the potential risk factors that were taken into consideration in this study were found not to be related to sports injuries, in contrast to what is often cited in the literature. Several possible explanations for this discrepancy exist. Regarding the design of our study it should be noted that the sports injury information was collected retrospectively; this process may have been hampered by factors such as recall bias and invalid injury description. Another point that needs attention is the relatively long time interval (6 years) between the assessment of the potential risk factors at age 21 and the occurrence of sports injuries some 5 to 6 years later at age 27. In this respect it would be better to assess potential risk factors as close as possible to the moment of injury. For instance, it is known that for the MOPER Fitness Test items the average interperiod correlation coefficient (IPC) between the 1985 and 1991 test scores was about .70, for both males and females (see also chapter 4), and that the IPC for organized sports activities over the same period was about .2 for males and .3 for females (see also chapter 9).

Our subjects were all relatively healthy, fit, and young. This may have consequences for the discriminating power of the potential risk factors that were taken into consideration in our study. For instance, it is known from a study by Marti et al. (1988) that the risk of sustaining a running injury is enhanced for runners with a BMI greater than 27. However, a BMI greater than 25 is a rare finding in nonelite sportspersons (Hølmich et al., 1989), which was also demonstrated in our subjects who had average BMIs of 21-22.

The design of most studies on the etiology of sports injuries are of a retrospective or a case-control nature. Neither of these two designs can distinguish between cause (potential risk factor) and consequence (sports injury). Also, most of the studies on the etiology of sports injuries lack a multivariate approach for analyzing the data, thereby leading to confounding results. Perhaps many associations found between sports injuries and potential etiological factors in univariate retrospective or case-control studies are the result of the previously mentioned methodological problems and are in fact nonexisting associations. If this is true, it may explain our "lack of results," since it is quite possible that our prospective design and our multivariate analyses have ruled out the detrimental influence of confounding factors.

Finally, it should be mentioned that only a fraction of all factors that are considered to influence the risk on sustaining a sports injury were taken into consideration in our study. This may have influenced our results.

Conclusions

• In this prospective study on sports injuries an overall 1-year person incidence of 27% was found; about 75% of the injuries were lower-extremity injuries.

• For all injuries after multiple regression analysis a significant final model was found combining the following variables: recalcitrance, emotion-focused coping, and extension disbalance. From these variables only recalcitrance proved to be an independent risk factor for sports injuries.

• Performing the same analysis for lower-extremity injuries only, a final model was found that combined recalcitrance and extension disbalance, but now with debilitating anxiety instead of emotion-focused coping. From these variables recalcitrance proved to be an even stronger independent risk factor for lower-extremity injuries, as was extreme extension disbalance, but only in males.

References

Agre J.A. Hamstring injuries: Proposed aetiological factors, prevention and treatment. Sports Med 2 (1985) 21-33.

Appels A., W. De Haes, J. Schuurman. Een test ter meting van het "coronary prone behaviour pattern" Type A. Nederlands Tijdschrift voor de Psychologie 34 (1979) 181-188.

Bouchard C., P.J. Stephard, T. Stephens. (1993). Physical activity, fitness and health: Consensus statement. Human Kinetics, Champaign, IL.

Galen W. van, J. Diederiks. (1990). Sportblessures breed uitgemeten; Uitg. De Vrieseborch, Haarlem.

Grace T.G. Muscle imbalance and extremity injury: A perplexing relationship. Sports Med 2 (1985) 77-82.

Hermans H.J.M. (1976). Prestatie Motivatie Test, Handleiding PMT, Swets & Zeitlinger, Lisse.

Hølmich P, S.W. Christensen, E. Darre, F. Johnsen, T. Hartog. Non-elite marathon runners: Health, training and injuries. Br J Sports Med 23:3 (1989) 177-178.

Hosmer D.W., S. Lemeshow. (1989). Applied logistic regression. Wiley, New York.

Jackson D.W., H. Jarret, D. Bailey, J. Kausek, J. Swanson, R.P.T. Majar, J.W. Powell. Injury prediction in the young athlete: A preliminary report. Am J Sports Med 6:1 (1978) 6-13.

Jansen M.E., D. Sikkel. Verkorte versie van de voegschaal. Gedrag en Samenleving 2 (1981) 78-82.

Kemper H.C.G., R. Verschuur. (1980). Measurement of aerobic power in teenagers. In: K. Berg, B.O. Erikson (eds.), Children and exercise IV. University Park Press, Baltimore.

Kemper H.C.G., R. Verschuur. (1985). Motor performance fitness test. In: H.C.G. Kemper (ed.), Medicine and sport science, vol. 20. Karger, Basel.

Loës M. de. Medical treatment and costs of sports-related injuries in a total population. Int J Sports Med 11 (1990) 66-72.

Luteijn F., J. Starren, H. van Dijk. (1985). Nederlandse Persoonlijkheids Vragenlijst. Handleiding, Herziene uitgave. Swets & Zeitlinger, Lisse.

Marti B., J.P. Vader, C.E. Minder, T. Abelin. On the epidemiology of running injuries. Am J Sports Med 16:3 (1988) 285-294.

Mechelen W. van. Running injuries: A review of the epidemiological literature. Sports Med 14:5 (1992) 320-335.

Mechelen W. van, H. Hlobil, H.C.G. Kemper. (1987). How can sports injuries be prevented? (Publication No. 25E) NISGZ, Papendal.

Mechelen W. van, H. Hlobil, H.C.G. Kemper. Incidence, severity, etiology and prevention of sports injuries: A review of concepts. Sports Med 14:2 (1992) 82-99.

Mechelen W. van, H. Hlobil, H.C.G. Kemper, W.J. Voorn, R.H. de Jongh. The prevention of running injuries by warm-up, cool-down and stretching exercises. Am J Sports Med 21:5 (1993) 711-719.

Mechelen W. van, H. Hlobil, M.G.H. Rep, W. Strobosch, H.C.G. Kemper. (in press). Running injuries and hamstring and quadriceps weakness and balance: A case control study. Sport, Medicine, Training, and Rehabilitation.

Sandelin J., S. Santavirta, R. Lättilä, S. Sarna. Sports injuries in a large urban population: Occurrence and epidemiological aspects. Int J Sports Med 8 (1987) 61-66.

Schlatmann H.F.P.M., H. Hlobil, W. van Mechelen, H.C.G. Kemper. Naar een Registratiesysteem van Sportblessures in Nederland. Geneeskunde en Sport 20:5 (1987) 179-184.

Vaillant P.M. Personality and injury in competitive runners. Percept Mot Skills 53 (1981) 251-253.

Velzen J.H.A. van, H.C.G. Kemper. Maximale momentswaarden isokinetisch gemeten tijdens extensie en flexie van het kniegewricht bij jongvolwassenen. Geneeskunde en Sport 21:2 (1988) 59-66.

Vingerhoets A.J.J.M., P.J.M. Flohr. Type A behavior and self-reports of coping preferences. Br J Med Psychol 57 (1984) 15-21.

Chapter 11

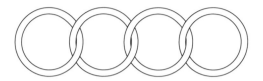

Tracking of Cardiovascular Risk Factors in Relation to Lifestyle

Jos Twisk, Han C.G. Kemper, & Jan Snel

Cardiovascular disease (CVD) is one of the most serious problems in public health. It is well understood that the origin of CVD lies in early childhood (World Health Organization, 1982). Therefore, it is important to identify individuals at risk as soon in life as possible so preventive strategies may be initiated early. To identify individuals at risk, it is necessary to follow the development of risk factors for CVD from childhood to discern how predictive early measurements are for values later in life. In epidemiology, the method that deals with this sort of problem is called *tracking*. No single definition of *tracking* seems to be generally accepted, but there are two concepts involved: The ability to predict future values from early observations (Rosner et al., 1977) and the maintenance over time of relative ranking (stability) within a distribution of values (Berenson et al., 1978; Clarke et al., 1978).

Risk factors for CVD can be roughly divided into biological parameters, like hypertension, hypercholesterolemia, body fat, and (low) cardiopulmonary fitness, and lifestyle parameters, like physical inactivity, smoking behavior, alcohol consumption, and Type A behavior. Furthermore, a family history of CVD or hypertension is often mentioned as an important genetic risk factor for CVD (Haynes et al., 1980; Manson et al., 1992; Webber et al., 1991a).

In relation to preventive strategies it is important not only to look at the longitudinal development of both the biological and lifestyle risk factors but also to quantify the influence of the lifestyle risk factors on the longitudinal development of the biological risk factors. There is evidence suggesting that the biological risk factors hypertension and hypercholesterolemia are not only influenced by some of the lifestyle risk factors but also by other biological risk factors, namely, cardiopulmonary fitness and body fat (Beaglehole, 1990). Relative to hyper-cholesterolemia, three factors seem to be important: high serum total cholesterol (TC), low high-density lipoprotein (HDL) cholesterol, and a high TC:HDL-cholesterol ratio (Wallace & Anderson, 1987).

The purpose of this chapter is therefore to describe the tracking of the biological risk factors hypercholesterolemia (i.e., TC, HDL cholesterol, and the TC:HDL-cholesterol ratio), hypertension (systolic blood pressure and diastolic blood pressure), cardiopulmonary fitness, and body fat and the lifestyle risk factors daily physical activity, smoking behavior, alcohol consumption, and Type A behavior in a group of males and females as they progressed from age 13 to age 27.

We further focus on the relationship between the longitudinal development of biological risk factors, on the one hand, and other biological risk factors, the lifestyle risk factors, and family history of CVD or hypertension, on the other hand (Fig. 11.1).

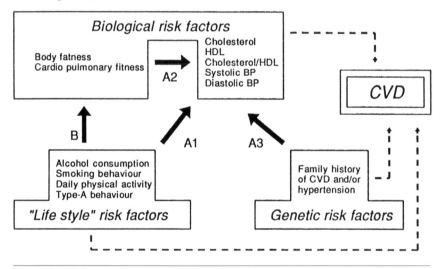

Figure 11.1   Diagram of the possible relationships among biological risk factors, life-style risk factors, and genetic risk factors for CVD. We are investigating the relationships between the risk factors connected by the solid arrows.

Methods

Subjects

All subjects—84 males (mean age 27.14 ± 0.79 years) and 98 females (mean age 27.07 ± 0.75 years)—were participants in the Amsterdam Growth and Health Study. This multiple longitudinal study started in 1977, when subjects were 13 years of age, and included four annual measurements (Kemper, 1985). A fifth measurement took place in 1985 (age 21), and a sixth in 1991 (age 27).

Biological Risk Factors

For the determination of TC in blood serum, approximately 10 ml of venous blood was taken from the vena antecubitis of each subject with a vacutainer. Blood sampling was done with subjects in a nonfasting state. Analysis of TC and HDL-cholesterol levels met the criteria of World Health Organization (WHO) reference laboratories. Systolic and diastolic blood pressures were measured using a sphygmomanometer with a standard pressure cuff. The subjects were measured at the left upper arm while seated. Two readings were made and the lower value recorded. Body fat was expressed as the sum of four skinfolds (biceps, triceps, subscapular, and suprailiac), measured according to the guidelines of the International Biological Program (Weiner & Lourie, 1969). Cardiopulmonary fitness was operationalized as maximum oxygen uptake ($\dot{V}O_2$max) expressed as milliliters per kilogram to the two-thirds power per minute, which can be used as a meaningful fitness index (Åstrand & Rodahl, 1986). $\dot{V}O_2$max was measured by a direct method using a running test on a treadmill with constant speed and increasing slope till exhaustion (Kemper, 1985).

Lifestyle Risk Factors

Daily physical activity was measured by a standardized activity interview covering a period of 3 months prior to the interview. Duration of specified activities was combined with intensity, classified into three levels (light, medium-heavy, and heavy activities), to form a weighted physical activity score. This score was expressed in METs (the ratio between the work metabolic rate and basal metabolic rate) per week (Verschuur, 1987). Alcohol consumption was measured as part of a dietary recall, a modification of the cross-check dietary history interview (Post et al., 1987). Information about smoking behavior was gathered by a questionnaire that asked each subject whether he or she smoked and, if so, how much. Type A behavior was expressed as the total score on the Jenkins Activity Survey (JAS)(Appels et al., 1979). The family history of CVD and hypertension was measured as part of a health questionnaire in which the subjects (in 1991, at age 27) were asked whether first-order relatives were suffering from CVD or hypertension.

Analysis

For both the biological and lifestyle risk factors, Pearson correlation coefficients were calculated between the first measurement at age 13 and the five following measurements (interperiod correlation coefficients, or IPCs). Next, tracking was described by means of percentile ranking. The subjects were divided into quartiles and those in the highest risk quartile at the first measurement in 1977 were selected. The percentage of subjects who stayed in this high-risk quartile was calculated separately for all the five following measurements. Relative high-risk values correspond with high values of TC, the TC:HDL-cholesterol ratio, systolic blood pressure, diastolic blood pressure, body fat, alcohol consumption, smoking behavior, and Type A behavior and with relatively low values of HDL cholesterol, daily physical activity, and cardiopulmonary fitness. Because of the distribution of smoking behavior and alcohol consumption (at age 13 most subjects did not smoke or drink alcohol), tracking of these two variables was described only by means of percentile ranks. Tracking of family history of CVD and hypertension was, of course, not described at all.

So far, tracking was only described based on one measurement (at age 13), but tracking correlations probably can be increased by using as an initial value the mean value of several measurements, with relatively short time intervals, (Gillman et al., 1991; Rosner & Willett, 1988). To verify this idea, the mean of the first four measurements, made between 13 and 17 years of age (the adolescent period), was calculated and used as an initial value to describe tracking. All tracking analyses were done for males and females separately.

To assess the influence of the lifestyle risk factors, the biological risk factors body fat and cardiopulmonary fitness, and family history of CVD and/ or hypertension on the longitudinal development of TC, HDL cholesterol, the TC:HDL-cholesterol ratio, and systolic and diastolic blood pressures, multiple logistic regression (MLR) was used. The same analysis was done for the relation between the lifestyle risk factors and body fat and cardiopulmonary fitness (see Fig. 11.1).

In order to create a dichotomous dependent variable, for all the biological risk factors the population was split into high-risk and low-risk groups. The high-risk group consisted of subjects above P_{50} during the whole measurement period (for HDL cholesterol and cardiopulmonary fitness beyond P_{50})—which means that they had to score high on the mean of the adolescent-period measurements, the young-adult period measurement (age 21), and the adult period measurement (age 27). The low-risk group was formed in the same way and consisted of subjects who scored below P_{50} (for HDL cholesterol and cardiopulmonary fitness, above P_{50}) at all three measurements.

In the MLR analysis the following independent variables were treated as continuous: daily physical activity, cardiopulmonary fitness, body fat, and Type A behavior. For all these variables, the mean value of the measurements during the adolescent period and the measurements of the young-adult and adult periods were used to calculate the mean value of the whole measurement period.

Alcohol consumption was handled in the same way, but because of distribution problems (many subjects did not drink any alcohol throughout the whole period), alcohol consumption was treated as a categorical variable. Subjects were classified as nondrinkers, light drinkers, or heavy drinkers. The separation between light and heavy drinkers was based on more or less than P_{50} of the whole group of drinkers. Smoking behavior was also treated as a categorical variable. Because of the way smoking behavior was queried, the total amount of tobacco smoked from age 13 to age 27 could be calculated. Based on that value, subjects were classified as nonsmokers, light smokers (below P_{50} of the whole group of smokers), or heavy smokers (above P_{50} of the whole group of smokers). Family history of CVD and hypertension was scored dichotomously.

To control for gender, this variable was an independent variable in the MLR models for each risk factor. For the same reason, HDL cholesterol was an independent variable in the TC model, and TC was an independent variable in the HDL-cholesterol model. The same was done for the systolic blood pressure and diastolic blood pressure models. All variables were treated as continuous and were calculated in the same way as daily physical activity, cardiopulmonary fitness, body fat, and Type A behavior.

Decisions on whether to put variables into the MLR models were based on the significance of the variables as well as the deviance of the whole model (Hosmer & Lemeshow, 1989). Gender was forced in all the final models. To assess the goodness of fit of the final models the Hosmer and Lemeshow C statistic was calculated. The lower the C (the higher the p-value), the better the fit of the model (Lemeshow & Hosmer, 1982).

Results

The IPCs between the first measurement at age 13 and the following five measurements and the IPCs between the mean value of the first four measurements (during the adolescent period) and the following two measurements for all the observed risk factors are shown in Table 11.1. The IPCs between two measurements 1 year apart for the lipoproteins were around .7 to .8. With longer interperiods they were a bit lower, but with an interperiod of 15 years the correlations were still above .5. The IPCs between the measurements of systolic and diastolic blood pressures and $\dot{V}O_2$max were lower over the whole measurement period.

During the adolescent period, the IPCs for the measurements of body fat were very high (around .8), but they decreased fast (especially for males) when the interperiods were longer. Daily physical activity showed not only low correlations with short interperiods but also the lowest IPCs with the longer interperiods.

If the mean value of the measurements during the adolescent period is taken as the initial value for describing tracking, all correlations are higher than the correlations when just the first measurement is taken as initial value.

In general, females showed higher IPCs than males, but only for the TC:HDL-cholesterol ratio and $\dot{V}O_2$max was this true throughout the whole measurement period.

Tables 11.2 (biological risk factors) and 11.3 (lifestyle risk factors) give the percentages of subjects who stayed in the high-risk quartile during follow-up. Although there was a lowering trend with increasing interperiods, this is not as obvious as with the IPCs.

When the mean value of the adolescent period measurements is taken as initial values to describe tracking, most of the percentages are higher than the percentages when just the first measurement is taken as initial value. When the mean value of the measurements of daily physical activity during the adolescent period is taken as initial value to describe tracking, the percentages that stayed at high risk are *not* higher than the percentages when just the first measurement is taken as initial value. The proportion of subjects who stayed in the high-risk

**Table 11.1 Interperiod Correlation Coefficients
for Biological and Lifestyle Risk Factors**

	Comparison between measurement at age(s)						
	13					13-17 (avg. value)	
	14	15	16	21	27	21	27
Total cholesterol (TC)							
Males	.71	.73	.66	.71	.62	.83	.72
Females	.84	.77	.75	.62	.52	.68	.60
HDL cholesterol							
Males	.70	.68	.61	.38	.52	.47	.56
Females	.66	.74	.63	.55	.62	.69	.71
TC:HDL							
Males	.72	.73	.70	.61	.54	.70	.60
Females	.78	.79	.76	.74	.67	.74	.75
Systolic BP							
Males	.61	.50	.31	.40	.39	.53	.53
Females	.57	.48	.57	.34	.46	.45	.41
Diastolic BP							
Males	.39	.41	.44	.37	.18	.63	.44
Females	.47	.48	.31	.30	.31	.65	.56
$\dot{V}O_2$max							
Males	.57	.57	.49	.35	.30	.54	.37
Females	.71	.62	.61	.42	.36	.58	.53
Body fat							
Males	.87	.76	.84	.49	.22	.57	.22
Females	.89	.82	.77	.55	.51	.65	.56
Daily physical activity							
Males	.47	.38	.44	.20	.05	.27	.10
Females	.64	.55	.58	.18	.17	.24	.21

Note. BP = blood pressure.

groups with longer interperiods was below 50% for both daily physical activity and alcohol consumption. Smoking behavior showed relatively high percentages (70%-80%).

For systolic and diastolic blood pressures it was very difficult, for the first four measurements, to divide the subjects into quartiles. Thus, we only used the mean value of these measurements as an initial value to describe tracking by means of percentile ranks. For the measurements in 1985 and 1991 as well there was not a perfect division into quartiles. The division was made as close to the P_{25} value as possible (Table 11.4). Only the percentage of females who stayed in the high-risk group for diastolic blood pressure at age 21 was below

Table 11.2   Percentages of Subjects at High Risk (P_{25}) for Biological Risk Factors

	Subjects at high risk at age(s)						
	13					13-17	
	Who stayed at high risk at age						
	14	15	16	21	27	21	27
Total cholesterol (TC)							
Males	62.5%	62.5%	58.3%	66.7%	58.3%	81.0%	71.4%
Females	71.4%	57.1%	50.0%	39.3%	42.9%	50.0%	57.1%
HDL cholesterol							
Males	59.1%	63.0%	68.2%	40.9%	50.0%	47.6%	57.1%
Females	60.0%	56.7%	56.7%	40.0%	46.7%	65.2%	65.2%
TC:HDL							
Males	63.3%	54.5%	50.0%	40.9%	31.8%	47.6%	38.1%
Females	62.5%	79.2%	58.3%	54.2%	62.5%	54.2%	62.5%
$\dot{V}O_2$max							
Males	57.1%	61.9%	52.4%	42.9%	33.3%	47.6%	38.1%
Females	62.5%	50.0%	70.8%	45.8%	45.8%	58.3%	54.2%
Body fat							
Males	76.6%	81.0%	76.2%	47.6%	52.4%	52.4%	57.1%
Females	87.5%	66.7%	70.8%	52.4%	45.8%	58.3%	45.8%

Table 11.3   Percentages of Subjects at High Risk (P_{25}) for Lifestyle Risk Factors

	Subjects at high risk at age(s)						
	13					13-17	
	Who stayed at high risk at age						
	14	15	16	21	27	21	27
Daily physical activity							
Males	61.9%	52.4%	57.1%	28.6%	28.6%	28.6%	23.8%
Females	53.8%	38.5%	57.7%	34.6%	30.8%	29.2%	41.7%
Alcohol consumption							
Males	—	—	—	—	—	33.3%	42.9%
Females	—	—	—	—	—	45.8%	37.5%
Smoking							
Males	—	—	—	—	—	73.3%	60.0%
Females	—	—	—	—	—	70.8%	58.3%

Table 11.4   Percentages of Subjects at High Risk at the Adolescent Period for Systolic and Diastolic Blood Pressures

| | Subjects at high risk at ages 13-17 who stayed at high risk at age | |
	21	27
Systolic BP		
Males	75.0% (P_{34})	55.0% (P_{26})
Females	58.3% (P_{26})	58.3% (P_{28})
Diastolic BP		
Males	57.1% (P_{23})	52.4% (P_{24})
Females	34.6% (P_{18})	61.5% (P_{32})

Note. Percentile values are those used to define the high-risk group.

50%, but this high-risk group was based on the 18th percentile point. All the other percentages are higher than 50%.

Type-A behavior was measured only in 1985 and 1991. The correlation between the two measurements was .58 for males and .55 for females. The proportions of subjects who stayed in the high-risk group over a six-year period were 58% for males and 46% for females.

As mentioned earlier, we divided the population for the biological risk factors into a high-risk group and a low-risk group. In Table 11.5 the mean values over the whole measurement period of 15 years for the biological risk factors TC, HDL cholesterol, the TC:HDL-cholesterol ratio, and systolic and diastolic blood pressures are given for both the high-risk and low-risk groups. For all the variables the high- and low-risk groups showed great differences.

The univariate relations between body fat and other biological risk factors are shown in Figure 11.2. All the low-risk groups for the biological risk factors had lower values for body fat (sum of skinfolds), except low-risk males for HDL cholesterol and diastolic blood pressure. However, only high-risk males for TC and the TC:HDL-cholesterol ratio and high-risk females for the TC:HDL-cholesterol ratio showed significantly higher values for body fat ($p < .01$).

Figure 11.3 shows that the low- and high-risk groups of all the biological risk factors seem to have had almost the same $\dot{V}O_2$max, but males at high risk for body fat had a significantly ($p < .01$) lower $\dot{V}O_2$max than low-risk males.

The relationships between the amount of daily physical activity and biological risk factors for CVD are shown in Figure 11.4. The low-risk group (both males and females) for $\dot{V}O_2$max had higher values of daily physical activity, but only for females was this difference significant ($p < .01$). The other risk factors revealed no differences in the amount of daily physical activity.

Figure 11.5 shows the relationships between alcohol consumption and the biological risk factors. For systolic and diastolic blood pressures, low-risk males

Table 11.5   Means and Standard Deviations of Biological Risk Factors for the High- and Low-Risk Groups

	Low risk	High risk
Total cholesterol (TC) (mmol/L)		
Males	3.91 ± .32	5.42 ± .35
Females	4.04 ± .29	5.46 ± .42
HDL cholesterol (mmol/L)		
Males	1.56 ± .10	1.08 ± .10
Females	1.71 ± .21	1.13 ± .11
TC:HDL		
Males	2.82 ± .30	4.42 ± .60
Females	2.78 ± .32	4.33 ± .57
Systolic BP (mmHg)		
Males	117.86 ± 3.74	137.69 ± 5.96
Females	116.58 ± 3.94	136.54 ± 6.07
Diastolic BP (mmHg)		
Males	71.68 ± 3.61	83.99 ± 4.76
Females	71.56 ± 2.75	83.49 ± 4.85

Note. BP = blood pressure.

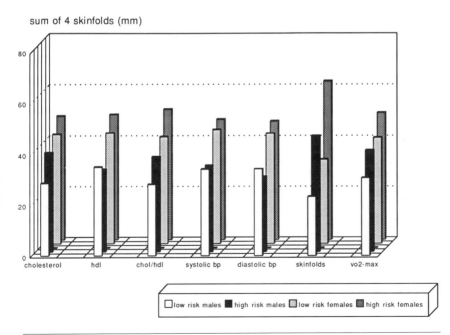

Figure 11.2   Mean values of the sum of four skinfolds measured over a period of 15 years for the high- and low-risk groups for the other biological risk factors.

maximum oxygen uptake (ml•min⁻¹•kg⁻²ᐟ³)

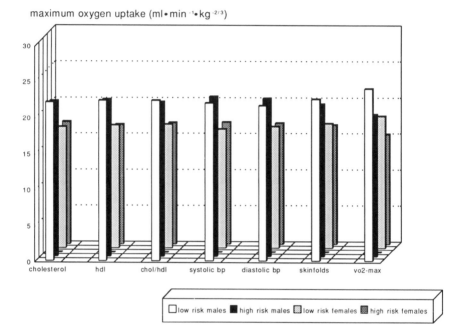

Figure 11.3   Mean values of V̇O₂max measured over a period of 15 years for the high- and low-risk groups for the other biological risk factors.

and females drank more than high-risk males and females, while for TC, the TC:HDL-cholesterol ratio, and body fat, low-risk males and females drank less than the high-risk groups. However, none of these differences were significant.

In Figure 11.6 the relations between smoking behavior and the biological risk factors for CVD are summarized. For TC, HDL cholesterol, the TC:HDL-cholesterol ratio, and V̇O₂max, the high-risk groups smoked more than the low-risk groups. For systolic blood pressure, the high-risk groups smoked less than the low-risk groups. Significant differences ($p < .05$) were found between the two risk groups for HDL cholesterol for females only and for systolic blood pressure and V̇O₂max for both sexes.

Figure 11.7 reveals that the low- and high-risk groups of all the biological risk factors for CVD showed no differences in Type A behavior.

In Table 11.6 the percentages of subjects with a family history of CVD and/ or hypertension are given for the high- and low-risk groups for the biological risk factors TC, HDL cholesterol, the TC:HDL-cholesterol ratio, and systolic and diastolic blood pressures. In the high-risk groups for TC, the TC:HDL-cholesterol ratio, and sysolic and diastolic blood pressures, the percentage of subjects with a family history of CVD and/or hypertension was higher than in the low-risk groups. For HDL, however, the percentage in the high-risk group was lower than in the low-risk group.

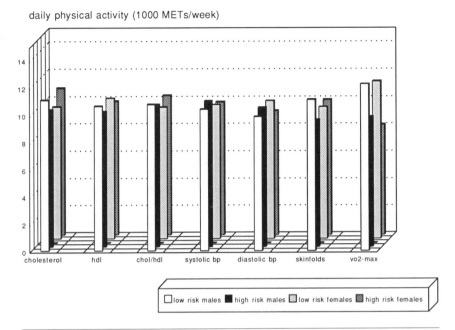

Figure 11.4   Mean values of the amount of daily physical activity measured over a period of 15 years for the high- and low-risk groups for the biological risk factors.

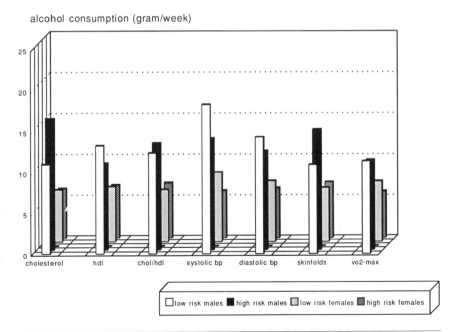

Figure 11.5   Mean values of alcohol consumption measured over a period of 15 years for the high- and low-risk groups for the biological risk factors.

smoking behaviour (gram tobacco/week)

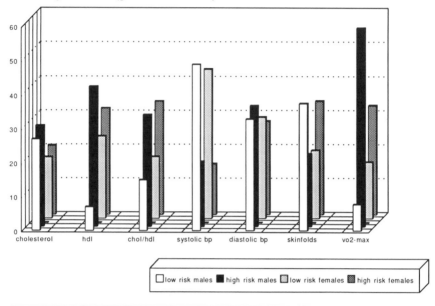

Figure 11.6   Mean values of the amount of tobacco smoked measured over a period of 15 years for the high- and low-risk groups for the biological risk factors.

type A-behaviour (score on JAS)

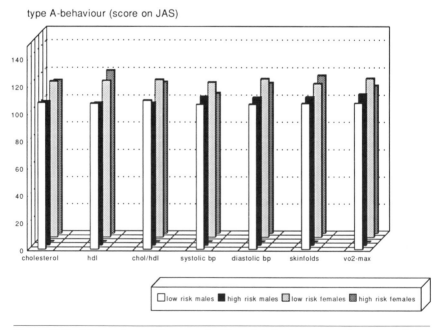

Figure 11.7   Mean values of the score for Type A behavior measured over a period of 6 years (1985-1991) for the high- and low-risk groups for the biological risk factors.

**Table 11.6   Percentages of Subjects With Family Histories
of Cardiovascular Disease and/or Hypertension
in the High- and Low-Risk Groups for Biological Risk Factors**

	Low risk	High risk
Total cholesterol (TC)		
Males	25.0%	33.3%
Females	34.4%	45.2%
HDL cholesterol		
Males	27.3%	26.3%
Females	45.2%	22.6%
TC:HDL		
Males	22.2%	30.8%
Females	30.0%	30.3%
Systolic BP		
Males	25.8%	37.5%
Females	31.0%	37.5%
Diastolic BP		
Males	28.6%	40.0%
Females	31.6%	38.2%

Note. BP = blood pressure.

The results of the MLR analysis are given in Tables 11.7-11.9. MLR analysis with continuous variables gives odds ratios based on one measurement-unit of change in the variable of interest. In order to meaningfully interpret the results, odds ratios were calculated for a 5-mm change in sum of skinfolds, a 1,000-MET change in daily physical activity, and a 10 ml · $kg^{-2/3}$ · min^{-1} change in $\dot{V}O_2$max.

Body fat seems to be related to all the lipoprotein variables, while smoking behavior is related only to HDL cholesterol and the TC:HDL-cholesterol ratio. Smoking behavior is also related (inversely) to systolic blood pressure. $\dot{V}O_2$max is influenced by the amount of daily physical activity and smoking behavior.

Discussion

Tracking

Both IPCs and the percentage of subjects who stayed in the high-risk quartile during follow-up were moderately high for the lipoprotein variables (with the exception of the correlation coefficient between the measurement of males' HDL cholesterol in 1977 and 1985 and the percentage of males who stayed in the high-risk group at the 1991 measurement of the TC:HDL-cholesterol ratio), indicating that early measurements of these risk factors are predictive of measurements later in life, even though the measurement period was as long as 15 years.

Table 11.7   Adjusted Odds Ratios, 95% Confidence Intervals (CI), and Goodness of Fit for the MLR Models for Lipoprotein Values

Model	Factor	Odds ratio	95% CI
Total cholesterol (TC) ($n = 105$)	Sum of skinfolds > 5 mm	1.66	1.29-2.12
	Goodness of fit: $C = 6.75$ ($p = 0.56$)		
HDL cholesterol ($n = 98$)	Sum of skinfolds > 5 mm		
	Males	0.80	0.50-1.29
	Females	1.26	1.01-1.58
	Smoking		
	Light smokers	2.13	0.74-6.08
	Heavy smokers	3.83	1.17-12.58
	Goodness of fit: $C = 10.69$ ($p = 0.22$)		
TC:HDL ($n = 108$)	Sum of skinfolds > 5 mm	1.73	1.33-2.24
	Smoking		
	Light smokers	1.41	0.50-3.95
	Heavy smokers	5.20	1.40-19.31
	Goodness of fit: $C = 2.65$ ($p = 0.95$)		

Table 11.8   Adjusted Odds Ratios, 95% Confidence Intervals (CI), and Goodness of Fit for the MLR Models for Blood Pressure (BP)

Model	Factor	Odds ratio	95% CI
Systolic BP ($n = 119$)	Smoking		
	Light smokers	0.46	0.16-1.38
	Heavy smokers	0.24	0.08-0.68
	Goodness of fit: $C = 9.98$ ($p = 0.27$)		
Diastolic BP ($n = 122$)	No relationship		

Comparison of our results with other studies in which the follow-up time and the age of the subjects at the start of the follow-up are comparable reveals that the values are similar for males but that ours are a bit higher for females (Clarke et al., 1978; Lauer et al., 1989; Orchard et al., 1983; Stuhldreher et al., 1991; Webber et al., 1991b).

The IPCs for systolic and diastolic blood pressures were much lower than those for the lipoprotein variables, especially since the scores of the measurements at age 13 were used as the initial values. Not only are low IPCs for blood pressure measurements found in other studies; higher coefficients for systolic blood pressure than for diastolic pressure are also found (Clarke et al., 1978; Lauer et al., 1989; Michels et al., 1987).

This lower tracking of systolic and diastolic blood pressure owes partly to the greater difficulty in obtaining reliable measurements during growth. Rapid changes in body size and proportions (e.g., changing upper-arm diameter) and the influence of measurement itself on blood pressure (Palti et al., 1988) are said to play an important role. To verify this, we calculated IPCs for the biological risk factors TC, HDL cholesterol, TC:HDL-cholesterol ratio, and systolic and diastolic blood pressures between the measurements at ages 21 and 27 (Table 11.10). The IPCs for systolic and diastolic pressures were more or less the same

Table 11.9   Adjusted Odds Ratios, 95% Confidence Intervals (CI), and Goodness of Fit for the MLR Models for $\dot{V}O_2$max and Body Fat

Model	Factor	Odds ratio	95% CI
$\dot{V}O_2$max ($n = 96$)	Smoking		
	Light smokers	1.22	0.40-3.70
	Heavy smokers	6.93	1.60-28.88
	Daily physical activity		
	1,000 METS	0.76	0.65-0.89
	Goodness of fit: $C = 3.26$ ($p = 0.92$)		
Body fat ($n = 101$)	No relationship		

Table 11.10   Interperiod Correlation Coefficients for Some Biological Risk Factors Between the Measurements at Ages 21 and 27

Total cholesterol (TC)	Males	.68
	Females	.64
HDL cholesterol	Males	.55
	Females	.66
TC:HDL	Males	.65
	Females	.76
Systolic BP	Males	.71
	Females	.67
Diastolic BP	Males	.56
	Females	.65

Note. BP = blood pressure.

as those for the lipoprotein variables, indicating that the problems of measuring blood pressure during growth were responsible for the low tracking.

Although tracking of daily physical activity over a 15-year period was very low (IPCs were less than .2, and the proportion of subjects who stayed in the high-risk quartiles was only a bit more than the random value of 25%), cardiopulmonary fitness and body fat showed moderate to high tracking. For all three parameters females tracked better than males. The IPC between the measurements of body fat with an interperiod of 15 years for males was low (.22), whereas the percentage that stayed in the high-risk quartile over the same period was moderate to high (52.4%). This indicates that the low IPCs were caused by the subjects' not belonging to the high-risk group; in relation to risk factors for CVD this low-risk group is not very interesting. This is one of the problems of describing tracking with correlation coefficients. In the epidemiologic literature there is little information about tracking of cardiopulmonary fitness, body fat, and daily physical activity. The few studies done on these subjects show comparable results (Beunen et al,. 1992; Casey et al., 1992; Lee et al., 1992).

To our knowledge no studies have been done to describe tracking of smoking behavior, alcohol consumption, or Type A behavior. In our study only smoking behavior tracked well, although both smoking behavior and alcohol consumption would be expected to track well because of the addictive character of tobacco and alcohol.

If we use the mean value of the four measurements of the adolescent period as the initial value to describe tracking, both the IPCs and the percentage of subjects who stayed in the high-risk quartile during follow-up are higher than when the single score at age 13 is used as initial value (see Table 11.1 and 11.2). This finding, also reported by Rosner and Willett (1988) and Gillman et al. (1991), may have important implications in relation to identifying subjects with high values of risk factors for CVD.

Influences on the Longitudinal Development of Biological Risk Factors

Before discussing the influences on the longitudinal development of biological risk factors, it needs to be noted that, especially for the systolic blood pressure and diastolic blood pressure models, it is questionable whether the "high-risk" group is really at high risk. For instance, subjects with a mean diastolic pressure, measured over a period of 15 years, of 83-84 mmHg (see Table 11.6) were classified in the high-risk group, which is, according to the WHO (1982), not extremely high. Because the same is true for systolic pressure, the analytical results for the blood pressure models have to be interpreted very carefully. This is probably the reason why no relationship between high risk for systolic and diastolic pressures and other risk factors was found, although in the literature body fat (Lauer & Clarcke, 1989) and alcohol consumption (Keil et al., 1991) are often mentioned as increasing both pressures. According to the summary statistics of goodness of fit, the models for the lipoprotein variables, cardiopulmonary fitness, and body fat fit the data well; although there are some difficulties in the interpretation of the MLR models for systolic and diastolic pressures, these models also seem to fit the data well.

• *Body fat*, measured as the sum of skinfolds, was highly related to high risk for TC, HDL cholesterol, and the TC:HDL-cholesterol ratio (see Table 11.7). The fact that body fat is related to lipoprotein levels is well established in cross-sectional studies (Bonora et al., 1992; Glueck et al., 1980; Jossa et al., 1991; Kikuchi et al., 1992), as well as in such longitudinal studies as the Framingham Heart Study (Hubert et al., 1983) and the Muscatine Study (Mahoney et al., 1991). The inverse relation between body fat and $\dot{V}O_2$max has also been shown (Jossa et al., 1991). Our results indicate that reduction of body fat has an important role in preventive strategies relative to hypercholesterolemia (Kemper et al., 1990).

• *Daily physical activity* and *cardiopulmonary fitness* were not present in the final MLR models of TC, HDL cholesterol, the TC:HDL-cholesterol ratio, and systolic and diastolic pressures, indicating that daily physical activity and cardiopulmonary fitness are not related to any of these biological risk factors. The fact that $\dot{V}O_2$max was not related to any of these risk factors is in agreement with some studies (Armstrong et al., 1991; Haskel et al., 1980), whereas other studies indicate that a lack of daily physical activity and low cardiopulmonary fitness are related negatively to HDL-cholesterol concentrations and positively to the TC:HDL-cholesterol ratio (Gibbons et al., 1983; Lakka et al., 1992). One of the reasons for the absence of any effects of daily physical activity and cardiopulmonary fitness on the studied biological risk factors may be that the relationship found in other studies can be explained by the inverse relationship between the amount of daily physical activity and cardiopulmonary fitness on the one hand and body fat on the other (Jossa et al., 1991).

The relationship between body fat and $\dot{V}O_2$max was also analyzed in our study by means of MLR. An increase of 5 mm in the sum of skinfolds gives an odds ratio of 1.43 (95% confidence interval = 1.13-1.81) for high risk for cardiopulmonary fitness; a decrease of 10 ml · $kg^{-2/3}$ · min^{-1} in $\dot{V}O_2$max gives an odds ratio of 0.64 (95% confidence interval = 0.49-0.85) for high risk for body fatness. Thus, an inverse relationship between the two variables was found, and although we did not find a direct relationship between the amount of daily physical activity and body fat, we did find one between daily physical activity and cardiopulmonary fitness. So perhaps daily physical activity and cardiopulmonary fitness have an indirect effect (through body fat) on high risk for TC, HDL cholesterol, and the TC:HDL-cholesterol ratio. Another possible reason for not finding any relationship between daily physical activity and the biological risk factors is the relatively low longitudinal stability (i.e., low tracking) of the amount of daily physical activity. Creating one value for an unstable variable over a longer period leads to a regression to the mean, which makes the difference between high and low daily physical activity relatively small.

• *Smoking behavior's* positive relation to a high risk for HDL cholesterol, the TC:HDL-cholesterol ratio, and cardiopulmonary fitness corresponds to results of other studies. In particular, the lowering effect of smoking on HDL-cholesterol concentrations has been shown numerous times (Handa et al., 1990; Jossa et al.,

1991; Mahoney et al., 1991; Willett et al., 1983). The preventive influence of smoking on high risk for systolic blood pressure looks perhaps a bit strange, but a similar relationship has been reported in other studies (Berglund & Wilhelmsen, 1975; Goldbourt & Medalie, 1977; Handa et al., 1990).

• *Alcohol consumption* was not related to the longitudinal development of any of the biological risk factors. These findings are in disagreement with other investigators, who report a positive effect of mild alcohol consumption on the concentration of the lipoproteins (Jossa et al., 1991a; Razzay et al., 1992). Results similar to ours, however, are reported by Webber et al. (1991a), who found no effect of alcohol consumption on the concentration of TC and HDL cholesterol. One of the reasons for the differing results is probably the age of the subjects. The two studies that report an effect of alcohol consumption on lipoprotein concentrations used subjects with mean ages of 40 to 50 years, whereas Webber et al. (1991a) studied subjects during adolescence and young adulthood, comparable to our subjects.

• *Type A behavior*, the score on the JAS, was present in none of the final MLR models. To study a possible relationship between Type A behavior and other risk factors for CVD, an MLR analysis was done with Type A behavior as a dependent variable. No relationship was found between Type A behavior and any of the other biological or lifestyle risk factors. Haynes et al. (1978), in the Framingham Heart Study, likewise found no relationship between Type A behavior and the other biological risk factors, although Type A behavior was not measured by the JAS. These and our results and the fact that Type A behavior seems to be related to CVD give support to the idea that Type A behavior is a possible independent risk factor for CVD.

• *Family history of CVD and/or hypertension* is said to be an important risk factor relative to lipoprotein levels and hypertension (Blonde et al., 1981). Although the proportions of subjects with a family history of CVD and/or hypertension were much higher in the high-risk group for TC and systolic and diastolic pressures than in the low-risk groups (Table 11.7), in none of our MLR models did this variable play a significant role. The reason for this is probably the way family history is measured. Only two questions, dealing with first-degree relatives, were asked of the subjects. To get a better idea about the influence of family history, we need to question the relatives themselves and, in addition, not only the first-degree relatives but also second- and even third-degree relatives.

Conclusions

The major results of our study, involving the relationships between lifestyle risk factors, genetic risk factors, and biological risk factors for CVD are summarized in Figure 11.8. Compared to our expectations (see Figure 11.1), no significant relationship between genetic risk factors and biological risk factors could be traced (Fig. 11.1, arrow A3). The possible relationships between lifestyle risk factors and biological risk factors (Fig. 11.1, arrows B and A1) and among

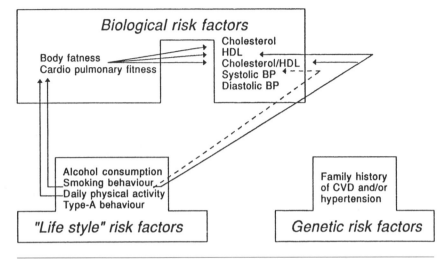

Figure 11.8   Relations between lifestyle risk factors, biological risk factors, and genetic risk factors for CVD. Solid arrows indicate a relation to high CVD risk. Dotted arrow indicates a relation to low CVD risk.

biological risk factors themselves (Fig. 11.1, arrow A2) are more or less present in this analysis.

We can conclude that in preventive strategies relative to the lipoproteins (decreasing TC, increasing HDL cholesterol, and decreasing the TC:HDL-cholesterol ratio), most attention must be paid to reducing body fat and smoking. Increasing cardiopulmonary fitness and the amount of daily physical activity can play a role in reducing body fatness.

References

Appels A., W. de Haes, J. Schuurman. Een Test ter Meting van het "Corornary Prone Behaviour Pattern" Type A; Ned. Tijdschrift v. Psychologie 34 (1979) 181-188.

Armstrong N., J. Williams, J. Badling, P. Gentle, B. Kirby. Cardiopulmonary fitness, physical activity patterns, and selected coronary risk factor variables in 11- to 16-year-olds. Pediatric Exercise Science 3 (1991) 219-228.

Åstrand P-O., K. Rodahl. (1986). Textbook of work physiology (3rd ed.). McGraw-Hill, New York.

Beaglehole R. International trends in coronary heart disease: Mortality, morbidity and risk factors. Epidemiol Rev 12 (1990) 1-15.

Berenson G.S., T.A. Foster, G.C. Frank, R.R. Frerichs, S.R. Srinivasan, A.W. Voors, L.S. Webber. Cardiovascular disease risk factor variables at the preschool age: The Bogalusa Heart Study. Circulation 57 (1978) 603-612.

Berglund G., L. Wilhelmsen. Factors related to blood pressure in a general population of Swedish men. Acta Med Scan 198 (1975) 291-298.

Beunen G., J. Lefevre, A.L. Claessens, R. Lysens, H. Maes, R. Renson, J. Simons, B. van den Eynde, B. van Reusel, C. van den Bossche. Age-specific correlation analysis of longitudinal physical fitness levels in men. Eur J Appl Physiol 64 (1992) 538-545.

Blonde C.V., L.S. Webber, T.A. Foster, G.S. Berenson. Parental history and cardiovascular disease risk factor variables in children. Prev Med 10 (1981) 25-37.

Bonora E., M. Zenere, P. Branzi, M. Bagnani, L. Maggiulli, F. Tosi, D. Travia, P. Cacciatori, M. Querena, R. Micciolo, M. Muggeo. Influence of body fat and its regional localization on risk factors for atherosclerosis in young men. Am J Epidemiol 135 (1992) 1271-1278.

Casey V.A., J.T. Dwyer, K.A. Coleman, I. Valadian. Body mass index from childhood to middle age: A 50-year follow-up. Am J Clin Nutr 56 (1992) 14-18.

Clarcke W.R., H.G. Schrott, P.E. Leaverton, W.E. Connor, R.M. Lauer. Tracking of blood lipids and blood pressures in school age children: The Muscatine Study. Circulation 58 (1978) 626-634.

Gibbons L.W., S.N. Blair, K.H. Cooper, M. Smith. Association between coronary heart disease risk factors and physical fitness in healthy adult women. Circulation 67:5 (1983) 977-983.

Gillman M.W., B. Rosner, D.A. Evans, M.E. Keough, L.A. Smith, J.A. Taylor, C.H. Hennekens. Use of multiple visits to increase blood pressure tracking correlations in childhood. Pediatrics 87:5 (1991) 708-711.

Glueck C.J., H.L. Taylor, D. Jacobs, J.A. Morrison, R. Beaglehole, O.D. Williams. Plasma high-density lipoprotein cholesterol: Association with measurements of body mass: The Lipid Research Clinics Program Prevalence Study. Circulation 62 (1980, Suppl IV) 62-69.

Goldbourt U., J.H. Medalie. Characteristics of smokers and ex-smokers among 10,000 adult males in Israel. Am J Epidemiol 105:1 (1977) 75-86.

Handa K., H. Tanaka, M. Shindo, S. Kono, J. Sasaki, K. Arakawa. Relationship of cigarette smoking to blood pressure and serum lipids. Atherosclerosis 84 (1990) 189-193.

Haskel W.L., H.L. Taylor, P.D. Wood, H. Schrott, G. Heiss. Strenuous physical activity, treadmill exercise test performance and plasma high-density lipoprotein cholesterol: The Lipid Research Clinics Program Prevalence Study. Circulation 62 (1980, Suppl IV) 53-61.

Haynes S.G., M. Feinleib, W.B. Kannel. The relationship of psychosocial factors to coronary heart disease in the Framingham Study. Am J Epidemiol 111:1 (1980).

Haynes S.G., S. Levine, N. Scotch, M. Feinleib, W.B. Kannel. The relationship of psychosocial factors to coronary heart disease in the Framingham Study. Am J Epidemiol 107:5 (1978).

Hosmer D.W., S. Lemeshow. (1989). Applied logistic regression. Wiley, New York.

Hubert H.B., M. Feinleib, P.M. McNamara, W.P. Castelli. Obesity as an independent risk factor for cardiovascular disease: A 26-year follow-up of participants in the Framingham Heart Study. Circulation 67:5 (1983) 968-977.

Jossa F., M. Trevisan, V. Kroghi, E. Farinaro, D. Giumetti, G. Fusco, R. Galaso, S. Frascatore, C. Mellone, M. Mancini. Correlates of high-density-lipoprotein cholesterol in a sample of healthy workers. Prev Med 20 (1991) 700-712.

Keil U., L. Chambless, B. Filipiak, U. Hrtel. Alcohol and blood pressure and its interaction with smoking and other behavioural variables: Results from the MONICA Augsburg Survey 1984-1985. J Hypertens 9 (1991) 491-498.

Kemper H.C.G. (ed.). (1985). Growth, health and fitness of teenagers: Longitudinal research in international perspective. Vol. 20 of: Medicine and sport science. Karger, Basel.

Kemper H.C.G., J. Snel, R. Verschuur, L. Storm-van Essen. Tracking of health and risk indicators of cardiovascular diseases from teenage to adult: Amsterdam Growth and Health Study. Prev Med 19 (1990) 642-655.

Kikuchi D.A., S.R. Srinivasan, D.W. Harsha, L.S. Webber, T.A. Sellers, G.S. Berenson. Relation of serum lipoprotein lipids and alipoproteins to obesity in children: The Bogalusa Heart Study. Prev Med 21 (1992) 177-190.

Lakka T.A., J.T. Salonen. Physical activity and serum lipids: A cross-sectional population study in eastern Finnish men. Am J Epidemiol 136 (1992) 806-818.

Lauer R.M., W.R. Clarcke. Childhood risk factors for high adult blood pressure: The Muscatine Study. Pediatrics 84:4 (1989) 633-641.

Lee A., R.S. Paffenbarger, C. Hsieh. Time trends in physical activity among college alumni, 1962-1988. Am J Epidemiol 135:8 (1992) 915-925.

Lemeshow S., D.H. Hosmer. A review of goodness of fit statistics for use in the development of logistic regression models. Am J Epidemiol 115:1 (1982) 92-106.

Mahoney L.T., R.M. Lauer, J. Lee, W.R. Clarcke. Factors affecting tracking of coronary heart disease risk factors in children: The Muscatine Study. Ann N Y Acad Sc 623 (1991) 120-132.

Manson J.E., H. Tosteson, P.M. Ridker, S. Satterfield, P. Hebert, G.T. O'Connor, J.E. Buring, C.H. Hennekens. The primary prevention of myocardial infarction. N Engl J Med 326:21 (1992) 1406-1416.

Michels V.M., E.J. Bergstrahl, V.R. Hoverman, W.M. O'Fallon, W.H. Weidman. Tracking and prediction of blood pressure in children. Mayo Clin Proc 62 (1987) 875-881.

Orchard T.J., R.P. Donahue, L.H. Kuller, P.N. Hodge, A.L. Drash. Cholesterol screening in childhood: Does it predict adult hypercholesterolemia? The Beaver County experience. J Pediatr 102 (1983) 187-691.

Palti H., R. Gofin, B. Adler, O. Grafstein, E. Belmaker. Tracking of blood pressure over an eight year period in Jerusalem school children. J Clin Epidemiol 41:8 (1988) 731-735.

Post G.B., H.C.G. Kemper, L. Storm-van Essen. Longitudinal changes in nutritional habits of teenagers: Differences in intake between schooldays and weekend days. Br J Nutr 57 (1987) 161-176.

Razzay G., K.W. Heaton, C.H. Bolton, A.O. Hughes. Alcohol consumption and its relation to cardiovascular risk factors in British women. Br Med J 304 (1992) 80-83.

Rosner B., C.H. Hennekens, E.H. Kass, W.E. Miall. Age-specific correlation analysis of longitudinal blood pressure data. Am J Epidemiol 106 (1977) 306-313.

Rosner B, W. Willett. Interval estimates for correlation coefficients corrected for within-person variation: Implications for study design and hypothesis testing. Am J Epidemiol 127:2 (1988) 377-386.

Stuhldreher W., R. Donahue, A. Drash, L. Kullrer, M. Gloninger, T. Orchard. The Beaver County Lipid Study: Sixteen-year cholesterol tracking. Ann N Y Acad Sci 623 (1991) 466-468.

Verschuur R. (1987). Daily physical activity and health: Longitudinal changes during the teenage period. Thesis, Universiteit van Amsterdam, de Vrieseborch, Haarlem SO 12.

Wallace R.B., R.A. Anderson. Blood lipids, lipid-related measures, and the risk of atherosclerotic cardiovascular disease. Epidemiol Rev 9 (1987) 95-119.

Webber L.S., S. Hunter, C. Johnson, S.R. Srinivasan, G.S. Berenson. Smoking, alcohol and oral contraceptives: Effects on lipids during adolescence and young adulthood: Bogalusa Heart Study. Ann N Y Acad Sci 623 (1991a) 135-154.

Webber L.S., S.R. Srinivasan, W.A. Wattigney, G.S. Berenson. Tracking of serum lipids and lipoproteins from childhood to adulthood. Am J Epidemiol 133:9 (1991b) 884-889.

Weiner J.S., J.A. Lourie. (1968). Human biology: A guide to field methods. Blackwell, Oxford.

Willett W., C.H. Hennekens, W. Castelli, B. Rosner, D. Evans, J. Taylor, E.H. Kass. Effects of cigarette smoking on fasting triglyceride, total cholesterol and HDL-cholesterol in women. Am Heart J 105:3 (1983) 417-421.

World Health Organization. (1982). Prevention of coronary heart disease (Technical Report Series 678). World Health Organization, Geneva.

Chapter 12

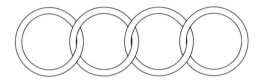

Effects of Weight-Bearing Physical Activity on the Development of Peak Bone Density

Han C.G. Kemper, Desiree C. Welten, & Willem van Mechelen

Osteoporosis is a major worldwide public health problem because it increases fracture risk in the aging population. In the United States, with a population 16 times that of the Netherlands, more than half a million vertebral fractures and a quarter of a million hip fractures occur (Peck et al., 1987) each year. In the Netherlands the annual number of hip fractures increased between 1972 and 1990 almost 3 times, from 4,500 to 12,000 (Health Consultancy, 1991). Osteoporosis is characterized by a significant reduction of bone mass. The reduction may occur during the growing years or be acquired later on in life. Because most available treatments of established osteoporosis do not significantly restore bone structure of previously lost bone, there is a growing emphasis on prevention of bone loss, particularly in the light of the constantly growing elderly population.

At present there are two approaches to the prevention of this disease: (a) reduction of the rate of bone loss during aging, especially in women after menopause, and (b) increasing peak bone mass at skeletal maturity (Matkovic et al., 1990). This chapter concentrates on the second approach: a strategy to increase bone mass during the growing years in order to reach maximal amount of bone mass at the time that peak bone density is achieved. Healthy lifestyles, such as high calcium intake from diet (see chapter 13) and high weight–bearing activities (Marans et al., 1992) are thought to influence peak bone density (Fig. 12.1).

Although considerable attention has been given to the onset of bone loss, the age at which peak bone mass is reached is not clear. Recent studies conclude that peak bone density may occur in early adolescence at age 17 in girls (Snow-Harter & Marcus, 1991) or in late adolescence following puberty (Gilsanz et al., 1988). Recker et al. (1992) demonstrated in a longitudinal study that gain of

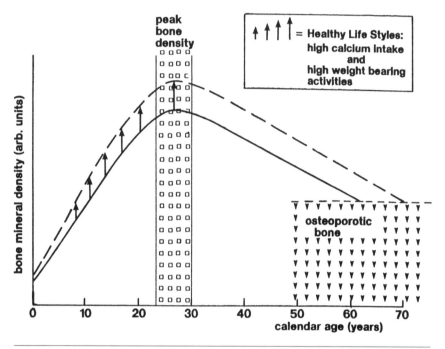

Figure 12.1   Model of the hypothesized influence of a healthy lifestyle, including high weight-bearing activities and high calcium intake during youth, upon peak bone density and attainment of critical values at older ages.

bone mass occurred in women in their late teens and 20s after linear growth had stopped in the entire skeleton and was completed by about age 30. This recent study indicates that peak bone mass is reached some time during the end of the second decade of life.

Bone is a dynamic tissue that continuously undergoes remodeling. Factors known to affect this process include age, nutritional and hormonal status, and physical activity (MacDougall et al., 1992). Although it has become axiomatic that physical activity benefits the skeleton, this idea is not supported by strong evidence. Most of the evidence is from cross-sectional studies that leave open the possibility of ascertainment bias: In most reports athletic subjects are compared with nonathletic subjects, or comparisons are made of the bone density of the playing and nonplaying arm in tennis players. In the few intervention studies examining the effects of exercise on bone density little attention has been given to understanding the type, intensity, duration, and frequency of exercise that are optimal for bone. Most of these studies concern trained postmenopausal women (Krolner et al., 1983; Smith et al., 1989), with a length of exercise intervention varying from 8 to 48 months.

In our own longitudinal study the male and female subjects reached ages 26 to 29 in 1991. Because the late 20s are thought to be the point at which peak bone density is reached, bone mineral density (BMD) of the lumbar region in this population was determined by dual X-ray absorptiometry. To demonstrate the proposed relationship between loading of the skeleton and bone density during youth over a long period, the weight-bearing activities of a group of healthy females and males were measured over a period of almost 15 years six times using cross-check interviews of their habitual physical activity (Verschuur, 1987). On the basis of differences in the amount of weight-bearing activities during the subjects' teens and twenties, a comparison was made of bone mineral density in the lumbar spine at a mean age of 28 years. The purpose of this comparison was to determine if weight-bearing activities during the growing years can affect the peak bone density of young adults.

Methods

A group of 98 females and 84 males were measured longitudinally from ages 13 to 18. Between 1977 and 1991 measurements were made six times of anthropometric, physiological, and psychological characteristics (see chapter 3). The subjects' lifestyles were also evaluated six times, by cross-check interviews of nutritional intake (Post, 1989) and habitual physical activity (Verschuur, 1987). In Table 12.1 the means, standard errors of the mean, and standard deviations of age, height, body weight, and percentage of body fat of the subjects in 1991 are presented. Percentage of body fat is estimated from body weight and four skinfolds (Durnin & Rahaman, 1967).

At age 27 the BMD of the lumbar region (L2-L4) of all subjects was measured by dual X-ray absorptiometry using a Norland XR-26. Scanning was performed in the Department of Nuclear Medicine of the Academic Hospital at Vrije Universiteit, Amsterdam, with subjects recumbent. A photomultiplier tube recorded transmission from a narrowly collimated X-ray source located under the scanning table. The whole procedure was finished within 10 to 15 minutes. Physical activity was measured longitudinally at six points in time: four annual measurements (1977-1980) covering ages 13 to 17 (the adolescent period), in 1985 at age 21 (young-adult age), and in 1991 at age 27 (adult age). We considered

Table 12.1   Statistics on Age, Height, Weight, and Percent Body Fat, Measured in 1991

| | Men (n = 84) | | | Women (n = 98) | | |
	M	SE	SD	M	SE	SD
Age (y)	27.1	0.09	0.79	27.1	0.08	0.75
Height (cm)	183.1	0.70	6.43	170.0	0.62	6.14
Weight (kg)	75.4	0.92	8.46	63.3	0.79	7.82
Body fat (%)	14.4	0.45	4.14	24.6	0.49	4.86

only activities that had a weight-bearing component (running; stair climbing; such sports activities as basketball and calisthenics). Weight-supported activities in which weight bearing was less important (such as bicycling and swimming) were neglected.

The weight-bearing activities (WBA) were selected from a cross-check interview measuring all habitual physical activities covering a period of 3 months prior to the interview. The activities were limited to those with a minimal intensity level of approximately 4 times the basal metabolic rate (4 METs) and with a duration of at least 5 minutes. The scored activities were subdivided into three levels of intensity: (a) *light*, equivalent to 4-7 METs; (b) *medium-heavy*, equivalent to 7-10 METs; and (c) *heavy*, equivalent to 10 METs or more. The total weighted activity score per week above a level of 4 METs was calculated as the product of time spent per level of intensity times a fixed value: 1 for light, 2 for medium-heavy, and 3 for heavy activities. The scores of the three levels were added to a total activity score in minutes per week.

From the longitudinal information on WBA, the males and females were divided into high- and low-WBA groups on the basis of quartiles (P_{75} and P_{25}). Three periods were considered: (a) the adolescent period, ages 13-17, (b) the period between ages 13 and 21, and (c) the total period between ages 13 and 27. For the adolescent period, the quartile with the highest WBA (P_{75}) of the four measurements was compared with the quartile of the lowest WBA (P_{25}), with respect to the mean of the BMD. In the second period, the division into quartiles was based on the sum of the mean value of WBA activities over the first four measurements and the fifth measurement. In the third period, the sum of WBA activities of the mean of the first four plus the fifth and sixth measurements was used for the quartile division.

Differences in BMD between the high- and low-WBA groups over the different periods were tested with two-tail *t*-tests at a 5% significance level.

Results

Among the 27-year-old males, the high-WBA groups showed higher BMD (1.2-1.3 g/cm^2) than the low-WBA groups (1.1 g/cm^2). The differences were significant ($p < .01$) and independent of the period over which the WBA groups were arranged (Fig. 12.2). Among the 27-year-old females, the high-WBA groups showed a higher BMD (1.2-1.3 g/cm^2) than the low-WBA groups (1.05-1.1 g/cm^2). The differences between WBA groups, however, were only significant ($p < .05$) when the quartiles were arranged on the basis of the WBA data of the adolescent period (Fig. 12.3).

Discussion

The most effective design for ascertaining the effects of an active lifestyle upon bone mass is the randomized intervention trial. However, these trials are difficult to perform on young people and, more importantly, cannot be continued over a

BMD and Weight Bearing Activities
Males

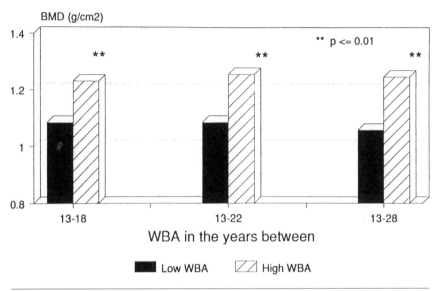

Figure 12.2   Means of bone mineral density (BMD) in males with relatively low and high weight-bearing activity (WBA). BMD was measured at age 27. WBA was measured over three periods.

long period. Our longitudinal study cannot be considered an intervention study; on the contrary, it was deliberately designed as a descriptive prospective study (Kemper et al., 1983). Because our longitudinal study covered a period of almost 15 years, descriptive data about the subjects' physical activity pattern became available during that relatively long period. When preparation for the Amsterdam Growth and Health Study began in 1974, a follow-up period of 15 years was not foreseen. However, the low dropout rate of the subjects in combination with continuing financial support from subsidizing bodies enabled us to continue the study. In 1974 dual X-ray absorptiometry measurements were not available; if they had been, we could have studied the change of BMD over time during the subjects' teens and 20s. Given this technical limitation it is possible to relate the WBA activities to the BMD measured at age 27 only. Even though it is not certain that at this age peak bone density is reached, BMD was measured in this normal healthy population of males and females. Some controversy exists about the age of peak bone density in youth. In general, it is assumed that maximal bone mass is reached at some time during the third decade of life. However, data indicating that peak bone density is reached much earlier exist (directly after puberty) (Snow-Harter & Marcus, 1991). The reasons for this controversy can be explained with reference to the studies of Sambrook et al. (1987), who

BMD and Weight Bearing Activities
Females

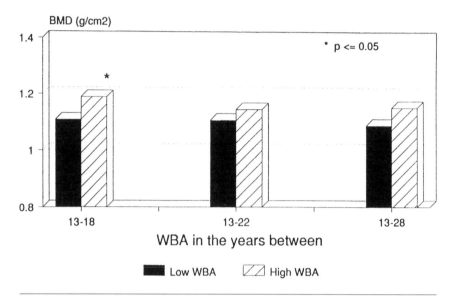

Figure 12.3 Means of bone mineral density (BMD) in females with relatively low and high weight-bearing activity (WBA). BMD was measured at age 27. WBA was measured over three periods.

explained using computer modeling that changes in BMD vs. age are confounded in cross-sectional studies because of inadequate sample sizes.

Our BMD measurements were taken in the lumbar region using dual X-ray absorptiometry. Because the detector recognizes all transmitted photons, estimates of bone density by this technique include not only the vertebral trabecular bone but also such cortical elements as spinous and transverse processes. The precision error of the technique is known to be less than 1% (Mazess, 1981; Sievänen et al., 1992).

Figures 12.4 and 12.5 provide frequency distributions of BMD for males and females compared with Dutch age-related norms. The results indicate that both distributions tend to shift to the right; i.e., to a higher BMD compared with Dutch age-related modus: Only two males and no females reached values lower then −2 standard deviations of the norm population. These data confirm that our population is a relatively healthy sample out of the Dutch population.

The same holds for the subjects' habitual physical activity pattern. In Table 12.2 the mean times per week given to light, medium-heavy, and heavy activities are summarized. During their teens (ages 13-17) boys and girls spent, respectively, about 8 h/wk and 7 h/wk in activities with an intensity of more than 4 METs (equivalent to walking). At ages 21 and 27 the total time spent on light activities

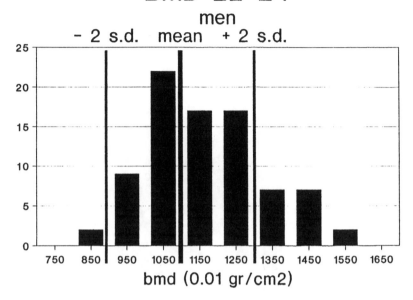

Figure 12.4   Frequency distribution of bone mineral density (BMD) in men. The mean and ±2 standard deviations of age-related norms in the Netherlands are indicated.

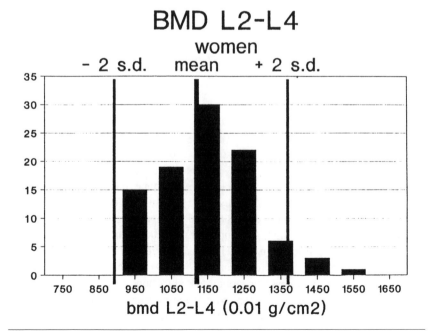

Figure 12.5   Frequency distribution of bone mineral density (BMD) in women. The mean and ±2 standard deviations of age-related norms in the Netherlands are indicated.

Table 12.2   Statistics on Physical Activities in Males and Females From Interviews Over the Three Measurement Periods

		Adolescent (13-18 years)		Young adult (21 years)		Adult (27 years)	
		Males	Females	Males	Females	Males	Females
Light (min/wk)	M	198.02	220.31	262.37	301.67	261.68	309.17
	SE	13.07	10.26	24.79	17.77	21.54	17.90
	SD	119.83	101.55	172.33	172.33	197.43	177.23
Medium-heavy (min/wk)	M	164.86	169.13	122.43	113.03	102.00	93.62
	SE	6.22	9.64	6.27	6.29	5.64	5.30
	SD	57.02	95.40	55.41	61.02	51.73	52.47
Heavy (min/wk)	M	103.49	18.06	75.81	24.16	66.81	28.58
	SE	11.69	4.17	9.54	4.88	7.48	4.65
	SD	107.15	41.31	84.23	47.36	68.60	46.03
Total (METs)	M	3680.5	2857.0	3355.5	2898.3	3074.6	2824.9
	SE	158.6	119.2	181.1	134.3	159.6	121.09
	SD	1453.8	1180.1	1599.7	1301.8	1464.4	1198.7
Weight-bearing activities: total activities (%)	M	87.5	81.5	87.7	84.6	87.5	85.2

Note. The activities were categorized as light, medium-heavy, or heavy.

increased, but the total time spent on medium-heavy and heavy activities decreased among males. The total amount of METs spent per week therefore decreased with age in males from about 3,700 to 3,000, but remained stable in females, at a level of 2,800 METs. The amount of WBA time as a percentage of total activity time also remains relatively stable over the years, at a percentage of 87% in males and between 81% and 85% in females.

The relationship between muscle strength and BMD has become an important research topic over the past few years as researchers have realized that there is a continuous interaction between muscle force and bone mass via muscle attachments to bone (Snow-Harter & Marcus, 1991). Results of correlations of BMD with muscle strength measurements show indeed positive relationships with explosive leg strength (standing high jump) and with static arm strength (arm pull). Our results were significant ($p < .01$) for explosive leg strength ($r = .31$) in females (Fig. 12.6) and static arm strength ($r = .29$) in males (Fig. 12.7).

Cardiorespiratory fitness appears unrelated to bone density: In both males and females we found no significant correlation between the directly measured maximal oxygen uptake ($\dot{V}O_2max$) (relative to body weight) and BMD. Although studies report significant correlations between estimated relative $\dot{V}O_2max$ and BMD, Nelson et al. (1988) and Dalsky (1988), who measured $\dot{V}O_2max$, did not

Explosive leg strength
women

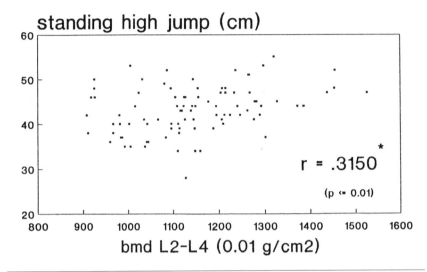

standing high jump (cm)

r = .3150 *

(p ← 0.01)

bmd L2-L4 (0.01 g/cm2)

Figure 12.6   Correlation diagram of explosive leg strength with bone mineral density (BMD) in women.

Static arm strength
men

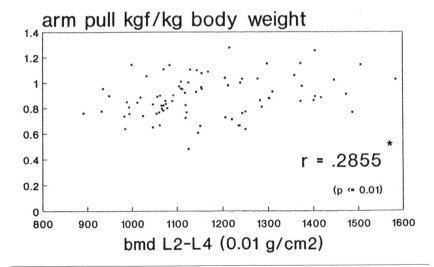

arm pull kgf/kg body weight

r = .2855 *

(p ← 0.01)

bmd L2-L4 (0.01 g/cm2)

Figure 12.7   Correlation diagram of static arm strength with bone mineral density (BMD) in men.

find significant correlations. These latter results lend more credibility to the hypothesis that endurance activities are not independent predictors of BMD and that the relationship is likely through the weight-bearing stimulation that these long-term activities provide to the skeleton.

There is also the possibility of an interaction effect between activity (as WBA) and nutrition (calcium intake) as stated by Kelly et al. (1990). In our study the comparison of WBA with lumbar BMD showed that the teenage period is an important decade for the construction of the maximal amount of BMD attained at the end of the third decade: Comparison of high- and low-WBA groups based on measurements between ages 13 and 17 resulted in significant differences in maximal BMD at age 27. That in males the differences in BMD are as large in the adolescent period as they are when WBA was measured at ages 21 or 27 and in females even larger when WBA were measured at ages 21 or 27 shows the importance of a physically active lifestyle early during adolescence.

Conclusions

From our results we can conclude that in a group of healthy males and females the lumbar BMD around age 27 is significantly and positively related to the amount of WBA carried out during their teens.

Our longitudinal study indicates that peak BMD may be influenced by a high level of WBA. The study stresses the importance of a sufficient amount of physical activity during growth and development in order to reach the highest peak bone mass at young-adult age and therefore to delay the attainment of critical minimal bone mass resulting in osteoporosis and fractures at an older age. These results, however, need to be confirmed in a true experimental design; in our study the differences in peak bone density can be explained by self-selection of activity level during puberty.

References

Dalsky G., K.S. Stocke, A.A. Ehsaui. Weightbearing exercise training and lumbar bone mineral content in post-menopausal women. Ann Intern Med 108 (1988) 824-828.

Durnin J.V.G.A., M.M. Rahaman. The assessment of the amount of fat in the human body from measurements of skinfolds thickness. Br J Nutr 21 (1967) 681-689.

Gilsanz D.T., T.F. Roe, M. Carlson. Vertebral bone density in children: Effect of puberty. Radiology 166 (1988) 847-850.

Health Consultancy: Commision Osteoporosis. (1991). Prevention of osteoporosis (Publication 91/21). Gezondheidsraad, Den Haag.

Kelly P.J., J.A. Eisman, P.N. Sambrook. Interaction of genetic and environmental influences on peak bone density. Osteoporos Int 1 (1990) 56-60.

Kemper H.C.G., H.J.P. Dekker, M.G. Ootjers, G.B. Post, J. Snel, P.G. Splinter, L. Storm-van Essen, R. Verschuur. Growth and health of teenagers in the

Netherlands. Survey of multidisciplinary longitudinal studies and comparison to recent results of a Dutch study. Int J Sports Med 4 (1983) 202-214.

Krolner B., B. Taft, S.P. Nielsen. Physical exercise as prophylaxis against involutional bone loss: A controlled trial. Clin Sci 64 (1983) 541-546.

MacDougall J.D., C.E. Weber, J. Martin, S. Ormerod, A. Chesley, E.V. Younglai, C.L. Gordon, C.J.R. Blimkie. Relationship among running mileage, bone density, and serum testosterone in male runners. J Appl Physiol 73:3 (1992) 1165-1170.

Marans R., B. Drinkwater, G. Dalsky, J. Dufek, D. Raab, C. Slemenda, C. Snow-Harter. Osteoporosis and exercise in women. Med Sci Sports Exerc 24:6 (1992) S301-S307.

Matkovic V., D. Fontana, C. Tominac, P. Goel, C.H. Chestnut. Factors that influence peak bone mass formation: A study of calcium balance and the inheritance of bone mass in adolescent females. Am J Clin Nutr 52 (1990) 878-888.

Mazess R.B. (1991). The noninvasive measurment of skeletal mass. In: W.A. Peck, (ed.), Bone and mineral research annual 1. Elsevier, New York.

Nelson M.E., C.N. Meredith, B. Dawson-Hughes. Hormone and bone mineral status in endurance-trained and sedentary postmenopausal women. J Clin Endocrinol Metab 66 (1988) 927-933.

Peck W.A., L.B. Riggs, N.H. Bell. (1987). Physician's resource manual on osteoporosis. National Osteoporosis Foundation, Washington, DC.

Post G.B. (1989). Nutrition in adolescence: A longitudinal study in dietary patterns from teenager to adult. PhD thesis, Wageningen, Vrieseborch, Haarlem.

Recker R.R., K.M. Davies, S.M. Hinders, R.P. Heaney, M.R. Stegman, D.B. Kimmel. Bone gain in young adult women. JAMA 268:17 (1992) 2403-2408.

Sambrook P.N., J.A. Eisman, S.M. Furlev, N.A. Pocock. Computer modelling and analyses of cross-sectional bone density studies with respect to age and to menopause. J Bone Miner Res 2:2 (1987) 109-114.

Sievänen H., P. Oja, I. Vuori. Precision of dual-energy X-ray absorptiometry in determining bone mineral density and content of various skeletal sites. J Nucl Med 33 (1992) 1137-1142.

Smith E.L., C. Gilligan, M. McAdam, C.P. Ensign, P.E. Smith. Deterring bone loss by exercise intervention in premenopausal and postmenopausal women. Calcif Tissue Int 44 (1989) 312-321.

Snow-Harter C., R. Marcus. (1991). Exercise, bone mineral density, and osteoporosis. In: Exercise and sport sciences reviews, ACSM Series vol. 19. William & Wilkins, Baltimore.

Verschuur R. (1987). Daily physical activity and health: Longitudinal changes during the teenage period. Thesis, Universiteit van Amsterdam, de Vrieseborch, Haarlem, SO 12.

Chapter 13

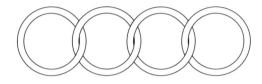

Bone Mineral Density and Dietary Calcium Intake

Desiree C. Welten, G. Bertheke Post, & Han C.G. Kemper

Osteoporosis is characterized by a reduction in bone mass, which increases susceptibility to hip fractures. Osteoporosis affects 25% to 30% of women over 65. It is a major health concern in the Netherlands because of the constantly increasing number of elderly people in the population. In 1980, 9.3% of the Dutch were aged 65 to 79 years, and 2.2% were aged 80 years or older. In 1991 the figures rose to 10% and 2.9%, respectively. It is expected that by 2010 the figures will rise to about 11.2% for ages 65 to 79 and 3.8% for ages 80 and over (Centraal Bureau voor de Statistiek, 1992).

There is a growing emphasis on osteoporosis prevention instead of treatment. Two preventive approaches can be made: (a) increasing the level of the peak bone mineral mass in early adulthood and (b) reducing the rate of bone loss, especially in women after the menopause. A maximal bone mass at skeletal maturity is considered to be the best protection against age-related bone loss and subsequent fracture risk (Matkovic, 1992). This chapter focuses on peak bone mass.

One of the determinants of peak bone mass is nutrition, with calcium as the most important nutrient. Although most studies have demonstrated that increased calcium intake has a positive effect on peak skeletal mass (Halioua et al., 1989; Johnston et al., 1992; Kanders et al., 1988; Matkovic et al., 1979; Matkovic et al., 1990; Metz et al., 1991; Picard et al., 1988; Recker et al., 1992; Sandler et al., 1985; Sentipal et al., 1991), this relationship is not supported by strong evidence: first, because the effect of calcium on peak bone density has not been extensively investigated (Chestnut, 1991; Cumming, 1990) and, second, because nearly all studies have ecological, cross-sectional, or retrospective designs. Ecological and cross-sectional studies are particularly prone to bias due to confounding. In retrospective studies the ability to recall the calcium intake in the distant past is limited. Finally, uncertainty remains concerning the age at which peak skeletal mass is attained. In the studies just mentioned, the assumptions regarding which period the peak is achieved in ranges from adolescence to the late 20s.

It has been suggested that several lifestyle factors interact with calcium intake and bone mass, including vitamin D, protein, fiber, caffeine, and alcohol, as well as physical activity and smoking. Insufficient exposure to daylight and the insufficient intake of vitamin D may impair calcium balance, and high protein and fiber intakes may have adverse effects on calcium balance. It is suggested that smoking and consumption of caffeine and alcohol are negatively correlated and physical activity positively correlated with calcium intake (Cummings, 1985; Toss, 1992). However, whether these lifestyle factors are of any significance for bone mass is still uncertain.

In this study only the interaction of protein intake and physical activity with calcium intake and bone mass is examined. In Dutch teenagers 80% of calcium intake is supplied by dairy products (Post, 1989). These foods are rich in calcium as well as in protein. Because the effects of a high calcium intake on calcium balance appear to be offset by the high levels of protein found in dairy products, the interaction of protein intake on the calcium intake and bone mineral density (BMD) is an important issue especially in our "dairy country." In chapter 12 a high amount of weight-bearing activity (WBA) during youth is reported to induce a significantly higher lumbar BMD. If WBA is also significantly related to calcium intake, then care must be taken in interpreting the effects of calcium intake on peak bone mass.

In our longitudinal study, observations were made over a 15-year period in youth. In 1991 the male and female subjects reached the age of 27. Although it is not certain that at this age peak bone density is achieved, we assumed that in the late 20s the peak occurs (see chapter 12). Therefore, in 1991 bone density of the lumbar spine was measured. Calcium intake was estimated six times during the 15-year period (Post, 1989). Thus, the purpose of the present study is, first, to examine the relationship between calcium intake during adolescence and young adulthood and the development of peak bone density in males and females at age 27. Second, the influence of protein intake and physical activity on this relationship is studied.

Methods

Subjects

The selection of the subjects as well as the study design is described elsewhere (see chapters 1 and 2). Between 1977 and 1991, 84 males and 95 females participated in this survey of calcium intake and peak bone mass. The mean, standard error, and standard deviation of age, height, weight, and body fat, measured in 1991, are shown for these subjects in Table 12.1, page 227.

Bone Densitometry

BMD of the lumbar spine (L2-L4) was determined by dual X-ray absorptiometry (Norland XR-26) in 27-year-old subjects. Scanning was performed in the Department of Nuclear Medicine of the Academic Hospital of Vrije Universiteit, Amsterdam, with subjects recumbent. The mean coefficient of variation of dual X-ray absorptiometry for repeated measurements of lumbar BMD is 1.7% (Sievänen, 1992).

Dietary Intake

Dietary intake was assessed longitudinally, six times. In the adolescent period (ages 13-17) four annual measurements were done, starting in 1977 and ending in 1980. The next measurement was at age 21, followed by a sixth assessment in 1991 in 27-year-old subjects. To minimize seasonal variation the measurements took place during the same months each year (February to June).

A modification of the cross-check dietary history interview was used to ascertain the nutrient intake. This food consumption method uses a quantitative food questionnaire that asks about the food eaten during meals as well as between meals. Data were collected separately for weekdays and weekend days. Only food items eaten at least once every 2 weeks were recorded. Amounts were recorded in household measures. All interviews were carried out by the same nutritionist (G.B. Post). Daily calcium and protein intakes were calculated using the computerized Dutch Food Composition Table (NEVO, 1989) and were related to body height.

Physical Activity

In our subjects WBA was measured six times over a period of 15 years by cross-check interviews of their habitual physical activities. A more extensive description of this process is given in chapter 12.

Statistical Methods

Subjects (males and females, separately) were divided into low and high calcium intake groups based on quartiles. Three periods were considered: (a) the adolescent

Table 13.1   Statistics on Bone Mineral Density (BMD) and Mean Calcium Intake

Characteristics	Men ($n = 84$)			Women ($n = 95$)		
	M	SE	SD	M	SE	SD
BMD (0.001 g/cm^2)	1,170	17	156	1,143	14	136
Ca intake (mg/day)						
Age 13-17	1,100	40	366	941	31	304
Age 21	1,403	67	591	1,112	51	484
Age 27	1,435	63	575	1,204	44	429

period (ages 13-18), (b) the period between ages 13 and 22, and (c) the total period between ages 13 and 28. In the adolescent period the quartile with the highest calcium intake (P_{75}) during the four measurements was compared with the quartile of the lowest calcium intake (P_{25}). In the second period the quartile division was based on the calcium intake of the mean value over the first four measurements and the fifth measurement. In the last period the sum of the calcium intake of the mean of the first four and the fifth and sixth measurements was used for the quartile division. Values for BMD of subjects grouped in the lowest quartile were compared with BMDs of subjects in the highest quartile of calcium intake. T-tests with a 5% significance level were used to test for differences in means. The same statistical methods were used for protein intake.

Results

The mean calcium intakes for the adolescent (ages 13-17) and for ages 21 and 27 are reported in Table 13.1 for both sexes, as is the BMD at age 27. The longitudinal results of the relationship between calcium intake and lumbar BMD at age 27 are presented in Figures 13.1 and 13.2. A relatively high daily calcium

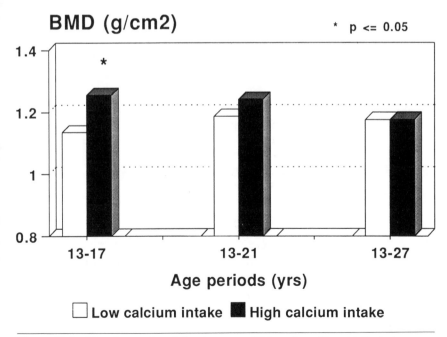

Figure 13.1   Mean bone mineral density at age 27 in males with a relatively low (< P_{25}) and high (> P_{75}) calcium intake for the age periods 13-17, 13-21, and 13-27 years.

Calcium intake
females

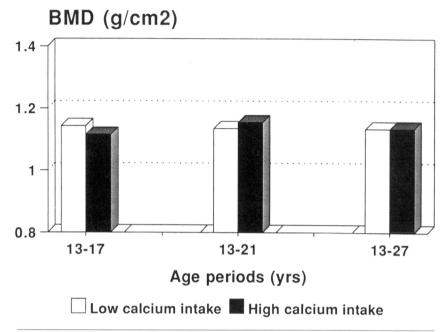

Figure 13.2 Mean bone mineral density at age 27 in females with a relatively low (< P_{25}) and high (> P_{75}) calcium intake for the age periods 13-17, 13-21, and 13-27 years.

intake (> P_{75}) in males during the adolescent period resulted in a significantly higher peak bone mass ($p < .05$) at age 27 compared with a relatively low daily calcium intake (< P_{25}). This relationship was not found in adolescent girls. When the groups were divided into relatively high and low calcium intake based on the age periods 13 to 21 and 13 to 27 years, no significant differences were found in peak bone mass at age 27 in either sex.

Discussion

The present study shows that a relatively high calcium intake in the nutrition of boys during their teens results in significantly higher lumbar BMD at age 27. This relation is not found in females. Analysis of distribution of BMD in 27-year-old men and women demonstrates that our study population is a relatively healthy sample of the Dutch population (chapter 12). Figures 13.3 and 13.4 show that the mean calcium intake in boys and girls during the adolescent period meets the current Dutch recommended dietary allowances (DRDA) for this age group. At ages 21 and 27 the mean calcium intake is above the DRDA for both sexes.

MALES

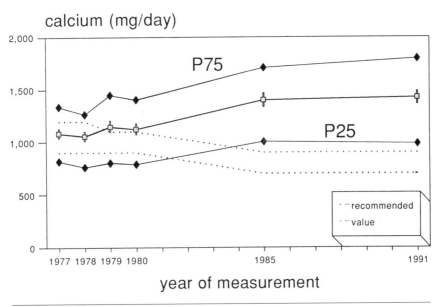

Figure 13.3   Mean calcium intake with corresponding P_{25} and P_{75} values in males over a period of 15 years. Indicated also is the Dutch recommended daily allowance for different ages.

Our results can be explained by the fact that especially in adolescent boys the low calcium intake group ($< P_{25}$) is far below the DRDA of 900 to 1,200 mg/day and in adolescent girls the low calcium intake group approximates the DRDA of 700 to 1,000 mg/day. At higher ages the low calcium intake group meets the DRDA of 700 to 900 mg/day in females and is even above recommended values in males.

Biological age, chronological age, and calcium intake are the main determinants of bone mass in adolescence (Sentipal et al., 1991). In our study the differences in skeletal age in adolescents are much greater than the 1-year difference in calendar age. The interindividual differences in skeletal age of boys and girls of the same calendar age can be as much as 5 or 6 years (Kemper, 1985). These differences result in relatively large differences in height. Therefore calcium intake, as well as protein intake, is related to height in order to account for these differences.

Physical activity is a positive determinant of bone mass. Kemper et al. (chapter 12 of this monograph) concluded that in a group of healthy males and females the lumbar BMD at age 27 is significantly and positively related to the amount of WBA carried out during their teens. There is possibly an interaction between mechanical stress and calcium intake (Kanders et al., 1988). Increased

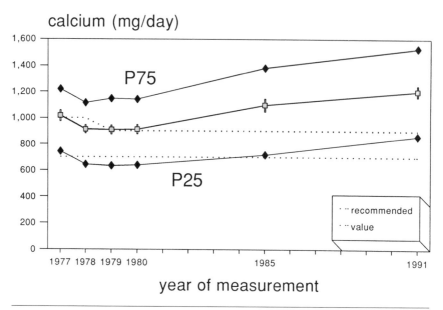

Figure 13.4   Mean calcium intake with corresponding P$_{25}$ and P$_{75}$ values in females over a period of 15 years. Indicated also is the Dutch recommended daily allowance for different ages.

physical activity may enhance energy intake, and calcium intake may increase secondarily (Toss, 1992). In our study, in the high calcium intake groups the mean values of WBA seem higher than in the low calcium intake groups at almost all age periods in both males and females (Figs. 13.5 and 13.6). The differences are significant in boys of ages 13 to 17 ($p < .01$) and in females during the age periods 13 to 21 years ($p < .05$) and 13 to 27 years ($p < .05$). These results can be explained from the different absolute levels in physical activity. In teenage boys, especially, the absolute level of physical activity is relatively high. A subdivision in high and low calcium intake groups results, therefore, in boys of ages 13 to 17 having the highest absolute activity differences. Because a high calcium intake coincides with high WBA and the amount of WBA is significantly and positively related to peak bone mass, it is suggested that in teenage boys a higher level of physical activity may be responsible for the higher BMD values in the high calcium intake group.

Additionally, protein intake may influence peak bone mass. It has been suggested that a high protein intake increases calcium excretion and has a negative correlation with the calcium balance (Cummings, 1985; Toss, 1992). The issue of whether a high protein intake is a risk factor for osteoporosis may be of interest when making a choice between calcium supplements and dairy

Calcium intake
males

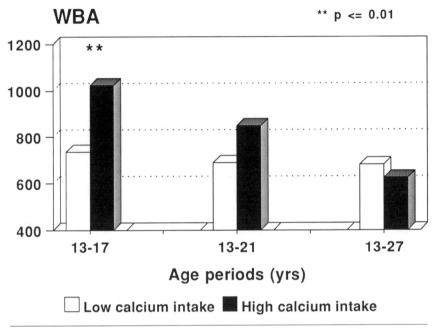

Figure 13.5   Mean weight-bearing activities (WBA) in males with a relatively low and high calcium intake for the age periods 13-17, 13-21, and 13-27 years.

products as a calcium source, given that dairy products are rich in protein. The high protein intake groups (> P_{75}) showed a significantly higher peak bone mass ($p < .01$) at age 27 compared with the low protein intake groups (< P_{25}) in boys during the adolescent period. This relationship was not found in adolescent girls. When the groups were divided into relatively high and low protein intake based on the age periods 13 to 21 and 13 to 27 years, no significant differences were found in peak bone mass at age 27 in either sex. These results can be explained by the fact that the calcium and protein intakes are highly interrelated. The intake of protein is significantly higher ($p < .01$) in the high calcium intake groups than in the low calcium intake groups in all age periods for both sexes. Therefore, the same relation was detected for calcium as well as protein intake during youth on the development of peak bone density. Because a negative relation between protein intake and BMD is not supported by our data, it may be that the effect of protein intake on the calcium balance depends on the protein source, as supported by Turnlund et al. (1992). They found that both calcium absorption and utilization appear to be more efficient with an animal protein diet than with a vegetable protein diet. In addition, our results suggest that dairy

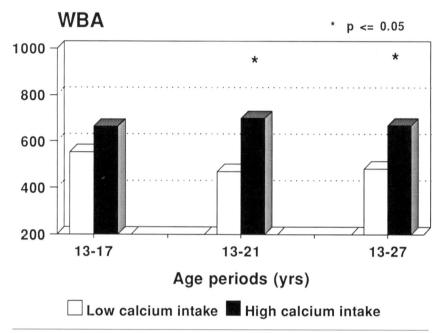

Figure 13.6   Mean weight-bearing activities (WBA) in females with a relatively low and high calcium intake for the age periods 13-17, 13-21, and 13-27 years.

products can be a good source of calcium intake for the attainment of peak bone mass.

Conclusions

The present longitudinal study on calcium intake and peak bone mass demonstrated that in adolescent boys a significantly lower peak bone mass at age 27 was found in the low calcium intake group than in the high calcium intake group. This could be explained by the fact that in these adolescents the calcium intake of the low calcium intake group was far below the DRDA. In adolescent girls and young adults comparison of high and low calcium intake did not result in significant differences in maximal bone density, possibly because the calcium intake met the DRDA.

In the prevention of osteoporosis, this study suggests the following recommendations for promoting the attainment of peak bone mass. First, although our results do not support a major role for calcium intake in determining maximal bone density, there should be adequate calcium intake, approaching the DRDA. This can be achieved by the consumption of dairy products. Second, because a high calcium intake coincides with high WBA and the amount of WBA is significantly and positively related to peak bone mass, regular WBA should be integrated into the daily lives of teenagers and adults.

References

Centraal Bureau voor de Statistiek. (1992). Statistisch Jaarboek 1992. Den Haag: SDU/Uitgeverij, CBS-publikaties.

Chestnut C.H. Theoretical overview: Bone development, peak bone mass, bone loss, and fracture risk. Am J Med 91 (1991) 25-45.

Cumming RG. Calcium intake and bone mass: A quantitative review of the evidence. Cal Tissue Int 47 (1990) 194-201.

Cummings S.R., J.L. Kelsey, M.C. Nevitt, K.J. O'Dowd. Epidemiology of osteoporosis and osteoporotic fractures. Epidemiol Rev 7 (1985) 178-208.

Dutch Food and Nutrition Table (1989). NEVO tabel. Stichting NEVO, Voorlichtingsburo voor de voeding.

Halioua L., J.J.B. Anderson. Lifetime calcium intake and physical activity habits: Independent and combined effects on the radial bone of healthy premenopausal Caucasian women. Am J Clin Nutr 49 (1989) 534-541.

Johnston C.C., J.Z. Miller, C.W. Slemenda, T.K. Reister, S Hui, J.C. Christian, M. Peacock. Calcium supplementation and increases in bone mineral density in children. N Eng J Med 327 (1992) 82-87.

Kanders B., D.W. Dempster, R. Lindsay. Interaction of calcium nutrition and physical activity on bone mass in young women. J Bone Miner Res 3:2 (1988).

Kemper H.C.G. (ed.). (1985). Growth, health and fitness of teenagers: Longitudinal research in international perspective. Vol. 20 of: Medicine and sport science. Karger, Basel.

Matkovic V. Calcium and peak bone mass. J Int Med 231 (1992) 151-160.

Matkovic V., D. Fontana, C. Tominac, P. Goel, C.H. Chestnut III. Factors that influence peak bone mass formation: A study of calcium balance and the inheritance of bone mass in adolescent females. Am J Clin Nutr 52 (1990) 878-888.

Matkovic V., K. Kostial, I. Simoovic, R. Buzina, A. Brodarec, C. Nordin. Bone status and fracture rates in two regions of Yugoslavia. Am J Clin Nutr 32 (1979) 540-549.

Metz J.A., P. Gallagher, J.J.B. Anderson. Determinants of bone mass in twenty-four to twenty-eight year-old Caucasian women. Clin Res 39:22 (1991) (abstract).

Picard D., L.G. Ste-Marie, D. Coutu, L. Carrier, R. Chartrand, R. Lepage, P. Fugére, P. d'Amour. Premenopausal bone mineral content relates to height, weight and calcium intake during early adulthood. Bone Miner 4 (1988) 299-309.

Post G.B. (1989). Nutrition in adolescence: A longitudinal study in dietary patterns from teenager to adult. Doctoral dissertation, Wageningen, de Vrieseborch, Haarlem, SO 16.

Recker R.R., K.M. Davies, S.M. Hinders, R.P. Heaney, M.R. Stegman, D.B. Kimmel. Bone gain in young adult women. JAMA 268:17 (1992) 2403-2408.

Sandler R.B., C.W. Slemenda, R.E. LaPorte, J.A. Cauley, M.M. Schramm, M.L. Barresi, A.M. Kriska. Postmenopausal bone density and milk consumption in childhood and adolescence. Am J Clin Nutr 42 (1985) 270-274.

Sentipal J.M., G.M. Wardlaw, J. Mahan, V. Matkovic. Influence of calcium intake and growth indexes on vertebral bone mineral density in young females. Am J Clin Nutr 54 (1991) 425-428.

Sievänen H., P. Oja, I. Vuari. Precision of dual-energy x-ray absorptiometry in determining bone mineral density and content of various skeletal sites. Nucl Med 33 (1992) 1137-1142.

Toss G. Effect of calcium intake vs. other life-style factors on bone mass. J Int Med 231 (1992) 181-186.

Turnlund J.R., A.A. Betschart, M. Liebman, M.J. Kretsch, H.E. Sauberlich. Vitamin B-6 depletion followed by repletion with animal- or plant-source diets and calcium and magnesium metabolism in young women. Am J Clin Nutr 56 (1992) 905-910.

Chapter 14

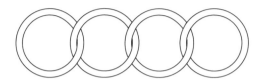

Effects on Adult Health of Physical Condition and Lifestyle Measured From Adolescence Through Adulthood

Jan Snel, Jos Twisk, Willem van Mechelen, & Han C.G. Kemper

The assumption that regular physical activity and good physical fitness reduce the risk of disease has been widely accepted and promoted over the past decades (Paffenbarger, 1989). Hence, lack of physical activity may have detrimental effects on health. De Geus (1992) concluded that aerobic fitness is the expression of an underlying healthy constitution and that only marginal health effects may result from short-term exercise programs. Whether the assumed protective effect of good physical condition is valid in all cases may be questioned also in view of the suggestion that top athletes are more prone to illness than recreational athletes. Also, it is recognized that effects of exercise can be counteracted by stress or certain lifestyle factors, like smoking and alcohol consumption. Conversely, beneficial effects on health seem to come from an adequate coping style (Snel & Gosselink, 1989; Temoshok, 1983; Vingerhoets, 1985) and from social support (Rehm et al., 1993). Because social support requires the skills appropriate to establishing and sustaining social relationships, the extent of social inadequacy is of relevance here.

Indeed, the beneficial effect of good physical condition has been found for coronary heart disease (CHD) (Morris et al., 1990; Paffenbarger, 1989) and death rate (Paffenbarger et al., 1986). Also, the protective value of a more active life, as indicated by occupational activity, has been found for colon cancer (Vena et al., 1985), while inactivity is associated with an increased risk of bowel cancer in men (Ballard-Barbash et al., 1990) and colon cancer risk (Gerhardson et al., 1988; Verdiar et al., 1990). The role of physical inactivity seems to be established for at least mortality and dramatic illness in adults, as has been shown in epidemiology, but much less attention has been paid to its role in youngsters, who generally possess good health. In our view, the question of whether exercise has potentially protective value for health can be answered best by studying subjects longitudinally from adolescence through adulthood, since at an early age people diversify their consumption pattern to include certain substances like alcohol and nicotine, and they also become more socially involved.

The presumption is that effects of physical activity on health need a long time to be reflected in a change of health and that this change might interact with lifestyle factors. Another point is that studies intentionally planned to test exercise-health coupling do not do justice to the everyday observation that people—more specifically, healthy people—seem to self-regulate their habitual level of physical activity to increase or optimize their health and their sense of well-being (Ross & Hayes, 1988). In the present study we checked these observations.

Objectives

In this nonintervention 15-year longitudinal study, we tested the assumption that aerobic and musculoskeletal fitness of a foregoing period are predictors of adult health, while taking into account such lifestyle factors as physical activity, smoking, alcohol consumption, and social inadequacy. More specifically, because we followed the subjects from adolescence through adulthood, this assumption was tested separately for three periods: adolescence (ages 13-17), the combined periods adolescence and young adulthood (ages 13-21), and the period running from adolescence through adulthood (ages 13-27).

Subjects

In the Amsterdam Growth and Health Study we followed a group of healthy subjects from age 13 to age 27. The study was conducted in 85 males and 98 females. In high school the first four points of measurements had 1-year intervals. The fifth measurement was done 5 years later, at age 21, and the last measurement was done when the participants were 27 years old. At these two last measurements, up to 6 subjects came to our laboratory for 1 day from 9:00 a.m. to 5:00 p.m. During this day the order of the testing activities varied for each subject, except for blood sampling at around 9.00 a.m. Each test had its own experimenter.

Instruments

Physical Condition

Physical condition was measured as follows:

• *Aerobic fitness* was operationalized as maximal oxygen uptake ($\dot{V}O_2max$), measured directly using a standard running test on a treadmill at a constant speed of 8 km/h (Kemper & Verschuur, 1981). During the test the slope was increased every 2 minutes by 2.5% or 5%, depending on the subject's heart rate; oxygen uptake ($\dot{V}O_2$) was measured each minute by the open-circuit technique. This test was continued until exhaustion. $\dot{V}O_2$max was measured as the maximal amount of oxygen consumed per minute by the subject; it was expressed per kilogram of body weight to the two-thirds power (Kemper & Verschuur, 1987).

• *Musculoskeletal fitness* was assessed with the Motor Performance (MOPER) Fitness Test. This test has seven subtests: static arm strength, endurance arm strength, explosive leg strength, trunk/upper-leg strength, running speed, arm speed, and flexibility (Bovend'eerdt et al., 1980).

Lifestyle

Lifestyle involved the following parameters:

• *Physical activity* scores during the first 4 years of measurement were based on energy expenditure scores derived from data collected with an 8-level heart integrator, pedometer, and a questionnaire/interview (Verschuur, 1987). In young adulthood and adulthood the physical activity data were derived only from the interview. The scores are expressed in units of basal metabolic rate (METs per week). In this analysis only the score of the activity interview was taken into account.

• *Alcohol consumption* was assessed by a dietary history interview (Post, 1989). At each point of measurement alcohol consumption was determined for the past 2 weeks. The score was expressed in grams per day. Because of the presence of nondrinkers, in particular during adolescence, the group of subjects was divided into nondrinkers, light drinkers ($<P_{50}$), and heavy drinkers ($>P_{50}$).

• *Cigarette smoking* habits were assessed by an interview that inquired after the number of cigarettes smoked daily and during the weekend. The measure was stated in grams per week. To deal with the scoring of no smokers, the subjects were categorized as nonsmokers and smokers.

• *Social inadequacy*, a scale of the Dutch Personality Inventory (DPI; Luteijn et al., 1985), is defined as neurotic shyness, uncomfortable feelings in social situations, and the avoidance of unfamiliar people or situations. The scale intercorrelation of the DPI-youth (DPI-y) and DPI-adult (DPI-a) version is .89.

Adult Health

Three categories of health status were defined at the age of 27 years.

1. *Physical health*

   • *Skinfold thickness.* The amount of body fat was estimated on the basis of the sum of two skinfold measurements taken at the trunk (subscapularis and crista suprailiaca) and two at the upper arm (biceps and triceps).

   • *Blood pressure.* Systolic blood pressure and diastolic blood pressure were measured indirectly with a standard pressure cuff (32×12 cm). The lower of two readings was recorded.

• *Total cholesterol:HDL-cholesterol ratio.* For the determination of total cholesterol (TC) and the high-density lipoprotein (HDL) cholesterol fraction in serum, 10 ml of venous blood were taken. Sampling was done in a nonfasting state after a light breakfast. The HDL-cholesterol fraction was analyzed according to Burstein and Samaille's method (1960). HDL-cholesterol is said to lower and TC to increase CHD risk. TC was analyzed according to the methods of Huang et al (1961).

2. *Mental health*

• *Inadequacy.* The Inadequacy scale from the DPI was used. The 21 items with three response alternatives and a scoring range of 0 to 63 elicit vague physical and psychosomatic complaints, depressed mood, and vague feelings of anxiety and malfunctioning. The scale correlates from .72 to .83 with neuroticism and from .52 to .64 with neurosomatism in psychiatric patients, revalidating patients and applicants (Luteijn et al., 1985). The Cronbach's α reliability coefficient for DPI-y is .87, and for DPI-a, .86.

• *Vital exhaustion,* defined as feelings of depression, malfunctioning, apathy, and anxiety, was measured with the Maastricht Questionnaire (Appels et al., 1987) and by simple summation.

• *Mild health complaints.* The VOEG (Vragenlijst over Ervaren Gezondheid, or Checklist on Experienced Health) is an index of long-term health or physical malaise. Jansen and Sikkel (1981) have shown it to be responsive to situational stress. The 13 items are scored dichoto-mously and weighed. The total score correlates .65 with Inadequacy (on the DPI) in psychiatric patients and also .65 in student nurses; in our subjects (n = 182) the correlation was .58.

• *Negative life events.* The Life Event List (LEL), a translated version of the Life Events Survey of Sarason et al. (1978) has 89 life events in five domains of life. These domains are health (8 events), work (14), home/family (38), personal/social relations (23), and finances (6). Each event can be scored on seven intensities, ranging from −3 (very negative) to +3 (very positive). The subject is asked to indicate only those events that have been experienced during the past year and to rate them in terms of negative or positive impact. The summed score of the given negative impacts for the life domains, with the health domain excepted, was used as the negative life events score.

• *Negative health events.* To measure negative health events, we used the negative impact scores on the eight life events in the health domain of the LEL. The negative health score was found by summing these negative impacts.

• *Daily hassles*—irritations of day-to-day life—were scored with the Everyday Problem Checklist (EPCL; Vingerhoets et al., 1989). The score used in the present study is the number of the items checked. The EPCL appears to be a better predictor (r = .53) of psychosomatic symptoms than the LEL. The correlation of the EPCL frequency with the personality attribute Inadequacy is about .25.

 • *Coping style* was measured with the Dutch version (Vingerhoets & Flohr, 1984) of the Ways of Coping Checklist (WCC) (Folkman & Lazarus, 1980). The checklist has 67 dichotomous items, of which 40 items refer to emotion-focused coping. The score used was found by simple summation.

3. *Self-reported health*

 • *Subjective sleep quality.* The Sleep Quality Scale (SQS) contains 14 items asking for the general impression of the subject's appraisal of his sleep for the past half year (Mulder-Hajonides van der Meulen, 1980).

 • *Sleep-wake problems* were assessed with the Sleep Wake Experience List (SWEL) (Van Diest et al., 1989). The scale contains 14 items, asking for problems in falling asleep, sleeping through the night, waking in the morning, and functioning during the day.

 • *Health disorders* were scored as the summed incidence of all reported health inconveniences, such as vague stomach complaints, stomach pain, excitation, ulcer, intestinal complaints, migraine, heart irregularities, heart problems, dizziness, and respiratory disorders.

Data Reduction and Processing

Predictor Variables: Physical Condition

 • Standardization of $\dot{V}O_2$max (in terms of kilograms of body weight to the two-thirds power) was obtained by averaging the data of the first 4 years of measurement. In addition to this mean, the separate data of the fifth measurement (at young adulthood) and sixth measurement (at adulthood) were used for men and women separately.

 • The seven musculoskeletal fitness subtest scores were averaged for the first 4 years of measurement. Each subscale score was added to its parallel score at ages 21 and 27 and then ranked for men and women separately.

Confounding Variables: Lifestyle Factors

 • The reported amount of grams of tobacco per week and the time the subject had smoked were used to estimate the total amount of tobacco consumption for each of the three periods. The subjects were organized into two categories: nonsmokers and smokers.

 • Alcohol consumption data gathered from the interview were averaged for the first 4 years of measurement. This amount and those found for young adulthood and adulthood were used to classify the subjects as nondrinkers, light drinkers ($<P_{50}$), or heavy drinkers ($>P_{50}$) for each of the three periods.

• The social inadequacy and physical activity scores were averaged for the adolescent period to get one score for this period in addition to the scores of the two other periods for further analysis.

Dependent Variables: Health Status

For each of the three health definitions, those men and women of age 27 falling in the first and third tertiles were selected as having "good" and "bad" health, respectively. It should be noted that this distinction is relative, since our subjects are essentially healthy. Thus, *bad* properly means "somewhat less healthy," but for the sake of convenience we will use the word *bad*.

The general procedure for obtaining one score for each of the three health categories and for men and women separately was as follows. The scores of each parameter were ranked, summed and divided by the number of variables in each category. More specifically, for *physical health*, systolic and diastolic blood pressures were ranked, summed, and divided by 2. Subsequently, these ranks were added to the ranks of skinfold thickness and TC:HDL-cholesterol ratio and again ranked. For *mental health*, the scores of the included measures were ranked separately and totaled. A similar procedure was followed for the *reported health* category, with the data of the SQS and the SWEL summed and ranked, and subsequently summed to the ranked total incidence of health disorders.

Statistics

Because the present study describes the development of health and growth of a normal, nonpatient group—hence, the participants may be described as healthy enough to test the assumptions of the study—the analyses were done on the first and third tertile of health. The analytical procedure comprised three steps. The predictor variables and confounders measured during the three periods under consideration were used to ascertain their role in health as determined at age 27. The criteria of health were those described earlier for the three defined categories of health.

To analyze the relation between the predictor variables and the three categories of health, multiple logistic regression (MLR) analysis was used. Including predictor variables into the logistic regression models was based on both the significance of the variables and a significant change in goodness of fit of a model without that particular variable. Odds ratios, for all the significant predictor variables, were calculated for a 10% change in ranking. To determine the goodness of fit of the final models, the Hosmer and Lemeshow H statistic was calculated. The lower the H (corresponding with high probability), the better the fit of the model (Hosmer & Lemeshow, 1989).

Results

Defining health is a critical matter, since there are numerous possible definitions. According to the World Health Organization (WHO), health is the absence of illness and the presence of a sense of well-being. It is hard to imagine that even in our sample, which can be described as normal and healthy, perfect health can be found—that is, the total absence of symptoms. Considering this fact and the aim of the study and looking at the three health categories defined, in our view it is legitimate to use the operationalizations of health as we did. We would also like to emphasize that our aim was to assess the influence of health-related factors assessed at a young age on health in adults, and for that reason we preferred to take a wide-band approach over a more fine-tuned one in order to create the possibilities of refining this approach in due time.

Physical Health

The decision to contrast the first ($\geq P_{67}$) and third ($<P_{33}$) tertile of our subjects on the achieved adult health scores is justified by the finding that the selected health variables differ in the expected direction. Those subjects at the relatively positive side of physical or objective health show smaller skinfold thicknesses, lower blood pressure, and more favorable TC:HDL-cholesterol ratios. In Table 14.1 the mean values of the groups with "good" physical health ($\geq P_{67}$) and "bad" physical health ($<P_{33}$) are summarized. The factors that may play a role in this observation are physical activity, aerobic and musculoskeletal fitness, and social inadequacy. These were checked by MLR analysis (Table 14.2).

No interaction was found of predictor variables or confounders with gender, which means that the impact of the predictor variables applies equally well to men and women. Only musculoskeletal fitness measured from adolescence to young adulthood and to adulthood contributes significantly to physical health independently of the confounders smoking, drinking, and social inadequacy (Step 1). When these confounders are also incorporated into the model as a group (Step 2), the odds ratios for this measure of physical condition show only marginal changes. The conclusions are that the effect of musculoskeletal fitness on adult physical health is independent of smoking, drinking, and social inadequacy and that these confounders, taken separately, do not affect adult physical health. In other words, adult physical "health" neither benefits from an increase in aerobic fitness or physical activity nor does it deteriorate by smoking and drinking. Inspecting the data of Table 14.3 supports this impression, since the importance of the difference in the means when taking into account the size of the standard deviations does not reach statistical significance.

Mental Health

The second health category, mental health, includes the variables mentioned in Table 14.4. The means of these variables reveal a large and consistent contrast between those men and women in "bad" ($<P_{33}$) and "good" ($\geq P_{67}$) mental health. In particular, feelings of inadequacy and vital exhaustion and the incidence of mild health complaints are illustrative. Regarding stressful events, subjects with relatively "bad" health scored more negatively on health and life events and reported more daily hassles.

Table 14.1   Descriptive Data for Physical Health Variables in Two Contrasting Health Groups

	"Good" (≥ P_{67})					"Bad" (< P_{33})				
	n	M	SD	Min.	Max.	n	M	SD	Min.	Max.
Males (age 27)										
Sum of 4 skinfolds (mm)	34	26.76	6.72	18.06	53.92	20	43.62	8.48	28.09	59.68
Diastolic BP (mmHg)	34	77.15	5.90	63.33	91.25	20	78.39	6.73	64.17	91.67
Systolic BP (mmHg)	34	131.1	8.67	115.4	150.0	20	134.4	7.78	121.3	149.6
TC:HDL-cholesterol	34	3.34	.58	2.30	4.33	20	4.34	.76	3.42	6.70
Females (age 27)										
Sum of 4 skinfolds (mm)	26	33.98	6.79	25.86	52.10	40	54.10	13.19	30.40	85.19
Diastolic BP (mmHg)	26	76.21	3.55	70.42	84.58	40	80.66	6.50	66.67	101.7
Systolic BP (mmHg)	26	120.9	6.13	109.4	138.9	40	126.2	8.99	110.4	149.2
TC:HDL-cholesterol	26	2.89	.48	1.99	3.87	40	3.86	.72	2.70	5.77

Note. BP = blood pressure; TC = total cholesterol.

Table 14.2   Odds Ratios of Adult Physical Health at Age 27

	Age (y)					
	13-17		13-21		13-27	
	Odds ratio	95% CI	Odds ratio	95% CI	Odds ratio	95% CI
Step 1						
Musculoskeletal fitness			1.41	1.09-1.82	1.58	1.17-2.12
10% in ranking			$H = 5.11; p = .75$		$H = 6.77; p = .56$	
Step 2						
Musculoskeletal fitness			1.63	1.19-2.25	1.70	1.20-2.40
10% in ranking			$H = 4.70; p = .79$		$H = 3.82; p = .87$	

Note. Physical health defined as sum of skinfolds, systolic and diastolic blood pressures, and total-cholesterol:HDL-cholesterol ratio. Confounders are smoking, alcohol consumption, and social inadequacy. Step 1: physical condition without confounders; Step 2: confounders together with physical condition variables. H is the measure of goodness of fit.

An analysis of the differences in adult mental health for the role of the separate confounders musculoskeletal and aerobic fitness and social inadequacy (Step 1) does not reveal an impact on adult mental health. Also, when the confounders physical activity, smoking, alcohol consumption, and social inadequacy are taken into account (Step 2) the adjusted odds ratios do not demonstrate any effect of physical condition during the three periods on adult mental health. However, an evaluation of the role of these confounders as distinct explanatory variables reveals a protective effect of social adequacy on mental health, which increases with age (Table 14.5). From adolescence throughout adulthood the risk of belonging to the mentally less healthy group decreases progressively with a 10% lower ranking on social inadequacy.

During the adolescent period the risk of worse mental health in adulthood was 5.61 times higher for smokers than for nonsmokers. However, this risk was found only for this period and not for the periods to ages 21 and 27, which suggests that smoking cigarettes in the age range from 13 to 16 is of crucial importance for adult mental health. Regarding alcohol consumption, being a heavy alcohol consumer increased a subject's risk of falling into the less healthy category by factors of 4.95 and 4.29 for the two later periods, respectively. The broad range of the 95% confidence interval illustrates that the specific risk for each person may vary dramatically, possibly as a result of factors other than smoking and physical condition–related factors, since no interactions with these factors were found.

Table 14.6 brings into focus the remarkable changes in lifestyle from adolescence through adulthood. Although smoking and alcohol consumption were still

Table 14.3   Descriptive Data for Musculoskeletal Fitness Variables of Physical Health in Two Contrasting Health Groups

	Age (y)														
	13-17					13-21					13-27				
	n	M	SD	Min.	Max.	n	M	SD	Min.	Max.	n	M	SD	Min.	Max.
Males in "good" physical health ($\geq P_{67}$)															
Plate tapping (s)	34	11.17	.88	9.24	12.93	31	9.39	.97	7.5	11.3	34	8.81	.70	7.4	10.4
Flexed-arm hang (s)	34	32.42	14.11	7.25	61.75	31	45.26	15.69	16	90	34	42.47	15.20	15	82
50-m shuttle run (s)	34	17.23	.60	15.83	18.68	31	17.28	1.01	15.7	19.4	34	16.58	.85	14.7	18.5
Arm pull (kg/kg BW)	34	.96	.12	.67	1.15	31	.97	.15	.65	1.18	34	.92	.14	.64	1.25
Sit-and-reach (cm)	34	29.17	6.37	16.50	42	31	33.71	10.69	8	52	34	32.91	10.54	8	51
Standing high jump (cm)	34	44.74	4.04	37.25	56.25	31	55.00	4.78	46	64	34	57.32	6.10	47	74
10 leg lifts (s)	34	13.81	2.08	10.53	18.83	31	12.37	1.55	1.03	1.64	34	12.84	1.80	1.04	2.06
Males in "bad" physical health ($< P_{33}$)															
Plate tapping (s)	20	11.30	1.33	9.18	14.23	20	9.52	1.04	7.8	11.0	20	8.85	.89	6.6	10.5
Flexed-arm hang (s)	20	24.51	10.39	7.00	45.25	20	30.50	14.08	7	64	20	29.05	15.92	4	73
50-m shuttle run (s)	20	17.47	.71	16.15	18.75	20	17.34	.69	16.2	19.0	20	17.27	1.54	14.9	22.4
Arm pull (kg/kg BW)	20	.94	.15	.66	1.19	20	.96	.13	.72	1.19	20	.83	.14	.61	1.03
Sit-and-reach (cm)	20	30.14	8.58	10.50	42.25	20	35.95	10.15	11	50	20	34.05	9.21	15	51
Standing high jump (cm)	20	44.87	5.72	32.50	56.67	20	53.50	5.87	45	69	30	53.70	6.59	44	68
10 leg lifts (s)	20	13.47	1.50	11.85	16.55	20	12.56	1.72	10.2	18.0	20	12.75	1.34	10.8	16.0

Females in "good" physical health ($\geq P_{67}$)

Plate tapping (s)	26	10.54	.77	8.95	12.23	23	9.74	.83	8.2	11.3	26	9.23	.56	8.0	10.1
Flexed-arm hang (s)	26	20.28	12.69	5.00	51.25	23	17.74	12.79	1	49	25	22.52	14.52	4	52
50-m shuttle run (s)	26	18.18	.69	16.98	19.67	23	19.11	.86	17.7	20.7	25	18.95	.98	17.0	20.6
Arm pull (kg/kg BW)	26	.82	.14	.64	1.25	23	.75	.13	.53	1.19	26	.65	.13	.50	1.03
Sit-and-reach (cm)	26	37.91	4.81	30.0	46.25	23	41.65	4.85	32	53	25	40.06	4.85	33	51
Standing high jump (cm)	26	43.39	5.64	33.25	52.67	23	42.87	4.71	34	51	25	43.64	4.21	36	53
10 leg lifts (s)	26	12.81	1.26	10.9	15.7	23	12.55	1.34	10.6	15.9	25	13.29	1.92	10.1	17.9

Females in "bad" physical health ($< P_{33}$)

Plate tapping (s)	40	10.49	.70	9.18	12.5	39	9.70	.85	8.1	11.6	40	9.23	.56	8.4	10.7
Flexed-arm hang (s)	40	15.02	8.72	4.00	36.75	38	11.26	9.05	1	36	38	11.63	11.27	1	47
50-m shuttle run (s)	40	18.28	.82	16.30	20.58	39	19.46	1.23	17.0	23.0	37	19.37	1.20	16.9	22.2
Arm pull (kg/kg BW)	40	.79	.11	.62	1.10	39	.68	.10	.44	1.03	40	.61	.11	.40	.91
Sit-and-reach (cm)	40	.36	6.28	21.75	50.75	39	38.72	6.84	20	51	38	38.32	7.96	21	52
Standing high jump (cm)	40	42.82	5.15	32.75	55.50	39	41.44	5.85	31	57	38	42.74	5.63	28	55
10 leg lifts (s)	40	13.07	1.44	10.13	18.33	37	13.24	1.60	9.8	17.0	37	13.18	1.65	10.0	17.9

Note. BW = body weight.

Table 14.4 Descriptive Data for Mental Health Variables in Two Contrasting Health Groups

	"Good" (≥ P_{67})					"Bad" (< P_{33})				
	n	M	SD	Min.	Max	n	M	SD	Min.	Max
Males (age 27)										
Inadequacy	31	2.74	2.66	0	13	26	13.92	8.01	6	37
Vital exhaustion	30	1.10	2.59	0	12	26	11.04	9.61	0	39
Mild health complaints	31	.41	.81	0	2.61	26	4.94	3.16	1.10	11.48
Negative health events	31	-.61	1.58	-6	1	26	-1.04	2.71	-7	7
Negative life events	31	13.52	9.64	0	41	26	3.23	13.15	-28	23
Daily hassles	31	19.84	21.1	4	112	26	36.04	22.33	7	85
Emotion-focused coping	29	54.28	4.08	45	62	26	62.32	4.50	53	69
Females (age 27)										
Inadequacy	30	3.33	2.59	0	10	35	13.91	6.23	3	29
Vital exhaustion	30	1.60	1.94	0	8	35	13.57	8.43	0	36
Mild health complaints	30	.81	.99	0	3.54	35	5.53	3.26	1.13	13.86
Negative health events	30	2.23	2.65	-2	9	35	-1.11	2.91	-8	6
Negative life events	30	16.57	9.99	2	42	35	6.09	9.49	-14	25
Daily hassles	30	14.57	18.73	0	92	34	35.68	20.83	5	85
Emotion-focused coping	28	58.36	4.35	48	66	34	61.91	4.87	54	75

Table 14.5   Odds Ratios of Adult Mental Health at Age 27

	Age (y)					
	13-17		13-21		13-27	
	Odds ratio	95% CI	Odds ratio	95% CI	Odds ratio	95% CI
Step 3						
Alcohol < P50			1.94	0.66- 1.51	2.74	0.76- 1.16
> P50			4.95	5.76-16.24	4.29	9.91-15.82
Smoking	5.61	1.62-19.43				
Social inadequacy						
10% in ranking	1.42	1.30- 1.54	1.63	1.32- 3.31	1.84	1.41- 2.39
	$H = 4.61; p = .80$		$H = 6.18; p = .63$		$H = 8.78; p = .36$	

Note. Mental health defined as inadequacy, vital exhaustion, mild health complaints, negative health events, negative life events, daily hassles, and emotion-focused coping. Confounders are alcohol consumption, smoking, and social inadequacy. Step 3: confounders as explanatory variables. H is the measure of goodness of fit.

at a socially acceptable level during the adolescent period, their increase in the period to young adulthood is dramatic and stays at a high, although strongly inconstant, level from young adulthood to adulthood. Also of interest is the consistent difference in consumption pattern between the mentally healthy and the less healthy throughout the three age periods. This phenomenon also accounts for the level of social inadequacy. In both mental health categories social inadequacy diminishes in time at a similar pace from age 13 to age 27.

Self-Reported Health

Self-reported health variables (Table 14.7) showed a consistent difference in the expected direction of the severity of complaints on self-reported health variables. Compared with the mental health category, the present category stresses more manifest physical complaints, so one might expect that the lifestyle factors are of a relatively high importance for this category.

Two lifestyle factors appear to be of importance (Table 14.8). First, a 10% decrease in social inadequacy enhanced one's chances of belonging to the relatively more healthy category at age 27 with a stable 37% to 38% through all three periods under study. Again, as seen in the mental health category, this effect might be expected to be manifest in all subjects individually when improving their social skills. Second, the independent explanatory power of smoking is of impressive importance. Smoking cigarettes during the adolescent period increases the risk of a worse self-reported health at adult age more than 12-fold. In particular, this period seems to be of essential importance for good health in adulthood, since the odds ratios for the later periods diminish progressively, although they

Table 14.6   Descriptive Data for Confounding Variables of Mental Health in Two Contrasting Health Groups

								Age (y)							
			13-17					13-21					13-27		
	n	M	SD	Min.	Max.	n	M	SD	Min.	Max.	n	M	SD	Min.	Max.
Males in "good" physical health ($\geq P_{67}$)															
Drinking (g/day)	31	1.04	2.30	0	9.52	30	5.59	6.47	0	26.07	31	10.80	11.01	0	45.08
Smoking (g/day)	31	.40	2.02	0	11.25	31	13.97	39.61	0	182.2	31	19.31	40.49	0	145.7
Social inadequacy	29	20.14	3.90	15.00	28.25	28	13.32	3.78	8.50	23.88	29	10.24	3.55	5.67	18.67
Males in "bad" mental health ($< P_{33}$)															
Drinking (g/day)	20	4.11	12.36	0	55.26	20	8.29	12.00	.00	49.91	20	11.07	10.78	.00	38.61
Smoking (g/day)	20	6.53	29.12	0	130.25	20	24.24	60.15	0	253.2	20	26.20	56.18	0	235.9
Social inadequacy	19	24.40	4.56	17.00	33.00	19	17.52	5.65	9.17	30.25	19	13.73	4.78	6.78	23.67
Females in "good" mental health ($\geq P_{67}$)															
Drinking (g/day)	30	.44	.64	0	2.23	28	2.54	3.10	0	10.25	30	4.78	5.36	0	15.59
Smoking (g/day)	30	.81	2.63	0	12.50	30	13.50	25.09	0	95.00	30	15.78	27.42	0	87.33
Social inadequacy	30	23.08	6.20	14.50	32.75	28	15.33	5.81	7.88	29.75	30	12.82	5.61	5.42	27.83
Females in "bad" mental health ($< P_{33}$)															
Drinking (g/day)	35	1.10	1.91	0	9.59	34	3.66	3.30	0	12.79	35	8.34	7.57	0	32.25
Smoking (g/day)	35	5.63	11.59	0	58.25	35	28.77	47.33	0	167.8	35	31.75	48.25	0	165.1
Social inadequacy	35	25.51	6.21	16.00	37.00	34	18.47	5.37	8.00	30.25	35	15.18	4.94	6.00	26.67

Table 14.7 Descriptive Data for Self-Reported Health Variables

Self-reported health	"Good" ($\geq P_{67}$)					"Bad" ($< P_{33}$)				
	n	M	SD	Min.	Max.	n	M	SD	Min.	Max.
Males (age 27)										
Sleep quality discontent	28	.29	.66	0	2	24	4.13	3.10	0	13
Sleep complaints	28	0	0	0	0	24	1.08	.97	0	3
Health disorders	28	.29	.46	0	1	24	2.33	1.55	1	6
Females (age 27)										
Sleep quality discontent	32	.19	.47	0	2	42	3.57	3.05	0	13
Sleep complaints	32	.06	.25	0	1	42	1.10	1.34	0	4
Health disorders	32	.41	.50	0	1	42	3.90	1.54	1	8

Table 14.8   Odds Ratios of Adult Self-Reported Health at Age 27

	Age (y)					
	13-17		13-21		13-27	
	Odds ratio	95% CI	Odds ratio	95% CI	Odds ratio	95% CI
Step 3						
Smoking	12.16	3.83-38.58	6.60	2.60-16.80	4.31	1.79-10.41
Social inadequacy						
10% in ranking	1.37	1.16- 1.62	1.38	1.14- 1.67	1.37	1.13- 1.66
	$H = 11.98$; $p = .15$		$H = 2.49$; $p = 96$		$H = 8.79$; $p = .36$	

Note. Self-reported health defined as subjective sleep quality, sleep-wake problems, health disorders. Confounders are smoking and social inadequacy. Step 3: confounders as explanatory variables. H is the measure of goodness of fit.

still remain at a high level. The conclusion is that smoking has its greatest effect on self-reported adult health when practiced during the adolescent period. The 95% confidence intervals of the odds ratios, ranging from 1.79 to 38.58 reveal that smoking may have varied tremendously among the subjects, probably due to differences in the amount of cigarettes smoked or to compensating factors not included in this study. Estimating the amount of tobacco in one cigarette at 1 gram means that the number of smoked cigarettes per day for the maxima, noted in Table 14.9, runs from 2 to 41 (about two packs/day) in men and from 1.5 to 28 (about 1 pack/day) in women.

Discussion

Our discussion is divided in two parts. In the first part we comment on aspects of the entire study; in the second part we highlight and discuss the results relative to the objectives of the study.

General Comments

In this study we determined the effect on adult health of physical condition and a number of life factors measured from youth through early adulthood. Because a generally accepted definition of *health* is lacking, we operationalized health in three ways. One might criticize this approach by saying that these definitions have been chosen rather arbitrarily. In our opinion, however, this approach is defensible, because we selected measures that fit in well with the health category intended.

An issue critical to the outcome of studies such as this is data reduction. The ranking procedure was needed to obtain a single measure for each of the three

Table 14.9   Descriptive Data of Confounding Variables of Self-Reported Health in Two Contrasting Health Groups

			Age (y)												
	13-17					13-21					13-27				
	n	M	SD	Min.	Max.	n	M	SD	Min.	Max.	n	M	SD	Min.	Max.
Males in "good" self-reported health (≥ P_{67})															
Smoking	28	.65	2.73	0	14.25	28	20.12	53.11	0	193.7	28	21.61	51.39	0	200.2
Social inadequacy	27	21.80	5.50	15.00	34.0	26	14.90	5.39	7.5	27.0	27	11.60	4.96	5.67	23.70
Males in "bad" self-reported health (< P_{33})															
Smoking	24	4.39	11.72	0	45.50	24	36.95	66.20	0	289.9	24	47.95	60.73	0	238.3
Social inadequacy	23	23.75	5.08	15.75	33.75	19	16.68	4.94	8.63	24.25	23	14.24	4.71	6.67	24.25
Females in "good" self-reported health (≥ P_{67})															
Smoking	32	3.34	9.63	0	50.00	32	23.02	49.10	0	197.0	32	22.46	45.30	.00	193.7
Social inadequacy	32	21.81	5.94	14.00	32.75	31	14.98	5.29	7.88	29.13	32	12.43	4.86	5.42	23.42
Females in "bad" self-reported health (< P_{33})															
Smoking	42	6.81	7.36	0	32.25	42	36.88	51.03	0	167.8	42	39.92	52.2	.00	181.3
Social inadequacy	42	24.41	5.97	16.50	37.00	42	17.12	5.60	9.00	29.75	42	14.35	5.27	6.50	27.83

health definitions. Ranking, however, involves a loss of information, especially for measures that show a wide range of absolute values; examples in this study were negative health and life events, daily hassles, smoking, and drinking. At present, the consequences of this ranking procedure for the findings of our study are unknown. One option for addressing this point is to select the best representative from the measures in a health category by principal-component analysis (see chapter 5).

One problem we had to solve was which parameter for aerobic fitness should be selected to include into the analysis. We studied three possibilities. One of the best known parameters for exercise capability is $\dot{V}O_2$max. The traditional approach is to relate $\dot{V}O_2$max to whole body weight, but because females gain more body fat than men, correction for body weight does not do justice to the true aerobic power of women; hence this measure might be an undercorrection. In our study this step revealed an effect for gender, showing that with a 10% increase of $\dot{V}O_2$max per kilogram of body weight, men had a 5-times greater chance of belonging to the more physically healthy third of the sample; for the women the result was nonsignificant. In particular, for young subjects the process of maturation may confound $\dot{V}O_2$max data.

Kemper and Verschuur (1987) developed a second method. Using 200 male and female teenagers, they compared various $\dot{V}O_2$max indices corrected in different ways. Because $\dot{V}O_2$max has the dimension of a second power, $\dot{V}O_2$max divided by height (h) squared takes this dimension into account (Asmussen et al., 1955); from this, Kemper and Verschuur (1987) concluded that $\dot{V}O_2$max corrected for height squared was to be preferred. The values for girls remained fairly constant, and in men an increase was noted above that which might have been expected from an increase in body size. In view of the same age of our subjects we followed this conclusion. It was found, independently of gender, that the chance of belonging to the physically healthier group ($\geq P_{67}$) *diminished* about one third when there was a 10% increase in the $\dot{V}O_2$max/h^2 ranking. This is a rather unsound finding. It suggests that taking account of body size by dividing by height squared is an overcorrection and does not take into account the effects of the increase of body weight—i.e., fat mass.

As a third step, we entered body weight into the $\dot{V}O_2$max calculation by dividing by weight to the two-thirds power (i.e., ml $\cdot$ kg$^{-2/3}$ $\cdot$ min^{-1}). This measure does justice to the dimensional approach and the body weight approach. For these reasons, this method might be preferred to the other two. Analyzing the data with this measure did not show any effect on adult health. Our cautious conclusion is that $\dot{V}O_2$max corrected for height squared is an overcorrection, whereas $\dot{V}O_2$max corrected for body weight is an undercorrection; the proper measure might be $\dot{V}O_2$max corrected for body weight to the two-thirds power. Future research should test the validity of this assumption.

Comments on Findings

Regular physical activity is said to be an important factor in maintaining and promoting good health (Laporte et al., 1985; Paffenbarger, 1989; Verschuur,

1987) and psychological well-being (Ross & Hayes, 1988). The present study shows that physical activity expressed in units of energy expenditure and aerobic fitness do not affect adult physical, mental, or self-reported health either separately or in interaction with aerobic fitness or musculoskeletal fitness. The only significant finding was that the chance of good adult physical health increased 50% with a 10% increase of musculoskeletal fitness ranking between young adulthood and adulthood. Of course, whether in the long run physical exercise and aerobic fitness may enhance health is something we cannot verify from our data.

Stephens (1988) pooled data from four large-scale cross-sectional surveys with almost 46,000 people and analyzed the data of men and women older than and younger than 40 years. Good mental health was defined as positive mood, general well-being, and relatively infrequent symptoms of anxiety and depression. Physical activity was focused on leisure time and assessed by interview or questionnaire in four ways, each of which revealed similar relationships to age, sex, and socioeconomic status, suggestive of at least construct validity. Besides the general finding that active people scored as mentally healthier and vice versa, of special interest for the interpretation of our findings is that the physical–mental relationship was weaker for the younger age group and stronger for the older, and stronger for women than for men. Again, as was said before, the potential for physical activity or aerobic fitness to accomplish a favorable change in health may be a question answerable only across the long term. If so, it might explain why, within the age range of our subjects, we could find neither these potential effects nor a differential effect for gender.

The idea that drinking and smoking are harmful to health is widely accepted. In our subjects we did not find a significant effect of these habits on the odds ratios referring to adult physical health. However, heavy drinking alone (up to 9 drinks/day in men and up to about 6 drinks in women) increased the risk of falling within the class of relatively bad mental health at age 27, with a factor 5 when measured at young adulthood and with 4 at adulthood. Mental health as we defined it can be seen as representative of a strong complaining tendency (see chapter 8). For example, one scale of the mental health definition, inadequacy, correlates from .72 to .83 with neuroticism and from .52 to .64 with neurosomatism in different groups of subjects (Luteijn et al., 1985). Indeed, the odds ratios for drinking may mean that drinking leads to complaints. Another interpretation is that people who drink are made aware of the potential harmfulness of alcohol, expect to have poorer health, and report more complaints.

Smoking, the other health-confounding consumption habit, is the subject of many health campaigns, with particular attention paid to its cancer-promoting risk. In this study we did not find any effect on adult physical health (cf. Raab & Krzyvanek, 1965). However, smoking induced higher odds ratios for worsened mental health and self-reported health at adult age (see Tables 14.5 and 14.8). These ratios demonstrate almost 6 times higher risk compared to nonsmokers for adult mental health when smoking started in adolescence, and a decreasing but still significant higher risk for adult self-reported health from adolescence on. Similarly to the interpretation for drinking, it may mean that the social pressure to stop smoking, especially for young people, may result in a strong tendency to express complaints at adult age, whereas this social pressure fades away in the periods of young adulthood and adulthood. It may explain why no relationship is found between smoking and adult mental health.

The study revealed no effect on adult health of the interactions among the predicting physical condition measures, lifestyle factors, and gender. The absence of interaction effects fits in with the findings of Blair et al. (1989) but deviates from the study by Rehm et al. (1993). Blair et al. (1989) showed in 13,344 men and women above 40 years of age with a different index of aerobic fitness (the total time spent on a maximal treadmill running test) that aerobic fitness was an important factor in mortality but independent of gender. Rehm et al. (1993) studied the effect of lifestyle factors similar to ours on mortality in 1,430 subjects ages 35 to 65 and found a significant interaction of gender and smoking and drinking. Men drank and smoked more and ran a higher risk of mortality than women.

The dissimilarity with our findings might be based on age-related differences in lifestyle. Older subjects in general have a longer history of smoking and drinking than younger people, and consumption patterns among them have had much more time to diverge (see Tables 14.6 and 14.9). The start of such divergence of habit in consumption of stimulants can be observed in our data. The amount of alcohol consumption at the adolescent age is similar for men and women, but in men consumption increases steadily and eventually doubles that of women. For smoking a different pattern emerges. From adolescence to young adulthood there is a huge increase of consumption in both men and women, but after that it tends to level off for the adult women. Another point is that long-term effects of smoking and drinking on morbidity may become manifest the longer one practices these habits. This plausible possibility together with the supposedly increasing divergent consumption pattern in men and women may explain the difference between findings of studies with young subjects and with older ones.

An interesting finding concerns the role of social inadequacy. For both mental health and self-reported health, a lower level of social inadequacy results in beneficial effects on adult health. Social inadequacy increases its effect on adult mental health increasingly (Table 14.5) through the three age periods considered, whereas for adult self-reported health its odds ratio remains at a constant 1.37 (Table 14.8). Parallel to these results the social inadequacy level itself diminishes at a steady pace (Tables 14.6 and 14.9). We conclude that having adequate social skills is protective for adult health, particularly for mental and self-reported health. Because the psychometric quality of the social inadequacy scale is without doubt (see chapter 5), we ascribe much value to this conclusion.

For a clear understanding and a possible implementation of the findings so far, it should be taken into consideration that statistical significance depends on the magnitude of effect size (that is, relative risks), as well as on sample size (cf. Rosenthal & Rosnow, 1984). If our sample size for males and females were doubled and the effect amounted to the same size, more effects would show statistical significance. In other words, even with the relatively small sample size and the relative, not absolute, defined difference in health in our healthy subjects, the findings are of interest for measures aimed at promoting adequate social skills, stimulating musculoskeletal fitness, and preventing smoking and drinking in young people to increase the chances of good health at adult age.

Conclusions

In this study we measured longitudinally, over 15 years, physical condition and the lifestyle factors of physical activity, drinking, smoking, and social adequacy. These measures were associated with physical, mental, and self-reported health at adult age in men and women. We started from the idea that people, and more specifically healthy people, may self-regulate their lifestyles to increase or optimize their health and psychological well-being. The findings on physical activity and aerobic fitness did not support this assumption. It was shown, however, that for both men and women musculoskeletal fitness was beneficial for adult physical health (cf. Arraiz et al., 1992). It was also demonstrated that drinking and smoking may jeopardize mental health, as shown from an increase in psychosomatic-like complaints, and that smoking is a potential adverse factor in adult self-reported health. The importance of adequate social skills was illustrated by showing that an improved social adequacy from young age on enhanced the chance for good mental and self-reported health in adulthood.

References

Appels A., P. Höppner, P. Mulder. A questionnaire to assess premonitory symptoms of myocardial infarction. Int J Cardiol 14 (1987) 15-24.

Arraiz G.A., D.T. Wiggle, Y. Mao. Risk assessment of physical activity and physical fitness in the Canada Health Survey Mortality Follow-up Study. J Clin Epidemiol 45:4 (1992) 419-428.

Asmussen E., K. Heebøll-Nielsen. A dimensional analysis of physical performance and growth in boys. J Appl Physiol 7 (1955) 593-603.

Ballard-Barbash R., A. Schatzkin, D. Albanes, M.H. Schiffman, B.E. Kreger, W.B. Kannel, K.M. Anderson, W.E. Helsel. Physical activity and risk of large bowel cancer in the Framingham Study. Cancer Res 50 (1990) 3610-3613.

Blair S.N., H.W. Kohl III, R.S. Paffenbarger, D.G. Clark, K.H. Cooper, L.W. Gibbons. Physical fitness and all-cause mortality: A prospective study of healthy men and women. JAMA 262:17 (1989) 2395-2401.

Bovend'eerdt J., H.C.G. Kemper, R. Verschuur. (1980). The MOPER Fitness Test: Manual and performance scales. De Vrieseborch, Haarlem.

Burstein M., J. Samaille. Sur un dosage rapide du cholesterol lié aux alpha- et aux beta-lipoprotéines du serum. Clin Chim Acta 5 (1960) 609-611.

Diest R. van., H. Milius, R. Markusse, J. Snel. De Slaap-Waak Ervaring Lijst. T Soc Geneeskunde 10 (1989) 343-347.

Folkman S., R.S. Lazarus. An analysis of coping in a middle-aged community sample. J Health Soc Behav 21 (1980) 219-239.

Gerhardson M., B. Floederus, S.E. Norell. Physical activity and colon cancer risk. Int J Epidemiol 17 (1988) 743-746.

Geus E. de. (1992). The effects of fitness training on physiological stress-reactivity. Dissertation, Vrije Universiteit, Amsterdam.

Hosmer D.W., S. Lemeshow. (1989). Applied logistic regression. Wiley, New York.

Huang T.C., P.C. Chen, V. Wefler, A. Raftery. A stable reagent for the Lieberman-Buchard reaction. Anal Chem 33 (1961) 1405-1407.

Jansen M.E., D. Sikkel. Verkorte versie van de voegschaal. Gedrag & Samenleving 2 (1981) 78-82.

Kemper H.C.G., R. Verschuur. Maximal aerobic power in 13- and 14-year old teenagers in relation to biological age. Int J Sports Med 2 (1981) 97-100.

Kemper H.C.G., R. Verschuur. Longitudinal study of maximal aerobic power in teenagers. Ann Hum Biol 14:5 (1987) 435-444.

Laporte R.E., H.J. Montoye, C.J. Caspersen. Assessment of physical activity in epidemiologic research: Problems and prospects. Public Health Rep 100 (1985) 131-146.

Luteijn F., J. Starren, H. van Dijk. (1985). Nederlandse Persoonlijkheids Vragenlijst. Handleiding, Herziene uitgave. Swets & Zeitlinger, Lisse.

Morris J.N., D.G. Clayton, M.G. Everitt, A.M. Semmence, E.H. Burgess. Exercise in leisure time: Coronary attack and death rates. Br Heart J 63 (1990) 325-334.

Mulder-Hajonides van der Meulen W.R.E.H., J.R. Wijnberg, J.J. Hollanders, I. de Diana, R. van den Hoofdakker. (1980). Measurements of subjective sleep quality. Paper presented at the Fifth European Congress on Sleep Research. Amsterdam.

Paffenbarger R.S. Jr. Contributions of epidemiology to exercise science and cardiovascular health. Med Sci Sports Exerc 20:5 (1989) 426-438.

Paffenbarger R.S. Jr., R.T. Hyde, A.L. Wing, C.C. Hsieh. Physical activity, all-cause mortality and longevity of college alumni. N Engl J Med 314 (1986) 605-613.

Post B. (1989). Nutrition in adolescence. A longitudinal study in dietary patterns from teenager to adult. Dissertation, Sportwetenschappelijke Onderzoekingen, vol. 16, de Vrieseborch, Haarlem.

Raab W., H.J. Krzyvanek. Cardiovascular sympathetic tone and stress response related to personality patterns and exercise habits. Am J Cardiol 16 (1965) 42-53.

Rehm J., M.M. Fichter, M. Elton. Effects on mortality of alcohol consumption, smoking, physical activity, and close personal relationships. Addiction 88 (1993) 101-112.

Rosenthal R., R.L. Rosnow. (1984). Essentials of behavior research. McGraw-Hill, New York.

Ross C.E., D. Hayes. Exercise and psychologic well-being in the community. Am J Epidemiol 127:4 (1988) 762-771.

Sarason I.G., J.H. Johnson, J.M. Siegel. Assessing the impact of life changes: Development of the Life Experience Survey. J Cons Clin Psychol 46 (1978) 932-946.

Snel J., H. Gosselink. Health, personality and physiological variables as discriminators of the Type A behavior pattern in young adults. Journal of Psychophysiology 3 (1989) 291-299.

Stephens T. Physical activity and mental health in the United States and Canada: Evidence from four population surveys. Prev Med 17 (1988) 35-47.

Temoshok L. (1983). Emotion, adaptation, and disease: A multidimensional theory. In: L. Temoshok, C. van Dyke, L.S. Zegans (eds.), Emotions in health and illness. Grune & Gratton, New York.

Vena J.E., S. Graham, M. Zielezny, M.K. Swanson, R.E. Barnes, J. Nolan. Lifetime occupational exercise and colon cancer. Am J Epidemiol 122 (1985) 357-365.

Verdiar M.G., G. De Steinek, U. Hagman, A. Rieger, S.E. Norell. Physical activity and colon cancer: A case-referent study in Stockholm. Int J Cancer 46 (1990) 985-989.

Verschuur R. (1987). Daily physical activity and health: Longitudinal changes during the teenage period. Thesis, Universiteit van Amsterdam, de Vrieseborch, Haarlem, SO 12.

Vingerhoets A.J.J.M. (1985). Psychosocial stress: An experimental approach—life events, coping and psychobiological functioning. Dissertation, Swetz & Zeitlinger, Lisse.

Vingerhoets A.J.J.M., P.J.M. Flohr. Type A behavior and self-reports of coping preferences. Br J Med Psychol 57 (1984) 15-21.

Vingerhoets A.J.J.M., A.J. Jeninga, L.J. Menges. The measurement of daily hassles and chronic stressors: The development of the Everyday Problem Checklist (EPCL) II. Gedrag & Gezondheid 17:1 (1989) 10-17.

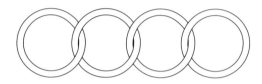

Conclusions of the Amsterdam Growth Study

Han C.G. Kemper, Willem van Mechelen, G. Bertheke Post, Jan Snel, Jos Twisk, & Desiree C. Welten

The Amsterdam Growth and Health Study concerned a 15-year follow-up period of 182 males and females age 13 to age 27. Here we make recommendations for changes in lifestyles and for preventive strategies that can help people enhance health and avoid diseases later on during their adult years. For future young populations in particular, some of our advice can be of potential benefit when implemented earlier in life, during an age period that is more critical to health-promoting activities (Dishman, 1994).

In considering these conclusions it must be kept in mind that this very extensive and multidisciplinary study has been performed using a specific Dutch sample. Although dropout effects appeared to be small and did not affect most measurements, one should be cautious with broad generalizations, for two reasons. First, the longitudinal group of subjects originated from one secondary school in the city of Amsterdam. Second, the children's intellectual as well as their socioeconomic status were slightly above the average of their peers in the Netherlands.

The obvious purpose of longitudinal research is to study the natural course of the aging process by descriptive methods (Part II). An age span of almost 15 years can be considered substantial and special, particularly when one takes into account the specific age group that is involved. At the starting point at age 13, all of the boys and most of the girls are pre- and circumpubertal—they haven't experienced their growth spurt—while at the last point of measurement they are adults in their late 20s. Between these two points in time physical growth has finished, sexual maturation has occurred, and education has been completed.

Growth, Body Composition, and Physical Fitness

Our study was initiated as part of a descriptive study, and we have now collected successive sets of anthropometric data of the same variables in the population, from ages 13 to 27.

Growth in height was completed in girls and boys by age 21. Median values were 170 cm for females and 183 cm for males. These values are close to the national height standards established in a nationwide cross-sectional sample in 1985 (Roede et al., 1985).

The percentage of fat relative to total body mass increased in both sexes with age, resulting in values of 20% fat in males and 28% in females at age 27. The gender difference was caused by the two arm skinfolds (biceps and triceps); the two skinfolds at the trunk (subscapularis and crista suprailiaca) did not differ at adult age between males and females. If we accept as a risk value 20% fat in males and 30% fat in females, one third of our population demonstrated over-weight. The body mass index (BMI) as an indirect estimate of fatness increased from 18 at age 13 to 22 at age 27 in both sexes. There was an interaction, however, between the sexes, indicating that females had a higher BMI during adolescence than males; at adult age, however, the reverse is true.

Systolic blood pressure (125 mmHg) and diastolic blood pressure (75 mmHg) did not differ significantly between girls and boys at age 13; both measures, however, increased with age. At age 27 in both sexes diastolic pressure reached a mean value of 80 mmHg. Systolic blood pressure increased 10 mmHg in males to a mean value of 135 mmHg, while in females it first decreased to 120 mmHg and then increased to 125 mmHg at age 27.

The longitudinal pattern of the changes in lipoprotein content in blood showed the typical pattern of sex differentiation over time: After a decrease in total cholesterol (TC) and high-density lipoprotein (HDL) cholesterol fraction levels during adolescence, in both sexes TC content increased; however, the HDL-cholesterol concentration increased only in males. This resulted in a higher TC:HDL-cholesterol ratio in males (4.2) than in females (3.4). Relative to age- and sex-related norms, the mean values for our cholesterol data are at about or are below risk values. However, 36% of the males and 53% of the females showed TC values that were above the cutoff for TC for moderate increased health risk. With regard to the TC:HDL-cholesterol ratio 57% of the males and 18% of the females surpassed the cutoff value for moderately increased CVD risk (Ruwaard et al., 1993).

Three of the seven physical fitness parameters (arm pull, 10×5-m run, and 10 leg lifts) showed an increase during adolescence, followed by a decrease at age 21 and a stabilization pattern at age 27. The other four (standing high jump, sit-and-reach, bent-arm hang, and plate tapping) showed a relatively steep increase, at least in boys, during adolescence followed by small increase at adult age. In females performance on the standing high jump and bent-arm hang did not change substantially over the 15 years. In most physical fitness tests, males performed better than females. Exceptions were that there were no differences in plate tapping and leg lifting, and that at all ages females are more flexible than males in the sit-and-reach test. Aerobic power was measured directly on a treadmill following the same protocol at all measurements. This made it possible to compare submaximal oxygen uptake ($\dot{V}O_2$) at the same running speed (8 km/h) at different slopes (0%, 2.5%, and 5%). The results show that $\dot{V}O_2$ per kilogram of body mass decreased 5 ml · kg^{-1} · min^{-1} during adolescence and an additional 2 ml · kg^{-1} · min^{-1} at adult age. This decrease in absolute values was similar for each slope. Males consumed significantly more oxygen than females (2 ml · kg^{-1} · min^{-1}) in the three submaximal running conditions and at all ages. Apparently, running economy increases with age and is higher in females compared to males throughout the age levels represented in our study.

As expected, maximal oxygen uptake ($\dot{V}O_2$max) increased with growth, and more in males than females. During adolescence $\dot{V}O_2$max increased from 2.7 L/min to 3.7 L/min in males and from 2.4 L/min to 2.7 L/min in females. Relative to body mass, however, this increase was not confirmed; on the contrary, in males a decrease from 59 ml · kg^{-1} · min^{-1} to 51 ml · kg^{-1} · min^{-1} was found, while in females the change was from 51 ml · kg^{-1} · min^{-1} to 40 ml · kg^{-1} · min^{-1}. To make clear which part of the changes can be ascribed to the oxygen transport systems and which part to body mass, we expressed the longitudinal course of $\dot{V}O_2$max per kilogram of body mass to the two-thirds power. During adolescence, males demonstrated an increase in $\dot{V}O_2$max measured this way, followed by a continuous decrease until age 27. In females a continuous decrease was apparent until age 21; $\dot{V}O_2$max then remained constant. The stability of the scores on physical fitness parameters was assessed by inspection of the interperiod correlations (IPCs; r) over three time periods—5, 10, and 15 years. In both males and females over the 15-year period the highest stability was seen in the sit-and-reach ($r = 0.6$) and the standing high jump ($r = 0.71$). The lowest stability was found in males in the arm pull ($r = 0.3$), flexed-arm hang ($r = 0.3$), and $\dot{V}O_2$max ($r = 0.2$) and in females in $\dot{V}O_2$max ($r = 0.3$).

Psychosocial Characteristics

Personality traits were measured using the Achievement Motivation Test (AMT) and the Dutch Personality Inventory (DPI). Although youth and adult versions of these inventories had to be used, the IPCs reflect a high and progressively increasing consistency of personality traits from adolescence through adulthood. Shifts in the traits of Dominance, Rigidity, and Social Inadequacy started earlier in women than in men. This is in line with the later biological development of boys compared to girls (e.g., peak height velocity begins roughly 1-1/2 years later in boys).

The evaluation of changes in personality profiles with time revealed that both sexes are characterized by a change from fearfulness and insecurity in their teens to social assertiveness at adult age. Again, this change was found earlier in girls than in boys and may result in adult women who become more firm.

Associations that are often considered as existing between physical and psychological characteristics were neither substantial nor consistent in our study. In particular, aerobic power, an oft-mentioned aspect of physical fitness, failed to reflect this relationship in a longitudinal perspective. Because aerobic power is a physical characteristic that is measured very reliably (and the personality questionnaires used are of proven reliability and validity), we cannot help but have serious doubts about this association put forward in the literature. The reason for our divergent findings may be that these associations result from cross-sectional studies, which can be seriously biased by self-selection, the result of the participation of relatively highly fit subjects. The saying *mens sana in corpore sano*, illustrating the ancient belief in the close relation of body and mind, was not shown in longitudinal perspective.

Lifestyle Characteristics

An important aspect of this longitudinal study was the repeated assessment of several aspects of lifestyle over 15 years, including nutritional intake, physical activity, and behavioral patterns like stress and coping style. These are described in part III.

From adolescence to adulthood nutritional intake showed significantly higher energy and nutrient intakes in males than in females. These higher absolute values are not surprising in view of the greater height and weight of males. Mean energy intake in females corresponded to the Dutch recommended dietary allowances (DRDA). In males during the young adult period, the intakes were significantly higher than the DRDAs. However, it was also observed that after the period of growth—in both females and males—the percentage of body fat gradually increased during their 20s. This suggests that the official recommendations for daily energy intake are either not taken seriously or are too high. In females, especially, higher-than-recommended intakes introduced a positive energy balance resulting sooner or later in overweight in adulthood.

In absolute value and over the whole period, nutrient intake levels comprised too few carbohydrates and too many fats. The contribution of polysaccharides was too low and the fats contained too few polyunsaturated fatty acids. On a long-term basis, both components are thought to contribute to the development of cardiovascular diseases (CVD) (National Research Council, 1991).

On the other hand, the evidence gathered did not indicate that a high energy intake or a high percentage of energy from fat was related to two well-known and accepted CVD risk factors: percentage of body fat and TC. The absence of this relationship can be explained partly by the relatively low absolute values of these risk factors due to the group's young age.

In general, in both sexes no relationship between nutritional intake and CVD risk factor could be demonstrated. The one exception was that in males, a high alcohol intake was significantly correlated with a higher percentage of body fat and with a tendency to a higher TC level.

Although the reliability of our cross-check dietary history questionnaire proved to be sufficient, the absence of clear relationships with CVD risk factors may be due to the unifactorial approach: Apart from nutrition, other CVD risk–related lifestyles (such as physical activity and stress/coping) could have masked the dietary effects.

The pattern of habitual physical activity over a period of almost 15 years was monitored by structured interviews performed six times. The following conclusions may be drawn.

In males there was a tremendous decrease in the amount of time spent in physical activities (above the intensity level of 4 METs). The decrease from age 13 to age 27 was, on the average, 75%. When physical activities were weighted according to their energy expenditure, the decrease over the total period was also considerable: about 42%. Even more important is the fact that most of the decrease took place during the first 5 years of the adolescent period (between ages 13 and 18). In females the decrease was only manifest when the weighted activity score was used, giving a 17% decrease over the whole period.

Surprisingly, when only the energy expenditure of the physical activities is taken into account, males showed significantly higher activity patterns than females. The differences are not significant when the total amount of time spent on physical activities is compared. These results emphasize that it is crucial not only to measure the total time that youngsters are active but also to make a distinction between the different intensities of the activities. The males chose more intensive activities than females.

The extent of tracking of the pattern of physical activity from age 13 to age 27 appears to be negligible in both sexes. Only shorter periods of time (5-year intervals) resulted in tracking coefficients that vary between .3 and .4 in males and between .25 and .6 in females. Tracking was also better when the four adolescent measurements were averaged and correlated with the scores at ages 21 and 27. After the strong decrease in physical activity during the adolescent period, the participation in organized sports activities became more important. From a preventive point of view, in our opinion it seems critical to apply strategies that encourage young people to participate in sports and continue their participation throughout the adult years because the amount of energy spent in other activities (work, leisure, transport) appears to be very low at adult age (ACSM, 1990).

Concerning psychosocial behavior, data were collected on the subjective impact of stressors such as life events and daily hassles, the use of an adequate coping style, the presence of coronary-prone behavior (Type A behavior), and health-related symptoms (such as sleep and health complaints). We found that from ages 21 to 27 there was a stable pattern of intercorrelations among the three components stress, coping, and health.

It is interesting to note that Type A behavior is seen by men as a stressor but that women interpret this behavior as a complaint-like variable belonging to the health component. This confirms the general finding that women complain more than men; in other words, women are apparently more aware of their health and at an earlier stage than men. Further, a significant association could be found in both sexes between neuroticism and the experience of health problems. Since neuroticism is a stable personality trait, it may potentially contribute to the early identification of high-risk groups. A continued follow-up of the subjects could verify this assumption in the future.

Relations Between Lifestyle and Health

In the last part (Part IV) analyses were made to discover relationships between different aspects of lifestyle and health over the 15-year period. Since there is epidemiologic evidence that physical inactivity can be described as an important risk factor for CVD, the longitudinal physical fitness data of males and females were analyzed by comparing the relatively physically active subjects with the relatively inactive ones during the 15 years of follow-up. A division in tertiles showed that on the average the activity scores of the bottom tertile (low actives) in both sexes is one third of the activity of the top tertile (high actives); the total range of activity scores of each of the two tertiles did not even overlap.

Both males and females who during the 15-year period consistently ranked in the upper tertile became significantly more fit than the subjects in the tertile with the lowest activity pattern. These interaction effects are predominantly present after the adolescent period and are reflected in the fitness parameters VO_2max, muscle endurance, explosive muscle strength, and flexibility. These results quite clearly demonstrate that a relatively high physical activity level between ages 13 and 27 is of utmost importance for the level of physical fitness at adult age in both sexes. That these activity effects first become apparent at adult age suggests that there is a rather long latent period in youth in which a high activity pattern is not accompanied by manifest effects on physical fitness. This can be explained by the fact that after the adolescent period the absolute levels of activity decrease considerably in both sexes.

The descriptive design of our longitudinal study does not justify the firm conclusion that physical activity is the cause. However, that the majority of the effects on physical fitness tended to increase with higher age and appeared to be related to the activity level during childhood and adolescence strongly supports the activity pattern itself, and not self-selection, as the important determinant. Strategies to promote exercise adherence therefore should be started not only in childhood to make children acquainted with all kinds of exercises (sports, recreational activities, and also activities in daily life such as walking, cycling, and stair climbing instead of physically passive forms of transportation and recreation) but should be continued after the school years to establish a habit of exercising during the years thereafter.

Because not much is known about the etiology of sports injuries in youth and because the injury rate relative to the amount of sports participation is thought to be high, we investigated the relationships of several risk factors and sports injuries in our population. We asked all subjects at age 27 about their sports injury history over the 12 months prior to the interview. We related these injury rates to the information on the physical, psychological, and psychosocial characteristics of the subjects measured 5 years before at age 21. In this way it was possible to study this relationship prospectively instead of cross-sectionally as is usually done in most studies. In the latter way cause (potential risk factor) and effect (sports injury) are measured at the same time. The data show that 1-year incidence rates are almost 3 times higher in males (42%) than in females (14%). More than two thirds of these injuries (72%) were located at the lower extremities.

In a stepwise multiple logistic regression (MLR) analysis with sex and sport participation as covariates, a significant final model was found to explain lower-extremity injuries. The model indicates two psychosocial variables (recalcitrance and debilitating anxiety) and one fitness variable (right/left leg extension disbalance). It indicates that the chance of lower-extremity injuries can be partly explained by high recalcitrance and high debilitating anxiety in combination with extreme extension disbalance (in males). That no further risk factors could be traced can be explained by the fact that a relatively young, healthy, and fit population was used and by the unique design, in which we took into account factors that can have confounded other cross-sectional results (Mechelen, 1993).

Predictability of Health and Risk Factors

Because CVD is a very serious problem in public health and because some of its causes originate in childhood, it is of great importance not only to identify those persons who run the risk of CVD but also to do so early in life. We therefore investigated the predictability and the maintenance over time of three well-known and accepted categories of CVD risk factors: (a) biological factors, such as hypertension, hypercholesterolemia, and body fat; (b) lifestyle factors, such as smoking, alcohol drinking, physical activity, and Type A behavior; and (c) a genetic risk factor—that is, family history of CVD or hypertension.

Contrary to our expectations no significant relationship between family history of CVD or hypertension and biological risk factors could be traced. Although the percentage of subjects with family history of hypertension was much higher in the high-risk groups for TC and systolic and diastolic blood pressures than in the low-risk groups, family history did not play a significant role in the explanation of biological risk factors. More extensive questioning in follow-up—not only of first-degree but also second-degree relatives—might result in more concrete findings regarding the relationship.

MLR analysis revealed that within the category of biological factors, body fat is significantly related to a high risk for hypercholesterolemia. Of the four lifestyle factors under review, smoking and physical activity showed significant relationships with biological risk factors. Smoking was related to low cardiopulmonary fitness and hypercholesterolemia. Low daily physical activity was, as expected, associated with a low cardiopulmonary fitness. The other two lifestyle factors, alcohol consumption and Type A behavior, did not emerge as significant in the MLR models. The analyses do suggest, however, that a healthy lipoprotein level is promoted by reducing smoking and body fat. Increasing physical activity and cutting down on smoking enhance cardiopulmonary fitness. Increased cardiopulmonary fitness can reduce body fat and thus indirectly lead to a healthy lipoprotein level—i.e., by lowering TC, increasing HDL cholesterol, and lowering the TC:HDL-cholesterol ratio. Our recommendation is that preventive strategies be aimed at lipoprotein profiles.

Osteoporosis is a major health concern because of an exponentially increasing incidence of this condition in elderly populations. Prevention is aimed at reducing the rate of bone loss during aging and increasing the level of peak bone mass in young adulthood. Because maximizing bone mass is considered to be the best protection against age-related bone loss and subsequent fracture risk, in our study peak bone mass was measured in the lumbar spine at a mean age of 27 and related to such lifestyle aspects as calcium intake from diet and weight-bearing activities in the 15 years of the study. The results show a marginal role for calcium intake in determining the peak bone density: Only in adolescent boys did the relatively low calcium intake group show a significantly lower bone mineral density compared with the relatively high calcium intake group. This was also the group with a calcium intake below the DRDA. The adequate calcium intake in the majority of our subjects is due to the relatively high consumption of dairy products (milk and cheese) in the Netherlands.

On the other hand, it appeared that in the same healthy males and females the peak bone mineral density of the lumbar spine is significantly and positively related to the amount of weight-bearing activities undertaken, preferentially during the adolescent years. This finding stresses the utmost importance of a sufficient amount of physical activity during youth for the optimal development of the adult skeleton (Welten et al., 1994).

In the last chapter a sophisticated analysis was conducted to gain insight into the assumption that aerobic and musculoskeletal fitness are predictors of adult health while taking into account the lifestyle factors physical activity, smoking, alcohol drinking, and social inadequacy. Adult health status was operationalized into three subcategories: (a) physical health (fatness, blood pressure, and serum cholesterol), (b) mental health (inadequacy, vital exhaustion, mild psychosomatic complaints, life events, and coping style), and (c) self-reported health (sleep quality and health disorders). We started with the idea that healthy people may self-regulate their lifestyles to optimize their health. The results on physical activity and aerobic fitness, however, did not support this assumption. Even so, musculoskeletal fitness appeared to be beneficial for adult physical health in both sexes. Drinking and smoking behavior may jeopardize mental health, and smoking was also negatively related to adult self-reported health. An interesting finding is the beneficial role of low social inadequacy on both mental health and self-reported health. These findings are relevant to measures aimed at promoting adequate social skills, stimulating musculoskeletal fitness, and preventing smoking and alcohol drinking in young people in order to increase their chances of good health during adulthood.

References

American College of Sports Medicine. The recommended quantity and quality of exercise for developing and maintaining cardiorespiratory and muscular fitness in healthy adults. Med Sci Sports Exercise 22 (1990) 265-274.

Dishman R.K. (ed.). (1994). Advances in exercise adherence. Human Kinetics, Champaign.

Mechelen W. van. (1993). Incidence and severity of sports injuries. In: P.O. Renström (ed.), Sports injuries: Basic principles of prevention and care. Vol. 4 of: Encyclopedia of sports medicine. Blackwell Scientific Publications, Oxford.

National Research Council. Diet and health implications for reducing chronic disease risk. Nat. Academic Press, Washington, 1989.

Roede M.J., J.C. van Wieringen. Growth diagrams 1980. Netherlands third nationwide survey. Tijdschrift voor Sociale Gezondheidszorg 63 (1985, Suppl.) 1-33.

Ruwaard D., P.G.N. Kramers. Volksgezondheid Toekomst Verkenning. Rijksinstituut voor Volksgezondheid en Milieuhygiëne, SDU uitgeverij, Den Haag, 1993.

Welten D.C., H.C.G. Kemper, G.B. Post, W. van Mechelen, J.W.R. Twisk, P. Lips, G.J. Teule. Weight-bearing activity during youth is a more important factor for peak bone mass than calcium intake. Bone and Min Res 9:7 (1994) 1089-1096.